THE
NEGRO COWBOYS

by Philip Durham and Everett L. Jones

University of Nebraska Press
Lincoln and London

First Bison Book edition: October 1983
Most recent printing indicated by the first digit below:
              7   8   9   10

Library of Congress Cataloging in Publication Data
Durham, Philip.
  The Negro cowboys.

  Reprint. originally published: New York : Dodd,
Mead, c1965.
  Bibliography: p.
  Includes index.
  1. Afro-American cowboys. 2. West (U.S.)—Social
life and customs. I. Jones, Everett L. II. Title.
F596.D8 1983   978'.00496073   83-6446
ISBN 0-8032-6560-3 (pbk.)

Published by arrangement with Curtis Brown, Ltd.

Preface

As teachers of English, the authors came upon this subject through a long-standing interest in the backgrounds of Western American literature. Pursuing this interest we discovered, to our surprise, an unimagined number of Negro cowboys, who had been dropped from the history of the West. Because our approach was through "literature," we drew on the histories and memoirs of such historians as Walter Prescott Webb, Ramon F. Adams, J. Evetts Haley, J. Frank Dobie, and Wayne Gard, who wrote from a personal knowledge of the West. The more we read, the more we realized that the subject demanded treatment.

In undertaking this work, we have been aided by the staffs and libraries of the Newberry Library, the UCLA Library, the William Andrews Clark Library, and the Huntington Library, as well as by the staff members of the Nebraska State Historical Society, the Barker Texas History Library, the California State Library, the Montana Historical Society, the State Historical Society of Colorado, the University of Kansas Library, and the University of

Texas Memorial Museum. This work has been made possible, too, because of past support to related projects by the John Simon Guggenheim Memorial Foundation and the American Council of Learned Societies.

In doing research and preparing the manuscript we have been aided by James Mink, Wilbur Smith, and Brooke Whiting, all of the Department of Special Collections of the UCLA Library. Marjorie Griffin, Violet Jordain, Jane Ruml, and Pauline Ward labored patiently and criticized tactfully while typing innumerable revisions of the book. Gwen Staniforth devoted hours to checking and correcting footnotes and bibliography. UCLA colleagues John Espey and Leon Howard read the manuscript and made many suggestions for its improvement. And, finally, Western historians Ray Allen Billington, William Brandon, and John Caughey gave generously of their time in reading and criticizing every chapter. All these good friends have done much to improve the book, but they are in no way responsible for its shortcomings.

The authors wish to thank the editors of *The American West* and the *Pacific Historical Review* for permission to reprint material earlier published in those journals.

PHILIP DURHAM

EVERETT L. JONES

University of California, Los Angeles

Contents

To Jeanne and Boots

Prologue

Now they are forgotten, but once they rode all the trails, driving millions of cattle before them. Some died in stampedes, some froze to death, some drowned. Some were too slow with guns, some too fast. But most of them lived through the long drives to Abilene, to Dodge City, to Ogallala. And many of them drove on to the farthest reaches of the northern range, to the Dakotas, Wyoming and Montana.

They numbered thousands, among them many of the best riders, ropers and wranglers. They hunted wild horses and wolves, and a few of them hunted men. Some were villains, some were heroes. Some were called offensive names, and others were given almost equally offensive compliments. But even when one of them was praised as "the whitest man I've ever known," he was not white.

For they were the Negro cowboys.

They rode with white Texans, Mexicans and Indians. All the real cowboys—black, brown, red and white—shared the same jobs and dangers. They ate the same food and slept on the same ground; but when the long drives ended and the great plains were tamed and fenced, the trails ended too. The cattle were fenced in, the Negroes fenced out.

Years later, when history became myth and legend, when the cowboys became folk heroes, the Negroes were again fenced out. They had ridden through the real West, but they found no place in the West of fiction. That was peopled by tall, lean, tanned—though lily-white under the shirt —heroes who rode through purple sage made dangerous by dirty villains, red Indians and swarthy "greasers," only occasionally being helped by "good Indians" and "proud Spanish-Americans." Even the Chinese survived in fiction, if only as pigtailed caricatures who spoke a "no tickee, no washee" pidgin as they shuffled about the ranch houses. Although the stereotypes were sometimes grotesque, all but one of the races and nationalities of the real West appeared in fiction.

All but the Negro cowboy, who had vanished.

·◦⊰[1]⊱◦·

The Move West

Among the cowboys who went up the trails from Texas during the years following the Civil War, more than five thousand Negroes played a part and did a job—doing no more and no less than cowboys of other races and nationalities. The real story is not about one group alone, but about all the men who conquered the grassland of the "Great American Desert," a vast area which suddenly became the Western cattle empire. In perspective, that achievement must be seen as the work of many men engaged in a common enterprise. It is best understood as a movement of people driven by economic forces, excited by new challenges and eager for adventure.

An observer standing on a rise and watching a herd of cattle being driven up a trail could not differentiate one cowboy from another. He saw only a group of men doing a job in a cloud of dust. Unless he rode down and met them individually, he could not tell whether they were Texans or Mexicans, whites or Negroes. Yet as he watched the cattle pushing north, he was viewing the making of history.

This history was made primarily by white Southerners

who had worn the uniform of the Confederacy. With them rode men who had fought for the Union. With them, too, were a number of Mexican vaqueros, as well as an occasional German, Irishman, Englishman or Swede. But more numerous than Northerners or foreigners, frequently among the most capable men in the crew, were the Negro cowboys.

There had always been Negroes in the West. They had, indeed, been scattered throughout the Western Hemisphere since their first importation as slaves at the beginning of the sixteenth century. Estevánico, a Spanish slave from the west coast of Morocco, was a member of an unfortunate party of four hundred explorers who landed near Tampa Bay in 1528. After a series of disasters, all of the party were lost except Estevánico, his master and two companions, who were marooned on the Texas coast. They were enslaved by Indians and spent seven years freeing themselves and making their way across Texas and Mexico to the frontiers of New Spain. Once there, they told stories they had heard of the Seven Cities of Cíbola, and their reports were directly responsible for the Coronado expedition.[1] Estevánico continued his explorations, discovered the pueblos of New Mexico, and was killed by the Zuñis in 1539.[2]

More than two hundred years later, Negroes and Negro-Indian families helped to found what is now the largest city in the West. Their settlement was established to grow food for the military, and it was called El Pueblo de Nuestra Señora La Reina de Los Angeles. Negroes and descendants of Negroes were literally among the first families of Los Angeles just as they were among the first settlers in the Spanish colonies of New Mexico.[3]

Negroes also took part in American exploration of the

West. When Lewis and Clark commanded the first official attempt to extend the "geographical knowledge of our continent," a Negro went with them. Clark's slave, a man named York, accompanied the expedition from the time it hoisted sail near the mouth of the Missouri River in 1804 until it returned in 1806 after having crossed the Rocky and Bitterroot Mountains and pushed to the mouth of the Columbia River.[4] Nearly forty years later a free Negro, Jacob Dodson, accompanied John C. Frémont on his 1843 expedition to search for a new pass through the High Sierra. Another free Negro, Saunders Jackson, joined Frémont's fourth expedition in 1848.[5]

Several Negroes ranged through the Rocky Mountains searching for beaver. One was James P. Beckwith (sometimes Beckwourth), the son of a white father and a Negro slave, who in 1823 was the blacksmith for General William Ashley's fur brigade. In time, he became one of the most famous of the mountain men (as well as a famous storyteller), his exploits rivaling those of Kit Carson and Jim Bridger, with both of whom he associated. During the last years of his life he was a chief among the Crows, earning new fame as a warrior and horse thief. Even his early death before the middle of the century was a subject of legend: it was said that his own tribe poisoned him, using a poison so deadly that not even his own powerful medicine (a bag containing a hollow bullet and two oblong beads) could save his life.[6] Edward Rose was another such mountain man, "a morose, moody misfit of mixed blood and lawless disposition," who "eventually joined the Crow tribe and abandoned civilization entirely." [7]

The explorations of Lewis and Clark, Frémont and the mountain men helped open the way to Oregon. Ironically, although Negroes participated in these expeditions, they

were early barred from the Oregon frontier settlements.
Many of the first settlers of the Willamette Valley were
Southerners, and while they could not change the ruling
of the 1843 provisional constitution that prohibited slavery, they added a provision in 1844 which expelled all the
Negroes and mulattoes. So in that same year, when George
W. Bush, a free Negro, joined an expedition to Oregon,
he was refused settlement there. He moved north to Puget
Sound and took up a homestead, where he lived the rest of
his life. One of the earliest settlers, he helped later arrivals
with interest-free loans of grain and other foodstuffs, assisting hundreds of white newcomers to survive their first
months on the new frontier.[8]

Another free Negro worked at the start of the Oregon
Trail in Independence, Missouri. There Hiram Young operated wagon factories and engaged in a general black-
smithing business, at one time employing more than fifty
men on twenty-five forges. He also owned and employed
slaves.[9]

After 1848 many travelers of the Oregon Trail turned
south to California, where gold had been discovered.
Among them were Negroes, both slave and free, who
staked claims and formed mining companies. Negro prospectors and miners also joined in later developments in
Nevada, Idaho and Montana, and they were among those
who headed for Colorado to become part of the Pike's
Peak gold rush of 1858. Other Negroes appeared in the
West as muleskinners, hostlers, hotelkeepers and unskilled
laborers. Some worked for Russell, Majors and Waddell
and their Pony Express. Negro women cooked for hungry
trappers in isolated mountain forts and for travelers on
the Butterfield stages that rolled through Texas and Arizona.[10]

Negroes, even as slaves, were usually more fortunate than the American Indians. During slavery days, Negroes were valuable property, and after the Civil War they rarely challenged the ambition and greed of Western pioneers. But the Indians were always despised, fair game for treachery and murder. In the West, as in the East, Americans dishonored treaty after treaty, driving Indians from one area to another, systematically attempting to exterminate whole tribes. The Indians fought back, and as they fought they were sometimes opposed, sometimes aided, by Negroes.

In the Indian Nations (now Oklahoma) some wealthy Indians of the Five Civilized Tribes owned large plantations and hundreds of slaves. Others become slavers, kidnapping and selling Negroes "down the river." Still others lived with Negro friends and relatives, learning together to make a new life in the West after their violent removal from ancestral lands in Florida, Georgia, Alabama and Mississippi. Some of the Seminole Indians, for example, rode with Negroes all the way through Texas to take up land in Coahuila province in Mexico. There, under the command of John Horse, the son of an Indian father and a Negro mother, a band of about a hundred Negroes joined with Seminole and Kickapoo Indians in campaigns against Mescalero and Comanche Indians.

In Texas, as white settlers occupied new lands, both they and their slaves suffered from Indian reprisals. As early as 1839, Indians killed a Negro hauling lumber between Bastrop and Austin. Another died in the same year when his surveying party was raided. Comanche raiders killed eleven more Negroes the next year and carried off several as prisoners. From 1839 until long after the Civil War, Texas Negroes fought against Indians.

But some became renegades, riding with Comanches, sometimes leading attacks on white settlements. One Negro was with an Indian raiding party that attacked the Hoover family in 1861; another was with the Indians who raided the Friend home in Llano County, Texas, in 1866. A "big Negro" led a party of thirty-five Indians that killed rancher George Hazelwood and fought against Hazelwood's cowboys in 1868. He was perhaps the same one who in 1868 led an Indian attack on the Ledbetter Saltworks in Shackelford County. Still another Negro led a band of more than forty Indians in surrounding a dozen cattlemen and cowboys "near the borders of Young and Palo Pinto counties, not far from Fort Belknap, on May 16, 1869." He sat on a large rock, well out of gun range, and commanded his forces in their attack. He and his Indians hurt the cattlemen badly, killing three and seriously wounding five, but they were forced to retreat when the besieged group was relieved by a rescue party summoned and led by a Negro cowboy.[11]

References to Negro renegades are not uncommon in accounts of Indian fights in the West and Southwest. Some of these renegades were themselves part Indian—usually Seminole or Creek, but occasionally part Comanche or Sioux. Some had been captured as children and raised in the tribes. Others deserted from the Army: fled courts-martial or merely went over the hill. Such men, particularly if they had long Army experience, made invaluable allies for the Indians. Probably one such man was the Negro bugler who accompanied the Indians in a famous attack on a group of buffalo hunters at Adobe Walls in the Texas Panhandle in 1874.[12]

But for every Negro renegade who joined against the white men, a company of Negro soldiers fought Indians.

No story of the seizure and settlement of the West would be complete without including an account of the Negro soldiers in the 24th and 25th Infantry Regiments and the Negro troopers in the 9th and 10th Cavalry Regiments. Organization of Negro regiments in the Regular Army was first authorized in 1866. During the Civil War, 178,975 Negro soldiers wore the blue uniforms of the Union Armies, and Negroes took part in 449 engagements. More than 38,000 were listed as killed, wounded or missing in action. With such a record, Negroes proved their effectiveness as soldiers, and the federal government prepared to use them.[13]

The Congressional Act of July 28, 1866 (later modified by supplementary legislation in 1869), established two Negro infantry regiments and two Negro cavalry regiments. All four saw continuous service in the West during the three decades following the Civil War. Negro infantry served in both Texas and the Dakota Territory, and Negro cavalry fought in almost every part of the West from Mexico to Montana. Both General Miles and General Merritt, as well as other officers who commanded Negro troops during the Indian campaigns, praised their courage and skill: "I have always," wrote General Merritt, "found the colored race represented in the army obedient, intelligent and zealous in the discharge of duty, brave in battle, easily disciplined, and most efficient in the care of their horses, arms and equipment."

The story of either cavalry regiment alone would be an exciting history. The men were carefully picked, held to high standards of physical fitness and mental alertness, and were commanded by some of the Army's best white officers. (Three Negroes graduated from West Point in the years before 1900, and a few Negroes were commissioned as chaplains, but all other officers were white.)

The men took quickly to the routine of fort and camp, maintained excellent morale and proved to be excellent soldiers. Because few of them had received more than a smattering of education, a company commander's biggest problem was training men for the inevitable War Department paper work. The men believed that wearing the Army uniform was a privilege and an honor, and they equaled and sometimes surpassed white troops in the field. "Their desertion rate was lower, court-martial record better, and general physical fitness superior." [14]

During the years before the Spanish-American War, troops of the 9th Cavalry served in Texas, New Mexico, Kansas, Oklahoma, Nebraska, Utah and Montana. The 10th Cavalry served in Kansas, Oklahoma, Texas, New Mexico and Arizona. Negro troopers fought against Comanches, Apaches and Sioux. They fought against Crazy Horse and his warriors, and they captured Geronimo.[15]

The Indians called the Negro troopers Buffalo Soldiers because of the similarity between their tightly curled hair, generally short, and that of the buffalo. The white soldiers called them the Brunettes. The War Department knew they were efficient.

Frederic Remington posed a rhetorical question: "Will they fight?" And he answered it himself: "They have fought many, many times. The old sergeant sitting near me, as calm of feature as a bronze statue, once deliberately walked over a Cheyenne rifle pit and killed his man. One little fellow near him once took charge of a lot of stampeded cavalry horses when Apache bullets were flying loose and no one knew from what point to expect them next.

These little episodes prove the sometimes doubted self-reliance of the Negro." [16]

Negro soldiers and troopers were also called to keep the peace among white cattlemen and settlers. When Billy the Kid was trapped in a burning building in Lincoln, New Mexico, Negro troops surrounded him. When settlers tried to preempt lands in the Indian Nations, and when Sooners tried to sneak into Oklahoma Indian lands before they were officially opened for settlement, Negro cavalry stopped them.[17] When Wyoming cattlemen started the Johnson County War, only to find themselves outnumbered and pinned down by angry settlers, Negro cavalry rescued them.

The soldiers helped to make the expansion of the cattle empire possible. Sometimes with their help and sometimes without it, cattlemen drove through Kansas and Nebraska to the Dakota Territory or through New Mexico and Colorado to Wyoming and Montana. And with the Texas cattlemen came the Negro cowboys.

These cowboys crossed the Red River and the Cimarron to ride the streets of all the early cowtowns. They stood in the saloons and slept in the jails. They fought Indians and other cowboys, and some of them were buried on Boot Hill or in unmarked graves along the trail. At the end of the long drives, a few remained on northern ranges to become horsebreakers, ranch hands or even outlaws, but most of them drew their pay and rode back to Texas.

While the trail drives lasted, Negroes had a conspicuous place in the life of the cattleman's West. They fought with guns and bullwhips on the streets of Dodge City, and they roamed the streets of Cheyenne. They carried gold through outlaw country, and they took part in bloody range wars. If one got drunk, he could crash through a plate glass window, shoot up a saloon or land in jail. If he turned outlaw, he usually died young.

Negro cowboys hunched in their saddles during blizzards and thunderstorms, fought grass fires and turned stampedes, hunted wild mustangs and rode wild horses. Wolves threatened their cattle, and rattlesnakes crawled into their camps. Their lives were like those of all other cowboys—hard and dangerous.

The point of their history is not that they were different from their companions but that they were similar. They had neither peculiar virtues nor vices to be glorified or condemned. But they should be remembered.

·⋯⦊[2]⦉·⋯

Slaves on Horseback

One of the early Negro cowboys has been forgotten, and his name will probably never be recovered. He was a slave and a rather poor cowboy, hardly worth a place in history. But because he was inefficient, even lazy, he made his master famous.

He and his family lived on the San Antonio River in Texas, and they were owned by a lawyer, not a cattleman. In 1847, when the lawyer received four hundred head of cattle in payment of a debt, he entrusted them to the Negro and continued his practice and his business of land speculation.

The Negro neglected to do much branding, and the cattle roamed free, growing and multiplying on the open Texas range and straying far from their home ranch. Consequently the herd had scattered when the lawyer sold his land, cattle and brand in 1856.

The lawyer's name was Samuel A. Maverick, and the buyer of his ranch was A. Toutant Beauregard, an active and ambitious cattleman. Beauregard sent his men riding over several counties, searching for Maverick's cattle.

Whenever they found an animal unbranded, they claimed it as Maverick's. Thanks to a Negro cowboy's carelessness and Beauregard's enterprise, every wandering animal, unbranded and unclaimed, soon came to be called a maverick, and hunting for such animals was called mavericking. Even men, for that matter, were called mavericks if they were free and independent and wore no man's brand.[1]

Most of the first Negro cowboys were slaves, not mavericks. Brought by their masters from the old South, they arrived in a new country and were set to learning a new trade. Some were taught by Mexican vaqueros, some by their white masters, and others by Indians like those of the Caddo Confederacy, who had learned to herd and handle cattle.

At the beginning of the twentieth century, when old cattlemen and cowboys talked of their youth, they remembered how their parents had moved to Texas with families, goods, cattle and slaves. One slave, for instance, came with N. M. Dennis and Joe Dennis, who left Arkansas in November, 1845, with their wives, seventeen children, one ox-wagon and five hundred hogs. Two of the older boys and the slave made the trip on foot, driving the hogs through days and nights so cold that the poorly clad Negro nearly froze to death. Two of the hogs did freeze.[2] More slaves came with William G. Butler's family from Mississippi at a time "when Texas was young and raw and the bad man seemed ever ready to get the better of the good man, because there were more of them." [3] Another settler described a trek made by his family in 1852; he remembered "the start for Texas, father and mother, twelve children, and seven negro slaves, traveling in covered wagons, each drawn by two yoke of oxen." [4] R. T. Mellard recalled that his father had been a Mississippi slaveholder so impressed with the vast possibilities of Texas "that he sold his farm on the Pearl River, loaded his family and slaves in buggies and wagons and started." [5] So came many of the pioneer cattlemen, bringing with them their wives, children and slaves, as Texas colonists had done ever since the Austins, father and son, had promoted the colonization of Texas.

Some of the colonists speeded their start in the cattle business by trading slaves for stock. George Reynolds told of coming to Texas in 1847, when he was sixteen. His father purchased a large herd of cattle, "paying in part with a negro girl, valued at $1,000, and giving the difference in gold." [6] And George F. Hindes wrote, "We lived in Caldwell county until the fall of 1856, when my father sold a likely negro woman to Major Fields for stock cattle, and we started west to grow up with the country." [7]

Certainly the country grew rapidly, just as it had been growing for more than a decade before Mr. Hindes sold his Negro woman. When Texas entered the Union in 1845, it had about 100,000 white settlers and 35,000 slaves. By 1861, when Texas seceded from the Union, it had more than 430,000 white settlers and 182,000 slaves. Settlement was almost entirely east of the Pecos River and south of the Dallas–Fort Worth area. Although many of the settlers and most of the slaves were on plantations, growing and chopping cotton, many worked in the cattle business, for it has been estimated that nearly 4,000,000 cattle grazed on the Texas range at the start of the Civil War.[8]

Ranchers living west of the Nueces River employed comparatively few Negro slaves as cowhands. One reason was that proximity to Mexico and an established local population assured ranches of adequate numbers of skilled vaqueros, long experienced with ropes and branding irons.[9]

Still another reason was that the same proximity to Mexico made escape attractive. Across the border, slaves found sympathy and refuge; and despite all precautions, thousands of them escaped to freedom in Mexico before the Civil War. Even slaves as far north and east as Austin thought of Mexico as the Promised Land. As early as 1845 the Houston *Telegraph and Texas Register* reported the escape of twenty-five Negroes from Bastrop: "They were mounted on some of the best horses that could be found, and several of them were well armed. It is supposed that some Mexican has enticed them to flee to the Mexican settlements west of the Rio Grande." [10] There must have been many such enticements, for by 1854 the Austin *State Times* estimated that more than 200,000 Negroes had escaped to Mexico—an impossibly large estimate.[11]

To the east of the Nueces River, vaqueros taught other cowboys to operate in the heavy coastal brush. Here really wild cattle ranged through bleak, rough country. And here men nearly as wild did the roughest work cowboys can do. While men on easier ranges hunted wild cattle with catch dogs and neck oxen, the dogs trailing and baying the cattle and the neck oxen leading in roped outlaws, cowboys in the brush country rode in alone, roped wild cattle in scrub thickets and led out what they had roped.

Occasionally a Negro cowboy was spared some of the most dangerous work. Because he was himself valuable property, his owner protected him. Therefore white bronc busters frequently were hired to ride bucking outlaw horses; they sat in dangerous saddles, taking the shocks of bucking, sometimes bleeding from nose and mouth, sometimes fainting, risking rupture, mutilation, or death [12] while expensive Negroes watched from a corral fence. Thus Abel (Shanghai) Pierce, a white cowboy who became one of the greatest of the early cattlemen, was only nineteen when he was hired by Bradford Grimes in 1853 as a bronc buster on Grimes's ranch near Palacios. He was paid fifteen dollars a month.

Grimes owned a number of Negro cowboys, as well as many wild, unbroken horses. One day in 1853, when Grimes and Pierce were working with an all-Negro crew of cowhands, they started to break a particularly unruly stallion. A Negro roped him, and Abel Pierce held the horse's head while the horse was saddled and a Negro cowboy mounted. When the horse was released, it went off in high jumps, spinning and jolting its rider. Just then, according to one account, "a high-pitched voice called from the ranch house: 'Bradford! Bradford! Put Abel on the bad 'uns. Those Negroes are worth a thousand dollars apiece. One might get killed!' " [13]

Many another slaveholder shared this kind of prudence in guarding his property. It was carried to its logical extreme during the Civil War by an old slaveholder who wrote to his son: "I hear you are likely to have a big battle soon, and I write to tell you not to let Sam go into the fighting with you. Keep him in the rear, for that nigger is worth a thousand dollars." [14]

Negro cowboys were most numerous in eastern Texas; and between the Trinity River and the Louisiana border, all-Negro crews were common. There were even a few free Negroes running cattle in eastern Texas before the Civil War. In what are now Orange and Jefferson counties, for instance, Aaron Ashworth, a free Negro, owned 2,570 head of cattle in 1850, a herd larger than that of anyone else in his county. He also owned slaves and employed a white schoolmaster to tutor his four children. He had first come to Texas in 1833 and had obtained an order of survey from the Mexican government enabling him to locate and claim land. When, after the Texas revolution, the Texas Congress ordered all free Negroes out of the Republic, Ashworth's neighbors interceded for him and his two brothers, and a special act of the Congress granted him relief from the general banishment. Again, two years later, a special act of the Texas Congress confirmed him and several other free Negroes in the ownership of their lands.[15]

From one side of Texas to the other, Negroes worked in the cattle business before the Civil War. North of Texas in the Indian Nations, thousands of Negroes were neighbors or slaves of the Five Civilized Tribes—the Cherokees, Chickasaws, Choctaws, Creeks and Seminoles. For their Indian masters many of them worked in cotton fields, pigpens or pecan orchards; others herded cattle. Still farther north, in Kansas, there were very few Negroes before the Civil War. Although "Bleeding Kansas" was a prewar battleground between proslavery and antislavery forces, the census of 1860 showed fewer than seven hundred Negroes in the state.[16] These Negroes were not in the cattle business; cattle were bred and marketed by settlers with small herds, by men operating as they had in New England or Illinois. Cowboys were not needed on these fenced-in Kansas farms.

Most of the rest of the Great Plains was still "desert" where buffalo moved in mighty tides from Canada to the Staked Plains of Texas, followed by Indians who had not yet seriously been threatened by white civilization. That civilization, faced with the woodless, waterless flatland, had leapfrogged to the Rocky Mountains and the West Coast. Covered wagons had driven through to Oregon, California, Utah and Colorado, with hardly a stop along the way. There were few whites, fewer Negroes, in the

West between Kansas and Pike's Peak, between Minnesota and the Oregon Country.

Thus the story of the Negro cowboys began in Texas and the Indian Nations before the Civil War. There thousands of Negroes, most slaves, some free, learned to ride and rope and brand.

·❦ 3 ❧·

Free Men and Wild Cattle

While Negro slaves and white Texans learned to handle cattle, their masters and employers looked for markets. To the west lay the sparse settlements of Mexico, New Mexico and Southern California, already supplied with native stock; to the north, a thousand miles of unsettled plain; to the south, land's end, the Gulf of Mexico.

The only possible markets lay to the east, but to drive through Louisiana meant losing cattle in almost impassable country; and driving toward Arkansas or the Indian Nations meant pioneering in unknown country and fighting Indians and lawless whites. Many ranchers, despairing of a market for beef, slaughtered some animals for their hides and tallow and let the rest multiply. According to Jo Mora, "It soon got to the point where a Texas stockman's poverty was reckoned by the number of cattle he owned. The more he had, the poorer he was." [1]

Some drives did go through Louisiana in 1842, but the hardships along the way and the low New Orleans prices discouraged followers. Four years later a herd of a thousand head was driven to Ohio and sold as feeding stock to local farmers. In 1856 a few drovers reached St. Louis, where they "realized a moderate profit," [2] and in 1857 P. R. Mitchell, with three others, gathered 1,200 steers in southern Texas for a drive to Chicago. With Mitchell rode a Negro cowboy known as Big-Mouth Henry because "he was a great singer and could almost charm a bunch of Longhorns." Helped by luck and Big-Mouth Henry's voice, Mitchell drove through Arkansas and swam the herd across the Mississippi some twenty-five miles above St. Louis.[3]

The two decades before the Civil War saw other attempts to sell cattle. Some daring cattlemen risked the fifteen-hundred-mile trek to the California gold fields. The few who made it sold their stock for high prices, but their success attracted few imitators.[4] Others tried shipping stock from Gulf ports to New Orleans and Mobile, but high freight charges ate up their profits. One steamship company, the Morgan Line, "loaded on as many of these cattle as could be crowded between decks, when other and more profitable freight was lacking. The company itself paid for these and sold them in New Orleans and Mobile, for the freight charged to anyone outside the company was so prohibitive that it precluded all private shipment. The plantations of Cuba could use beef if it were cheap enough, and now and then a shipload of longhorns was sold in Cuban ports." [5]

Selling cattle by fits and starts was unsatisfactory. Texas herds multiplied, moving out over broad ranges. And Texas Negroes, their population swelled by steady importation of new slaves, also increased until Texas became one of the great slaveholding states. Most of the Negroes worked on cotton and sugar cane plantations, tending crops that could be shipped profitably from Gulf ports. Much of Texas prospered on the eve of the Civil War.

Then John Brown raided Harper's Ferry, and Abraham Lincoln won the election. Secessionist sentiment grew, winning over the opposition of Governor Sam Houston. On March 2, 1861, Texas seceded from the Union. Three days later it voted to join the Confederacy. One month later it was at war.

Although some Texans joined the Union forces, more than fifty thousand fought for the South, serving through battles at Mansfield, Chickamauga, the Wilderness and Gettysburg. Their senators and representatives sat in the Confederate Congress. Texas ranches and farms helped to feed Confederate troops. Texans fought the last battle of the war, winning a futile victory at Palmito Ranch more than a month after the surrender of General Robert E. Lee.

Though Texas never suffered the horror of having great battles fought on its soil, and though no Union army marched through Texas to the sea, firing buildings and laying waste the countryside, the end of the war found the state bankrupt and demoralized. Confederate money was worthless, and good money was scarce—though not so scarce as elsewhere in the South. Federal troops occupied the state, and the future looked uncertain.

The history of the Reconstruction in Texas is both complicated and controversial. The Negroes had been freed, but most of them were illiterate, unskilled field hands. Some were skilled artisans, others capable cowboys. A few intelligent and educated Negroes held responsible posts in Reconstruction and post-Reconstruction governments. Nine Negroes sat in the constitutional convention of 1869, and six in the convention of 1875–1876, which wrote the present constitution of Texas. Negroes served in the Texas legislature from 1871 to 1895.

Negroes also served in the newly organized state police,

as well as in units of the Army stationed in Texas. Some undoubtedly abused their new authority, just as others were abused by white Texans merely for doing their duty. The state police, the Freedman's Bureau, and the Union League were met by the Ku Klux Klan and illegal terror. In Texas as in other Southern states, Reconstruction left a bitter heritage of racial antagonism.

This bitterness was strongest in eastern Texas, where large numbers of Negroes were employed in farming. It was less marked in the cattle country, although it certainly existed. There some cattlemen protested that Negroes were "rambling around in idleness, and will either not work at all or demand four prices for what they but half do." Negroes were accused, according to Wayne Gard, "of getting drunk, flourishing weapons, stealing horses, and insulting the whites." [6]

The whites were easily insulted. One Negro was plowing a field when Jack Helms, the white cowboy sheriff of De Witt County, went riding by. The Negro left off plowing, climbed up on the rail fence and began to whistle "Yankee Doodle" as Helms passed. Helms drew his powder and ball Colt and shot the Negro between the eyes. Then Helms rode on, and the Negro's body lay where it fell until only the bones remained.[7] Other Negroes fell victim to outlaws like John Wesley Hardin, who was proud of his reputation as a "nigger killer." [8] Still others were murdered by Sam Grant, a hired gun who killed white men as well as black. One white man he wounded and nearly killed was Charlie Siringo, the early cowboy writer. Only the timely intervention of Lige, a Negro cowboy who "galloped into camp out of the heavy timber and brush," saved Siringo's life.[9]

A history of Texas postwar racial antagonism and its

resultant violence would make a long and bloody story. Racial warfare persisted far into the twentieth century. Many Negroes died, and frequently those who lived survived only by fighting or by becoming respectful Uncle Toms. All Negroes suffered in some degree from social, legal and economic sanctions.

Upon Negro cowboys, however, these sanctions fell less heavily than upon many other Negroes, for as cowboys they held a well-defined place in an early established social and economic hierarchy. A cattle outfit was an almost feudal organization with a chief who demanded and got personal loyalty. His men, particularly in larger outfits, were organized with military precision, with foremen as lieutenants and top hands corresponding to noncommissioned officers. In such a unit, tightly organized and operating in a womanless vacuum, the Negro cowboy was welcomed as a hand or even as a top hand, though rarely as a foreman. Jim Perry, who worked for more than twenty years as a great rider, roper and cook for the vast XIT Ranch, once said, "If it weren't for my damned old black face I'd have been boss of one of these divisions long ago." One of the white cowboys who rode with him agreed, saying "he no doubt would have." [10]

In lacking "upward mobility," to use the current jargon, the Negro cowboy resembled the Negro cavalryman, who could become a trooper or even a noncommissioned officer, but who was almost always officered by whites. The Negro cowboy differed from the cavalryman in that his outfit was usually integrated, with whites and Negroes working, eating and living together.

The working and living were rough. Cattlemen returned from the Civil War to find their millions of cattle scattered on the plains, lurking in the brush and hidden in the coulees. During more than four years of war, hundreds of thousands of calves had grown to wild cows and longhorned bulls—unbranded, unclaimed, untamed and dangerous.

Many were rounded up and slaughtered just for their hides and tallow. J. Frank Dobie, one of the great historians of the West and of the cattle business, has described the hide and tallow factories "that operated in Texas during the late sixties and early seventies, when cattle were hardly worth stealing and when a cow's hide was actually worth more than a live cow. That was when old steers with horn-spreads wider than the length of a man from his feet to the tips of his fingers on upraised arm were driven by the hundreds and thousands to such plants as that above Brazoria. Here Negroes shucked the hides off, tried out the tallow, and then skidded the meat down chutes into the Brazos River, where catfish gorged themselves and grew to gigantic size. A similar establishment at Quintana at the mouth of the Brazos so attracted sharks that people were afraid to go in swimming." [11]

While some Negroes skinned steers on the Brazos, others joined with white cowboys to ride into the brush and hunt for wild cattle. Each cowboy had a few horses, a bag of corn bread and dried beef, and a length of good rope as well as a number of shorter pieces for hog-tying animals. Once on a hunt, he led a "bleak, stark, wary life." [12]

Typical of such men was Henry Beckwith, a Negro cowboy who hunted cattle in thickets so dense that neither horse, man nor cattle could see for more than a few yards, where a cowboy and his horse found their way with ear and nose. Beckwith carried no bedding, slept on dried cattle runs or spread his horseblanket over sticks, drank black coffee mixed with chili juice and rode much of the time at night. Perhaps because of his nocturnal ways, the

Mexican cowboys who sometimes rode with him called him the Coyote.

Like a coyote, he needed little sleep. If it was cold he might build a very small fire and hunker down over it all night, drinking coffee and dozing. Or he might just "wallow a couple of times," and then go on to another day's work. As J. Frank Dobie said (and the story is his), the Coyote represented "intensely what brush and brush cattle could and did make of men." [13]

What men made of cattle was great empires. Down on the Santa Gertrudis spread, Richard King used the profits of wartime trade with Mexico to build the enormous King Ranch. Men like Colonel Goodnight and Shanghai Pierce rounded up thousands of cattle for drives to markets they hoped they could find.

George Saunders, an old trail driver, waited nearly fifty years before he wrote his description of Shanghai Pierce. "My first recollection of Mr. Pierce," he said, "was just after the Civil War when he bought fat cattle all over South Texas. I remember seeing him many times come to our camp where he had contracts to receive beeves. He was a large portly man, always rode a fine horse, and would be accompanied by a negro who led a pack horse loaded with gold and silver which, when he reached our camp, was dumped on the ground and remained there until the cattle were classed and counted out to him, then he would empty the money on a blanket in camp and pay it out to the different stockmen from whom he had purchased the cattle." [14] Charlie Siringo also remembered Shanghai Pierce, for he visited Shanghai's headquarters near Matagorda in 1871. "There were about fifty cowboys at the headquarter ranch," he wrote, "a few Mexicans and a few negroes among them. . . . 'Shanghai' Pierce and his crew of cowboys had just arrived from the Rio Grande River with three hundred wild Mexican ponies for the spring work. . . . Meals were made up of meat from a fat heifer calf, with corn bread, molasses, and black coffee. The negro cook, who drove the mess-wagon, generally had two kinds of meat, the calf ribs broiled before the camp-fire, and a large Dutch oven full of loin, sweet-breads, and heart, mixed with flour gravy." [15]

Charlie Siringo, like everyone else who met Shanghai Pierce, never forgot him. But Siringo also had good reason to remember many of the Negro cowboys he met in Texas, for one or another of them was always saving or trying to save his life. Lige had kept him from being killed by Sam Grant. Another Negro tried to help him when he stopped at Matagorda. While attempting to mount his horse, Siringo fell and was dragged with one foot caught in the stirrup. The horse was trailing a long hackamore rope fastened to its nose. "While being dragged on my back," Siringo later wrote, "I could see a negro cowboy, who was present, running his best, afoot, trying to catch the end of the rope. At one time he was within a few feet of the dragging rope. Then I felt hopeful. But when I saw the end of the rope crawling farther away from the negro, I lost hope, and began to wonder what kind of place hell was, and whether I should be treated with kindness." Fortunately for Siringo, his worries proved premature, because he managed to free his foot from the stirrup.[16]

But he remained accident-prone. In the same season, he reported, "I roped a large animal and got my horse jerked over backwards on top of me and in the horse getting up he got me all wound up in the rope, so that I couldn't free myself until relieved by 'Jack,' a negro man who was near at hand." [17]

Anyone who reads Charlie Siringo's *The Texas Cowboy,
or Fifteen Years on the Hurricane Deck of a Spanish Pony,*
the first factual memoir published by a cowboy, must be
impressed by the number of Negroes with whom Siringo
worked in Texas. In 1871 he and a Negro tried unsuccessfully to rope and capture an old horse thief.[18] During the
next few years he often swapped or raced horses with Negroes, and when he took jobs, they were frequently with
crews that included Negro cowboys.

Going to work for Charles Word on a ranch near Goliad
during the middle 1870's, Siringo joined a crew assigned
to the branding pen. It worked in pairs, roping and tying
down animals because the pen had no branding chute.
Siringo's partner was "Ike Word, an old Negro who used
to belong to the Word family, and who was the best roper
in the crowd . . ." At first Ike distrusted his new helper,
but Siringo soon proved that he had grown less awkward
and more skillful than he had been a few years earlier. He
demonstrated superior skill with a rope, and then he rode
a dangerous wild horse. From that time on, Siringo boasted,
"old Ike recognized me as a genuine cow-puncher." [19]

Just as Siringo remembered the Negro cowboys who
worked with him, so they remembered Siringo. One of
them later talked to J. Frank Dobie on a "coldish, misty
December day, toward sundown, in the year 1931, [when
Dobie] rode up to a ranch house on the San Bernard River,
in Brazoria County, Texas. A white man of advanced
years was out in a pen with three Negro cowboys." When
Dobie met the Negroes, he found that one of them was
named Jim Keller. He immediately remembered, he later
wrote, "that Charlie Siringo had spoken of a Jim Keller
who once loaned him a saddle horse. . . . We went inside

the house to drink coffee and talk. Somehow what he told me lit up the Charlie Siringo of mavericks, mustangs, mossy-horned steers, fenceless coastal ranges, hide and tallow factories and Shanghai Pierce's bellowing voice more than anything else I have met outside of Siringo's first autobiography." [20]

A book like Siringo's is full of references to Negro cowboys in Texas. So, too, are the short notes that old Texans wrote when they attempted to recollect the first stirrings of the postwar cattle business. J. B. Murrah, for instance, remembered moving to Bell County in 1866: ". . . myself and a negro helped my uncle drive two hundred head of horses through on the trip. This was my first trail work." [21] As Jo Mora wrote, the early Texas cowboys "were just a cross section of Texan pioneer humanity, and you couldn't create a type model for all of them no more than you can for college boys, or carpenters, or bell hops. There were a few large ranch owners who might even be town dwellers part of the time; smaller ranchers and stockmen; those of the back range Hill-Billy type; even poor white trash; and not a few negro hands." [22] Of these last, many were like Pete Staples, a Negro cowboy from whom J. Frank Dobie collected stories of lost mines and treasure. Staples came to Texas as a slave before the Civil War. He lived in the border country working as a cowboy among Mexicans, and took part in early drives to Kansas. In later years, after he had married a Mexican woman, he lived in Mexico or in western Texas, riding as a cowboy or cooking for cow camps.[23]

As the cattle range spread north and west in Texas after the Civil War, Negroes were among the cowboys who rode over it. They came out of the brush country and the coastal

plains as the cattle spreads moved west toward the Pecos
River and north toward the Staked Plains. They rode in
wild country where men used brutal language. In Texas
they were "niggers," and some men were known as "Nigger Joe," "Nigger Tom" or "Nigger Add." Wherever they
rode, the epithet followed and became an adjective: a "nigger horse" in Texas was, literally enough, a black horse;
and a horse whose toes turned out was "nigger heeled." A
dessert made of raisins in dough was "nigger in a blanket."
Perhaps the most insulting of these usages to Negroes, who
were among the best riders and horse trainers in the West,
was the use of "nigger brand" for "a galled sore on a horse's
back caused by careless riding." [24]

Then, as now, Negroes were frequently called "boys."
Even today, in the North as in the South, many a Negro
man discovers that a condition of his employment is being
called a "boy." As a man, he finds this usage insulting, as
frequently it is intended to be; historians find it ambiguous
or confusing when it appears in records or memoirs. In the
following story, for example, the age of the "boy" is difficult to determine:

"After the Civil War, Robert Hall, a noted Indian
fighter, was catching wild cattle on the Nueces. A Negro
boy came in one evening and reported that he had roped
a two-year-old maverick bull that morning and left him
tied in a thicket. For some reason nobody went to brand
the bull and release him. Exactly twenty days later Hall
while hunting panthers heard his dogs baying something.
Galloping up, he found them barking at the bull, which
was on his feet, attempting to get loose." [25]

Ironically enough, all cowhands—whether white or
black—early came to be called cow*boys*. Some of them enjoyed the title, but others, particularly Texans, resented it.

Jim Shaw, for instance, who trailed cattle from Texas to Wyoming, always objected to having his horses called "ponies" and his crews called "boys."

"Hell, man," he said, "they were horses and men." [26]

·◦[4]◦·

North to Abilene

At the end of the war the cowboys and cattle broke out of Texas.

Two great markets lay to the northwest and the northeast. Northwest were hungry miners, soldiers and reservation Indians, as well as northern range ranchers eager to buy breeding and feeder stock. Northeast were railheads leading to a beef-hungry East and Midwest. Neither market was easy to reach, but Texas cattlemen tried for both, and they drove through at almost the same time. Arbitrarily, then, let the story of the drives begin with those to the northeastern market.

The first route was the Shawnee Trail, which left Dallas and Fort Worth, crossed the Red River at Preston and proceeded through the Indian Nations nearly to Baxter Springs. There it branched, with trails leading through Missouri to St. Louis or Sedalia and with other trails leading through eastern Kansas to St. Joseph or Kansas City. The only difficulty with the Shawnee Trail, and that nearly insuperable, was that it led through the most populous part of the Indian Nations, through areas where Indian and

Negro settlers demanded beef or money in toll or tribute, to the borders of eastern Kansas or western Missouri, where herds might be stolen, stampeded or destroyed by angry farmers fearing damage to their crops or cattle fever carried by Texas stock. Kansas and Missouri had laws barring the entrance of Texas cattle, and both had bands of determined men prepared to stop any herds that crossed their borders. The Shawnee Trail, therefore, soon became known as a dead end or a disaster, and access to Eastern markets seemed to be blocked.[1]

A second trail was made possible and profitable by the initiative of Joseph G. McCoy, a young cattle dealer who established a market and shipping center on the western edge of the Kansas settlements. He took advantage of a loophole in the Kansas law barring Texas cattle: the law did permit their entrance into the western half of the state. And the loophole became valuable when the Kansas Pacific branch of the Union Pacific extended its track westward.[2] After making contracts for favorable shipping rates and for commissions on shipments, McCoy established a cattle center at the little town of Abilene. There he persuaded the railroad to build a hundred-car switch, and he built a shipping yard to hold more than a thousand cattle (as well as pens and feed lots that held several thousand more). From his shipping yard he could load a train of forty cattle cars in two hours.

McCoy did more than locate a shipping point; he established a marketplace to which buyers could come and at which cattlemen could sell their herds. He erected a hotel to house crowds of cattlemen and built a livery stable to handle large numbers of horses. Then he publicized Abilene widely, sending representatives into the Indian Nations and Texas. Thus he established the terminus of a great new trail in 1867.[3]

Now best known as the Chisholm Trail, taking its name from an early trader and guide who ran wagons and cattle from the Indian Nations to Kansas, the new trail once had many names. Among these, according to Wayne Gard, were the Kansas Trail, the Abilene Trail, and the Eastern Trail.[4] Whatever its name, however, it opened a way for Texas cattlemen.

Its main stem ran from the Rio Grande to Austin and Waco and Fort Worth. It was intersected and joined by innumerable feeder trails leading from east and west Texas. Wayne Gard quotes T. C. Richardson, who wrote, "A thousand minor trails fed the main routes, and many an old-timer who as a boy saw a herd of stately Longhorns, piloted by bandannaed, booted, and spurred men, lived with the firm conviction that the . . . Chisholm cattle trail passed right over yonder." [5]

The advantage of the Chisholm Trail was that north of Fort Worth it lay far west of the Shawnee Trail, moving into less heavily settled portions of the Indian Territory and into very sparsely settled portions of Kansas. Consequently trail drivers, although they had to guard against Comanche raids, were temporarily free from the blackmail of Indian and Negro settlements and from the active hostility of Kansas homesteaders. The grazing was good, the trail was well watered, the rivers—except when they were in flood—easily forded; good camps and bed grounds for cattle were frequent.

So beginning in 1867 cattlemen threw their herds onto this trail, and with their cowhands began driving toward Abilene. As the cattle moved up the Chisholm Trail—and as they were to move up other trails to Dodge, to Ogallala

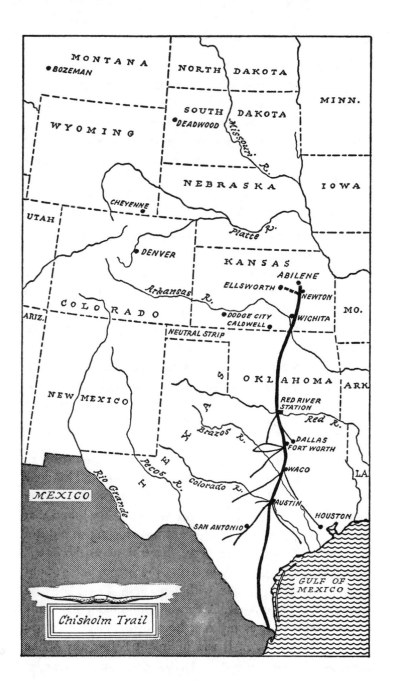

Chisholm Trail

and to the northern ranges—the cattlemen perfected the organization and operation of their trail crews.

The number of cattle in a single herd, it was early agreed, should not be much over twenty-five hundred.[6] To attempt to drive many more was to create a slow, unwieldy monster, hard to graze or bed down, and dangerous in a mill, stampede or water crossing. Herds of three thousand and even four thousand or more moved up the trail, but they proved hard to handle. One old trail driver, George W. Brock, reported his experience with a herd of four thousand three- and four-year-old cattle: they stampeded, and Brock ended up in a ditch. This is how he told it: "In this stampede my horse ran into a ditch that night. The cause of him doing this was because I was trying to point the cattle away from the ditch and a negro (Russ Jones) was on the opposite side of the herd trying to do the same thing, and the result was that instead of pointing them away from the ditch, we drove them straight into it." In this one stampede Brock's crew lost more than four hundred head of cattle, an expensive reduction in the size of the herd.[7]

Even larger herds went north. Dr. J. Hargis drove six thousand cattle up the trail in 1866. When he and his crew reached the Red River, it was in flood, overflowing its banks. They got the cattle across, but then they found that the Negro who owned the ferry at the crossing would not attempt to take the men over. "Several of us cowboys," Hargis wrote, "tried to swim across, the stream being about three hundred yards wide, with very high waves, but none were successful except R. C. Farmer and myself and I only upon second trial, as my first horse drowned and I was forced to another. . . . It was midnight before any of the others could cross over." So Hargis and Farmer were left to try to manage six thousand cattle until the rest of their crew could join them.[8]

"The largest trail herds," according to J. Frank Dobie, "were those massed for defense against Indians. The record—in so far as I have learned—was topped by 15,000 cattle started from the Brazos River, in lower Texas, for California, in 1869. They were owned by a number of ex-Confederate men dissatisfied with having to live under carpet-baggers who insisted on the equality of Negroes with white men. There were two hundred people with this outfit, many wagons, and 1200 horses. The cattle were driven in four divisions, but whenever there was danger of a night attack by Indians, they were bedded together in one vast herd." [9]

Exceptionally large herds rarely went up the Chisholm Trail. Herds smaller than twenty-five hundred were frequently seen, but they had the disadvantage of being more expensive to drive. Whenever possible, they were thrown together to make a more efficient operation. Any herd, no matter how small, required at least a minimum crew for a long drive. An average crew contained about eleven men: the trail boss, eight cowboys, a wrangler and a cook.

On a drive, the trail boss was like the captain of a ship, exercising complete authority and demanding and receiving loyalty and cooperation. He made all important decisions, controlling the speed of the herd, going ahead to find safe bed-ground, calculating distances between watering places and anticipating hazards. Frequently he owned the herd; sometimes he was a ranch foreman or a professional trail driver; and occasionally he was just one of the top hands.

The cowboys worked as a team. Usually two rode "on point," riding near the lead cattle to head them in the right direction and to slow or halt them when necessary. Four more rode "on swing," two patrolling on each side of the herd to keep it strung out and to keep cattle from straying too far off the trail. And the last two, riding "on drag," stayed with the stragglers at the rear and ate the dust of the herd.

How the cowboys operated depended in part on the cattle they drove. The commonest kind on long drives was the beef herd, all steers, headed for market or for the northern ranges. A beef herd traveled comparatively fast, sometimes as much as fifteen miles in a day, although no trail boss wanted to push his cattle so fast that they lost weight on the trail. A "wet herd," made up entirely of cows, traveled more slowly. It started as early in the spring as possible and grazed slowly up the trail, dropping calves almost every day. On comparatively short drives, one cowboy drove a calf wagon to carry the newborn, letting the calves out at night to join their mothers.

With mixed herds that traveled faster, it was frequently impossible to save the calves. Ed Nichols described how Ab Blocker, one of the most famous of the trail bosses, handled the problem: "A big six-foot Negro named Frank was known as Blocker's roper. He didn't work with the herd at night like the rest of the boys; he just did the roping. When they rounded up cattle to start on the trail there was generally a number of young calves. These were too young to travel and if there was no one to give them to Frank shot them and with the help of the other men drove the mothers off. When night come it was his job to rope and hobble these cows to keep them from going back. He had four good roping horses and was the best hand with a rope I ever saw." [10]

Ab Blocker hired large numbers of Negro cowboys. One

old trail driver remembered sitting in Doan's Store in 1879, some years after most drivers had abandoned the Chisholm Trail and had begun to use the Western Trail that led to Dodge City (Doan's Store was built at a then popular Red River crossing). As he sat there in the little adobe store, "someone struck up a lively air on a French harp and the door opened and in sailed a hat followed closely by a big black fellow who commenced to dance. It was one of Ab Blocker's niggers who had been sent up for the mail, giving first notice of the herd's arrival." [11] And Jack Potter wrote that his interest in old-time trail and range cooks began the day that Ab Blocker's Negro cook, Gordon Davis, rode into Dodge City mounted on his left wheel ox, fiddle in hand, playing "Buffalo Girls, Can't You Come Out Tonight?" [12] Blocker himself owed his dignity, if not his life, to his Negro roper Frank. A visitor to Blocker's camp wrote of arriving just as the outfit was nooning on the trail, with its chuck wagon stopped and coffee hot. Frank rode into camp, threw the bridle reins over his horse's head and climbed off to get a cup of coffee. Just then Ab Blocker, who had walked away from the camp, yelled for help. Frank looked up and saw Ab running with a steer after him. Frank "threw down his cup, ran to his horse, tossed the bridle over its head and jumped in the saddle. It was the quickest, prettiest thing I nearly ever saw. He turned his horse toward the steer, stuck spurs to him and began doing his rope as it ran. He made a loop not much bigger than the steer's horns was wide. The steer had tucked its head to hook Ab when Frank rode up behind it, whirled the rope around his head one time, and hollered, 'Hold on, boss, don't go no fu'ther.' He threw the rope over the steer's horns, the horse sat down and the steer changed ends. His tail was almost touching Ab." [13]

As a roping specialist, Frank was excused from night herding. All the other cowboys, however, rode night watch, usually riding two at a time. Sometimes, if the bed-grounds were secure, the cattle quiet, and the night calm, only one cowboy would take each shift. Telling time by the stars, he would wake another cowboy when his shift was finished. One of the common stories of the range, according to J. Frank Dobie, told of the tenderfoot Negro cowboy put on first night guard and instructed to call his relief when the North Star set. The next morning he rode in, tired and sleepy-eyed, to find his relief enjoying a cup of coffee after a good night's sleep. The tenderfoot complained that he had watched the star all night but that it had never moved. His first lesson in astronomy had been a hard one.[14]

A trail drive could take two or three long and arduous months. Without a certain basic understanding and agreement among the men, Abilene would have been as far away as Eldorado. Generally each crew developed an esprit de corps, an attitude not unlike that commonly thought of as the code of the West. The cowboy was both competitive and protective. His pride was such that he would not willingly let any man get the better of him in a physical act, but he found it unthinkable not to offer himself if a member of the outfit was in danger. Willingness to work almost day and night to the point of exhaustion, sometimes under the most strenuous conditions, was taken for granted. In an eleven-man crew that had a twenty-four-hour responsibility for twenty-five hundred longhorns, there were no standby man-hours. Everyone had to carry his own share; no one could let down or become too sick to work. In times of crisis the cowboy stayed in the saddle indefinitely.

Devotion could be carried too far, as one old-timer remembered when he described a death in the Texas Panhandle: "We had a negro cowboy named George," he wrote, "who was not very well clad because he liked to pike at monte too well to buy clothes. We all had colds and coughs till it was like a bunch of Texas pot hounds baying a 'possum when we tried to sleep. One bitter night I was near George on herd and tried to get him to go to the chuck wagon and turn his horse loose, but he was too game for that. His teeth were chattering as he said to me, 'I can stand it if the rest of you all can.' Presently I saw him lean over his saddle horn, coughing, and he looked like he was losing his breath. By the time I got to him he was off his horse, as dead as a mackerel and as stiff as a poker. He had simply frozen to death sitting on that horse. We placed his body in the chuck wagon on his bed and drove to the Palo Duro and on the highest hill we could find we planted the poor black boy, rolled in his blankets. The ground was sandy; so we could dig a grave deep enough that the coyotes would not claw into it." [15]

Few cowboys froze to death, but many rode long hours through wind and rain. George Chapman, a Texas trail driver, told of crossing the Guadalupe River at the start of a drive up the Chisholm Trail. "Just after nightfall," he wrote, "we had a severe storm with lots of thunder, lightning, and cold. It was so dark most of the hands left us and went to the chuck wagon except W. T. Henson, myself, and old Chief, a negro." With only three night herders left, the cattle drifted and scattered, and it took the whole crew more than two days to get them back together.[16]

A similar story was told by J. M. Hankins, who went up the trail in 1871. Near the Guadalupe River he experienced his first stampede. "Early in the night," he wrote, "it had rained, and I was on the watch. The herd began drifting, and the boss and several others came out to help with the cattle, and after the rain ceased we got them stopped, when Rany Fentress, a negro who had been in stampedes before, came to where I was in the lead and told me to move further away. About that time one of the boys struck a match to light a pipe, and the flare frightened the big steers and they began to run. I was knocked down three times, but managed to stay with the pony, and came out with the drags, which I stayed with until daylight." [17]

Hankins was forunate in that, having been warned, he survived and stayed with the herd. Some cowboys died in stampedes, and others were lost for hours or days. G. M. Carson described a stampede "one dark night" somewhere in the Indian Territory. During the confusion two cowboys—one of them "a Negro named Joe Tasby"—got separated from the herd and the rest of the crew for twenty-four hours.[18]

A stampede was only one of the hazards a cowboy faced on a long trail drive. As Joseph S. Cruze, another trail driver, wrote, "Everything was then tough, wild and wooly, and it was dangerous to be safe." [19] Every river was a potential killer when it was in flood, and dangerous river crossings claimed lives. Cowboys, if they could swim at all, were rarely strong swimmers, and the treacherous currents of high, muddy rivers were made even more dangerous by struggling cattle and horses, floating branches and debris, and hidden rocks and snags. Not all cowboys were so lucky as the Negro who had a narrow escape in a crossing of the flooding Canadian River. Near the middle his horse sank under him, leaving him stranded on a sandbar. S. B. Brite, another cowboy, rode to his rescue. Swimming his horse to the sandbar, Brite instructed the stranded cowboy to hang on to the horse's tail and then swam the horse back, pulling the man behind him. Once ashore, the rescued cowboy thanked Brite and told him that the horse's tail had been just like "the hand of Providence." [20]

Still another tale of a providential tail was told by R. F. Galbreath, of Devine, Texas, who remembered crossing the swollen Red River in 1873. One of his crew was Tony Williams, a Negro cowhand who got aboard a mule and rode point to lead the herd across. Williams made it well out into the river before a big wave knocked him off his mount. He disappeared into the river, far beyond reach of the other cowboys, who feared that he had drowned. But "in a little while," Galbreath wrote, "we discovered him holding on to the tail of a big beef steer, and when the steer went up the bank Tony was still holding on and went with him." [21]

Stampedes and river crossings, like Indian raids and meetings with outlaws or hostile settlers, were the occasional hazards of the trail. They punctuated the unending routine of drive and night herd, of saddle and hard ground, of coarse food and interrupted sleep. They even relieved the boredom and monotony, for cowboys were frequently forbidden relaxations and diversions possible for other men. Cattlemen who knew the dangers of dissension among their crews made their cowboys pledge not to drink, gamble or swear while on the trail. There is doubt that the cowboys kept their pledge not to swear, but drinking and gambling during the drives were uncommon. Only after a thousand miles of blistering sun, choking dust, drenching rain, filthy clothes and sweat-caked bodies did the boys arrive in Abilene for a day or two of don't-give-a-damn seeing the elephant. Their trail's-end pay of eighty or a hundred dollars could go in one wild night of drinking, gambling and whoring.

During the months on the trail a close relationship was

built up among all members of the crew—among the cowboys, the boss, the cook and the wrangler—that was little affected by differences of race and color. It would, of course, be ridiculous to say that there was no discrimination when men of different races worked together, particularly when most of them were Texans during the bitterness of Reconstruction and post-Reconstruction. But the demands of their job made them transcend much of their prejudice. On a drive, a cowboy's ability to do his work, to handle his share and a little extra, was far more important than his color. To be a good cowboy, one needed first of all to be a good man, for a wild longhorn had no more respect for a white Texan than for a Negro.

An old economic reality helped, too. When there are more jobs than men to fill them, there is less discrimination. And in the beginning, with literally millions of cattle and few experienced cowboys, trail bosses could not afford the luxury of unbridled discrimination. Many contemporary accounts show that some of the best riders, ropers, wranglers and cooks were Negroes.

George W. Saunders, at one time president of the Old Time Trail Drivers Association, estimated that from 1868 to 1895 "fully 35,000 men went up the trail with herds," and of this number "about one-third were negroes and Mexicans." [22]

When nationality or color is mentioned in accounts of the trail drives, far more Negroes than Mexicans are identified. It also appears that Mexicans, although many of them were excellent vaqueros, adapted themselves less well than Negroes to the long drives. They suffered from prejudices nearly as strong as those that worked against Negroes, and they had a language handicap. Unlike the Negroes, who could expect some protection from the law during

Reconstruction days, as well as active sympathy from some old Abolitionists in Kansas, Nebraska and other northern states, the Mexicans were despised foreigners in a strange land. Unlike the Negroes, who found that provisions for Negro troops had opened restaurants, saloons and even whorehouses to them, the Mexicans could expect to find themselves welcome only at the gambling tables. Small wonder, then, that Mexicans appear infrequently in accounts of the drives to Abilene, Dodge City and Cheyenne.

Yet even if all these evidences are discounted, and even if large numbers of Mexican vaqueros are assumed to have ridden the Chisholm Trail, the Western Trail and other trails north, it seems safe to assume that more than five thousand Negro cowboys rode north out of Texas during the three decades following the Civil War.

Understandably, most of the men who wrote of their days on the plains did not designate color or nationality among the cowboys with whom they rode. One finds reminiscences in which a cowboy is introduced by name as one of many others and then several pages later is identified, almost by chance, as a Negro. But from a sampling of writers who seemingly did note race or nationality with some consistency, one can infer that a typical trail crew had among its eight cowboys two or three Negroes. Its boss was almost certain to be white, although a few Negroes led crews up the trail. Its wrangler might be Negro or Mexican. Its cook was likely to be a Negro—usually an ex-cowboy.

A careful reader of Western reminiscences can note frequent references to Negro cowboys. Many of these, retold or quoted in various parts of this book, deal with stampedes, gunfights, snakebites, stomachaches, Indian attacks, jailbreaks and other adventures or misadventures. But some are simple listings. William G. Butler drove to Abilene in 1868 with a crew of twelve men that included Mexicans, white Texans and two Negroes, Levi and William Perryman.[23] On a similar trip, Joseph S. Cruze had Adam Rector, a Negro "who could ride and rope with the best," as his "main helper." [24] At least one Negro was in the crew that helped Richard Withers drive thirty-five hundred head to Abilene in 1870.[25] George Hindes rode in 1872 with eight Mexicans and one Negro, Jack Hopkins.[26] On drives to Kansas in 1873, C. W. Ackerman rode with seven white men and one Negro,[27] while R. F. Galbreath traveled with four white men and three Negroes.[28] In 1874, the same year that George Chapman rode through a stampede with old Chief, a Negro, L. B. Anderson was also in a crew with a Negro cowhand.[29] In early March of the same year, Jim Ellison went up the trail with all Negro hands.[30]

Other listings are typical. In the middle seventies near the Kansas line Charlie Siringo rode point with "Negro Gabe." [31] G. W. Mills trailed to Ogallala in 1877 with "the following boys, not a one over twenty-three years of age: W. M. Ellison, son of the boss; E. F. Hilliard, W. F. Felder, E. M. Storey, Albert McQueen, Ace Jackson, . . . two negro cowhands and a negro cook." [32] A story of a drive a year later mentions a Negro cowboy, Thad, only because he happened to find a large box of snuff in an area where "at least nine women out of ten" used it. He sold it for a good price at Red River Station.[33] Eight riders, "two of them colored," were engaged by George Gilland to take his herd from Texas to Wyoming in 1882.[34] And in 1885 Lytle & Stevens sent a herd up the trail "bossed by Al Jones, a negro." [35]

The catalog could continue for pages. Only now and then does a bare list or reference hint at an untold story.

What, for instance, is hidden in the laconic note written by Henry D. Steele in 1920? He wrote: "It has been just thirty-seven years since I went over the trail. I do not know what has become of the men who went with me on that trip. One of the hands, Charlie Hedgepeth, the negro, was hanged at Sequin by a mob some years ago." [36] Another Negro cowboy, George Glenn, is the only man identified in the crew that R. B. Johnson took from Colorado County, Texas, to Abilene in 1870. Shortly after reaching Abilene, Johnson died, his body was embalmed, and he was buried in Kansas. The following September the body was disinterred, and George Glenn took his old boss home. Because there were no railroads leading from Kansas to Texas, Glenn loaded the body in a Studebaker wagon and drove it back, making a trip that took forty-two days, sleeping every night in the wagon by the casket. [37]

Unlike the cowboys, the horse wrangler on a drive was rarely identified by name. It would be hard to make a long catalog of horse wranglers, either white or Negro, because the wrangler was the lowest man in the pecking order of the trail crew: frequently he was a mere boy. His job was important, but he became a cowboy as soon as he could.

The wrangler (perhaps, as Philip Ashton Rollins suggests, the word *wrangler* was a corruption of the Spanish *caverango*, a hostler) [38] was responsible for the crew's horses. On the trail, each cowboy needed fewer horses than he did on roundup, but still he might have as many as six mounts or as few as the two that Charles Goodnight, a pioneer ranchman, believed to be sufficient. [39] Thus the wrangler was responsible for herding a remuda of from twenty to nearly one hundred horses.

He usually rose early in the morning, called by the last night herder or the early-rising cook. He took his own horse, picketed near by, and rode off to bring in the remuda so that the cowboys could choose their first mounts of the day. Then he trailed the spares on the drive, normally going ahead of the herd, staying near the chuck wagon. At night he chose grazing grounds for his horses, picking spots well away from the herd, yet close enough that from camp he could guard against marauders or restlessness among his charges. Hobbled, his horses rarely strayed from the place he chose.

But sometimes they did roam. Alf Beadle described the experience of one Negro horse wrangler near the Pecos River. Waking early in the morning, Bob, the wrangler, found his horses missing and went after them. Later in the morning the crew woke to find both Bob and the horses gone. Not until six or seven hours later did they find him twelve miles up the river, where he had finally tracked down two of his horses.[40]

On the Chisholm Trail, wranglers were fortunate in working less rugged country than trans-Pecos Texas, but they faced recurrent threats from Indians as well as the natural hazards of a wild country. The Indians were usually as interested in horses as they were in cattle, and they were happy to steal either. Natural hazards included not only the horses themselves, some of which might be only half-broken and mean, but also an occasional wolf with a taste for horseflesh.

Always there were rattlesnakes that could spook the horses. Or even worse, they could bite the wrangler, who spent more time afoot than any other member of the crew except possibly the cook. Once bitten, he could expect rough and drastic treatment. In the early seventies a Negro wrangler named Dick came back to the wagon sucking his thumb; his hand and arm were already badly swollen. One of the cowboys immediately drew a knife and gashed—"almost hashed"—the thumb around the fang marks. Then he opened a pistol cartridge, poured powder over the wound, and lighted it with a match. Dick seems to have survived both the bite and the treatment.[41]

Even more surprisingly, he and most other wranglers survived their labors on the trail drives. Up before dawn, tending and driving horses all day, never off duty for more than a moment until the last night herder had cut his horse from the remuda and the other horses had been hobbled, the wrangler was also expected to rope wood or gather chips for the fire, help the cook load and unload the chuck wagon, and even wash dishes. He had good reason to want to be a cowboy, if only to escape the cook, who could be a tyrant.

According to Emerson Hough, the cook might be "a negro or a Spaniard or a 'Portugee,'" but almost certainly "hard-featured and unlovely, with a bad temper and perhaps a few notches on his knife handle." [42] Although the cook was sometimes called "the old woman," most writers agree that he rarely looked or acted like a lady. Everett Dick, perhaps echoing Hough, said the "cook often was a hard character with a record of his own. He might be either Spanish or Negro with a notch or two on his gun." [43] Ramon Adams agreed, adding that the cook "might be a Negro, a Mexican, or a white man from the dregs of the city." Occasionally he was a horse thief, who took a job as a cook to avoid suspicion.[44] Whatever the cook's race or nationality, most cowboys soon learned to agree that "crossin' a cook is as risky as braidin' a mule's tail." [45]

There is some evidence that the cook was often merely cranky rather than mean. He had many duties and responsibilities, and he had to enforce a kind of discipline in the camp. He depended on the wrangler and the cowboys for wood or chips, and he had to produce meals at all times, whether the day was calm or the wind blew. Normally he stopped with his wagon headed into the wind and then built his fire behind it. Jack Thorp remembered that "anyone riding up to the wagon was supposed to approach behind the fire so that no sand would blow into the skillets and ovens. Any green puncher who, not knowing this law, violated it, was likely to learn it soon enough, by being told the names of his ancestors and kinfolk." [46] Even a Negro cook, who was frequently forced by Texas mores to be more than ordinarily polite, was usually recognized as something of "an autocrat within his jurisdiction." Failure to treat him with consideration could be punished in too many ways: an erring cowboy found his coffee weak, his beans cold and hard, his meat full of gristle, his bedroll misplaced, his comfort disturbed by countless accidents.[47] Whether Negro or white, cranky or cheerful, the "old woman" was a very important member of the trail crew.

Normally one of the oldest men in the outfit, frequently an older cowboy who could no longer take the punishment of twelve to sixteen hours a day in the saddle, he was responsible not only for the crew's food but also for their bedrolls and personal possessions, which rode in his wagon. Often he was doctor, dentist and older brother, and it was he who dosed cowboys when they were ill, heard them when they were depressed, or amused them when they were bored.

His wagon was home. Each morning it pulled out ahead of the herd, carrying the food, the bedrolls and even the boss's papers; each night it stopped near the new bedground, where the cook built a fire and set out a fresh pot of coffee.

The chuck wagon was the product of long development. In the earliest cattle hunts and drives, each cowboy had carried his own food and prepared his own meals. Later, on the larger drives, a Negro or Mexican cook came along and carried his supplies on a horse or pack mule. Still later, after the use of chuck wagons became general, the few crews that persisted in using only pack animals were known as "greasy sack" outfits, and their mules were called "long-eared chuck wagons."

A true chuck wagon was a sturdy vehicle, usually one with iron axles and wide tires. It had a flat bed, under which was fastened a barrel large enough to carry a water supply for two days. A chuck box for holding food and cooking utensils was built onto the back of the wagon, and fastened to the box was a leaf which could be let down to form a work table for the cook. Stretched under the wagon was the "cooney," a loose-hanging piece of cowhide, tied by each of its four corners, which carried a supply of wood or chips for the cook's fire. In the wagon itself, which ordinarily was covered by a canvas sheet, were the flour, beans, sugar, coffee, bacon, salt pork, molasses, canned tomatoes— the bulky staples of the trail diet. There, too, were the bedrolls and other personal possessions of the crew, as well as rude medicines, a few tools and perhaps a little grain for the harness stock.[48]

The driver and master of the wagon was the cook, who had to be an expert mule skinner or bullwhacker as well as an artist with a dutch oven. Before he could cook, he led the way up the trail, driving over rough country and fording streams until he reached the bed-ground the boss had chosen. Then he made a new home for the crew. A good cook who could do these things, no matter how hard-bitten or temperamental he might be, was indispensable. If he also made a happy camp, he was a treasure.

While reminiscing with J. Frank Dobie, John Young remembered such a treasure: "The one man in our outfit that I recall most often and most vividly was Sam, the Negro cook. He always had a cheerful word or a cheerful song, and he seemed to have an affection for every one of us. When we camped in the vicinity of brush every cowboy before coming in would rope a chunk of wood and snake it up to the chuck wagon. That wood always made Sam grinning happy whether he needed it or not." [49]

Sam was also an entertainer. He carried along a banjo, which he played until one of the boys accidentally stepped on it. Then the crew chipped in and bought him a fiddle, which he also played, picking or sawing out airs like "Green Corn, Green Corn."

Carrying 225 pounds at thirty-five, Sam had become too heavy and a bit too old for the active life of a cowboy, but he was still a good rider; frequently one of the crew got him to ride and gentle an unruly horse. He was also part of the general hell-raising of a happy camp. One day, for instance, one of the boys looked at Sam's great bulk and said that Sam was "too big and strong for a man but not big enough for a horse. At that Sam said *he was a horse* and that he would give a dollar to any man in the outfit who could ride him without spurs." That night the crew camped in a sandy place, and the game began. Sam stripped, wearing only a bandanna around his neck for his riders to hold onto. Then one after another the cowboys took off their boots and mounted his back. One after another they were thrown into the soft sand by the human "horse" who could anticipate and bewilder the reactions of his riders. No one earned a dollar that night.[50]

Whenever a camp was established in one place long enough for the boys to do a bit of hunting, Sam provided some of the most "luscious eating" known on the plains. When he had time to barbecue antelope ribs or to roast buffalo steaks or wild turkey, the men had what Sam called a "wedding feast"—a wedding of dinner and supper. Then the cowboys waited eagerly for Sam to sing out for them to wash their faces, comb their hair, and come and get it "while she's hot and juicy." [51]

Sam had no need to fear men or horses. But he was badly frightened by a sudden darkness on a calm sunny afternoon in 1878 (probably August 19). The cattle were grazing quietly on the Texas plain while the crew loafed near the chuck wagon. Suddenly all the boys were startled by Sam's cry, a wild yell so unusual that some of them sprang to their horses and drew their guns. What had frightened Sam was the beginning of an eclipse, a blot on the sun that grew until the day was dark and the stars came out. No available newspaper had predicted it, and Sam—like many other frontier folk that day—had feared for a moment that the end of the world was coming. But enough of the boys knew about eclipses to explain what was happening.[52]

Sam's feats as a cook, a rider and a musician became known throughout the Southwest. Other cooks achieved temporary notoriety because of accident. A French Negro named Zeno, for instance, was long remembered by the men for whom he cooked on the trail in 1872. Because he kept his baking soda in one wide-mouthed pickle jar and a supply of calomel—"the universal medicine"—in another jar just like it, he confused the two when he was baking bread.

"We were a sick lot," one of the cowboys later wrote,

"for despite the more than peculiar taste, we ate Zeno's bread." [53]

Zeno and Sam were only two of the Negro cooks who went up the trail to Kansas. Some cooked meals that men remembered fondly for decades after: sourdough biscuits that floated, beef swimming in brown gravy, son-of-a-gun stew made from the heart, liver and brains of freshly slaughtered steers, and bread pudding sweetened with raisins and molasses. Other cooks became infamous for tough steaks, weak coffee and rocklike biscuits. Sometimes, like Ab Blocker's cook, Gordon Davis, they played the fiddle; or like Sam, they played the banjo and fiddle; or like Wash Adams, another cook, they sang "Oh Mary, My Mary" and other old plantation melodies.[54]

Usually cooks carried guns, for a chuck wagon driven in front of the herd was in a lonely and dangerous position. Some developed a healthy fear of Indians and a boastful pride in their superior skill as gunmen. One of these, a Negro cooking for an 1868 trail crew, demonstrated both at once. When J. L. McCaleb, one of the cowboys, found a five-dollar bill on the trail, the cook challenged him to a contest. This is how McCaleb told the story:

"One day at dinner the negro cook offered to bet me a two-year-old heifer he had in the herd against my five dollars that he could beat me shooting, only one shot each. I was good with a pistol, but I knew the cook was hard to beat. But I did not get nervous, as the two-year-old was about six to one if I won. One of the boys got a little piece of a board, took a coal out of the campfire, made a black spot about the size of a twenty-five-cent piece, stepped off fifteen steps (about 45 feet) and yelled, 'all ready, shoot.' I was to shoot first. I jerked my old cap and ball Navy out and just about one second before I pulled the trigger I saw the heads of six Indians just over a little rise in the ground coming toward the camp. This excited me so that I did not hit the spot, only about one-half of my bullet touched the board just to the right of the target. I yelled to the negro, 'Shoot quick! Look at the Indians!' By that time we could see them plainly on top of the rise. He fired, but never touched the board. So six big Osage Indians saved me my valuable find—the five-dollar bill." [55]

In this shooting match complicated by Indians, a Negro cook lost a heifer because of a hurried shot. Two years later, careless shooting won another Negro cook a place in the history of the West. For a few hours, at least, he became the first prisoner of Abilene's first jail.

As early as 1868 Abilene had become notorious. With thousands of cattle bawling in its pens and grazing on the surrounding plain, with trail hands riding into town to wash off sweat and dirt with tubs of hot water and liberal splashes of bay rum, with trail crews swinging from one saloon to another while the cattlemen stood at the hotel bar and sold their herds to commission men, with gamblers and whores competing for every cowboy's wages, Abilene was "the wickedest and most God-forsaken place on this continent." [56]

In 1870 the city began building a stone jail. Before construction had gone very far, Texas cowboys pulled down its walls. Then the town trustees hired a strong guard, and under its protection workmen completed the structure. The law was in business.

A Texas oufit camped on Mud Creek had a Negro cook who rode into town and quickly drowned his memories of smoking fires and hungry cowboys with heavy draughts of Abilene whiskey. Then he began shooting up the town—not doing much damage, but making a lot of noise. The town marshal came running and, as one account has it, "managed by some unaccountable good luck" to arrest the cook and throw him into jail.[57]

There the cook stayed until his hungry trail crew learned where he was. They mounted, rode into town, drove the marshal into hiding, shot the lock off the door and freed the cook. Then "they galloped past the office of Theodore Henry, chairman of the town trustees, and shot it full of holes." Finally, having rescued one of their own men and expressed their contempt for the town's government, they rode back to camp.[58] Thus a Negro posted two records: he was the first man thrown into the new jail, and the first man to break out.

The Abilene trustees promptly sent for a new marshal from the outside. And while they waited, more cattle came up the trail, pouring into Abilene's shipping pens; and hundreds of cowboys came up the trail to crowd Abilene's streets, saloons and rebuilt jail.

·≫[5]≪·

Trailing to Dodge

Meanwhile, back at the ranch . . .

It is no accident that this hackneyed phrase, this pathetic admission that somehow the story has got away from the writer, should have become a cliché of Western stories. For in Western history something is always happening in the back room of the saloon or back at the ranch or farther west or farther north. Men and cattle are simultaneously going thataway—and thataway—and thataway—and twenty other ways.

So it was with the cattle drives to the north. Even as Abilene became the first great market and shipping center for Texas cattle, other towns challenged its preeminence. In less than five years, by the summer of 1872, it had become merely a sleepy farmers' market. Although the mayor then complained that the village seemed "desolate, forsaken, and deserted," many of his constituents disagreed. Like the editor of the local paper, they rejoiced that "hell" had moved and now "was more than sixty miles away." [1]

"Hell"—the cowboys, the cattle, the gunfire, the saloons, the gamblers and the whores—was sixty miles away in Ellsworth. Hell was also farther south in Wichita, brought by the completion of a short-line railroad. There, after sunset, a Negro mounted a high elevation and sang plantation melodies to bring a crowd to an auction room; other Negro entertainers sang and played guitars in the saloons; a band played in a beer garden; and gambling halls and bawdy houses ran wide open.[2] There, too, hell roared by day when Texans were drunk and angry, shooting and killing. A typical murder was that of Charley Saunders, a Negro hod carrier who had an argument with a Texas cowboy one evening in 1874. Both men were arrested by the town officers. Two days later, after they had been released, the cowboy got the backing of some of his friends, walked down Main Street to where Saunders was working, and shot the unarmed laborer twice—in the ear and in the breast. Then he rode out of town, leaving Saunders dying in the street.[3]

The boom was also short-lived in Wichita. The drives moved farther west, pushed out of central Kansas by hostile settlers and new legislation. They were forced beyond the more populous parts of the Indian Nations by Indian tolls and grazing fees. As early as 1867 the Cherokee Nation Council met and set a toll of ten cents a head for all cattle driven through their territory. This action helped to turn the drive from the Shawnee Trail to the Chisholm Trail, which ran through the sparsely settled Cheyenne and Arapaho reservations where Indian tolls could be paid with a sore-footed steer or two. Most of the scattered population of this part of the Indian country was found in small, friendly Negro settlements. Thus J. H. Baker, a prominent cattleman of Palo Pinto County, made the following entry in his 1869 journal of a drive: "Sept. Fri. 17: It is foggy and misting rain this morning. We passed several Negro settlements on our route today before reaching [Fort] Arbuckle. Water

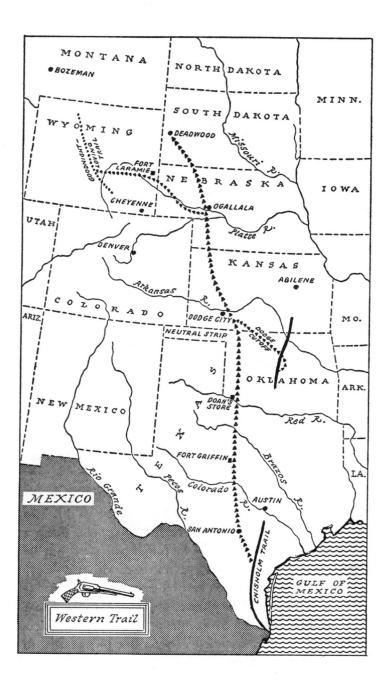

MONTANA

● BOZEMAN

NORTH DAKOTA

SOUTH DAKOTA

MINN.

WYOMING

● DEADWOOD

Missouri R.

IOWA

GOODNIGHT LOVING TRAIL

FORT LARAMIE

NEBRASKA

CHEYENNE

● OGALLALA

UTAH

Platte R.

DENVER ●

KANSAS

ABILENE ●

COLORADO

Arkansas R.

ARIZ.

DODGE CITY

MO.

NEUTRAL STRIP

DODGE CUTOFF

OKLAHOMA

ARK.

NEW MEXICO

DOAN'S STORE

Red R.

FORT GRIFFIN

Brazos R.

El Pecos R.

Colorado R.

LA.

Rio Grande

MEXICO

AUSTIN ●

SAN ANTONIO ●

CHISHOLM TRAIL

GULF OF MEXICO

Western Trail

is fine. . . . Fine grass and water. A good looking country." [4]

The greatest force pushing drives west was that of the Kansas settlers, who tired of having their crops trampled by great herds of longhorns. They threw up fences and clamored for new laws to keep out the drives. By 1876 the Kansas Legislature had moved the quarantine line far enough west to wipe out Wichita and Ellsworth as market centers for Texas cattle. So the trail drives turned toward western Kansas, toward the new "Gomorrah of the plains," Dodge City. Drivers still followed the Chisholm Trail through the Indian Nations to the crossing of the Cimarron River, but then they cut northwest to Dodge.

Typical of those who herded their cattle on the Chisholm Trail to the Dodge City cutoff was George Henry Gilland, who bought a herd of fifteen hundred one- and two-year-old steers in Dallas, hired a cook and eight cowboys, and began a drive north. During the first few days he rode through settled country, moving the herd over narrow, poorly fenced roads. Near St. Jo, a small Texas town about twenty miles south of the Red River, the country opened up somewhat, so that the steers could graze. But then, during a storm "on a night so dark no object could be seen," the herd stampeded.

The next morning the trail crew began rounding up the scattered cattle. Taking Hamm Harris, one of his two Negro hands, Gilland trailed one bunch straight down a lane to a closed corral. There he found his cattle, but he also found a dozen men lined up on the fence.

"Are these your cattle?" one of them asked.

When Gilland said they were, the farmer claimed that the steers had trampled his cornfield. Backed by his fence-sitting friends, he demanded fifty dollars in damages to release the herd.

Gilland went out to inspect the corn. He found cattle tracks all right, but they were old ones. And he knew that he had followed fresh tracks directly to the corral. So he refused to pay.

Instead, he and Harris—they were both armed—rode straight to the corral gate. The Negro cowboy opened it and guarded it while Gilland drove out the steers. The farmer and his friends made threats, but no one reached for a gun. Later Gilland learned that the farmer, who was also a part-time preacher, had made a regular practice of letting down his fences and trying to collect damages from trail drivers.

From St. Jo to the Red River was a long one-day drive. The Red was swift and high, and the crossing difficult, but the herd finally made it after Gilland lassoed a lead steer and dragged it bawling into the river. Swimming his horse, he half-led, half-pulled the steer across, while the rest of the herd followed.

Safely across the Red River, he and his crew were in the Indian Territory (now Oklahoma). Then they crossed the Arapaho and Chickasaw nations, ordinarily using lamed or crippled animals to pay the tolls demanded by the Indians. They crossed the Washita River, the south and north branches of the South Canadian River, and the Cimarron. "The Washita," Gilland later wrote, "offered no difficulties, but when we reached the South Canadian we were detained twenty-four hours by a flood which caused it to overflow its banks; when this subsided we crossed without much difficulty. The north branch was dry and its wide bed of alkali deposits could be seen for miles, glistening white in the sun like snow. The Cimarron was wide but the cattle had become trail broken and were not afraid to cross, so we reached Dodge City . . . without further incident." [5]

Armed cowboys like Hamm Harris were not the only Negroes on the trail. There were always Negro settlers in the Indian Territory, and during the great exodus from the South in 1879, vast numbers of Negroes walked on the Chisholm Trail. When Charlie Siringo came through the Indian Territory that year, he found the trail "lined with negroes, headed for Topeka and Emporia, Kansas, to get a free farm and a span of mules from the State Government. Over my pack," Siringo continued, "there was a large buffalo robe, and on my saddle hung a fine silver-mounted Winchester rifle. These attracted the attention of those green cotton-field negroes, who wore me out asking questions about them. Some of these negroes were afoot, while others drove donkeys and oxen." [6]

No such crowds cluttered the newer Western Trail, which by 1876 had become the route followed by more than a third of the cattle driven north. This trail went through Fort Griffin to Doan's Store on the Red River and then along the border of the Texas Panhandle, through the Cherokee Strip and straight north to Dodge City.

On the unsettled plains of north central Texas were buffalo rather than settlers, and Fort Griffin was a center for perhaps fifteen hundred buffalo hunters, whose piles of hides covered acres of ground. Farther north, where the trail crossed the Red River at Doan's Store, cowboys found only a few people and a few shacks. Still farther north, where the trail went toward Dodge through the western-most part of the Indian Territory, early drivers wrote of adventures with wild animals. E. A. Robuck and a Negro cowboy, Emanuel Jones, rode into a herd of buffalo and roped two of them.[7] Other cowboys tried to rope buffalo, not always successfully, and one who attempted to ride down an antelope had no success at all. Neither did Monkey

John, a Negro cook who tried to flood a prairie dog out of its hole.[8]

D. S. Combs, who drove north from San Antonio in 1876, believed that his crew was the first to pioneer the Western Trail.[9] By 1877 the trail was pretty well marked, though the settlement at the Red River crossing was then only "three buffalo hides and a wagon sheet." [10] A year later C. F. Doan and his uncle J. Doan established Doan's Store at the crossing, providing a last Texas outpost where trail outfits could get supplies and mail. (A post office was established there in 1879.) "Many a sweetheart down the trail received her letter bearing the postmark of Doan's and many a cowboy asked self-consciously if there was any mail for him while his face turned a beet red when a dainty missive was handed him." [11] Cowboys were less self-conscious about asking for whiskey: W. F. Thompson remembered a "little trouble" there. He wrote, "Zack Stucker, our boss, had gone ahead to look for a crossing on the river, as it was very high from spring rains, and when he came back he ordered me to get ready to cross at two o'clock in the evening. I informed him that all the boys were drunk as old man Doan had some wagon-yard whiskey, and that we had better not cross as the men would have to swim, and a drunken man cannot swim. I told him to move camp up the river and wait until the next day, which we did, and we crossed all right." [12]

Doan's Store was also a place to get news of the long trail ahead. There the trail drivers might be warned of troublesome Indians, raiding bandits or swollen streams. One group of white and Negro cowboys, for instance, spent several restless days and nights after crossing at Doan's Store, having been warned of a band of thieves who were stampeding and stealing horses. For a few nights the cowboys started out of their bedrolls every time the bean pot bubbled. They lost a lot of sleep, but no horses.[13]

Hundreds of miles due north of Doan's Store lay Dodge City, the head of the trail. Frequently a crew positioned the chuck wagon each night so that its tongue pointed to the North Star and showed the direction of the next day's drive. In the morning the cook fed the men and washed the dishes while the lead steers grazed slowly up the trail, nudged in the right direction by the point riders. Then the cook packed the chuck wagon, started up the trail and passed the herd. One Negro cook was so impressed by the way the lead steers followed his wagon that he said he thought the herd would follow him to the North Pole if he just kept going.[14]

Every cook was grateful for an uneventful drive. During emergencies he could be drafted as a rider or night herder, and then his life became much more strenuous. Sometimes, of course, he volunteered for extraordinary duties like the one described by James Gibson: "It was on this trip one night that a severe thunderstorm came up. The horses had been turned loose on the tableland when, just before the storm started, a deer jumped up in front of the herd and caused them to stampede. They ran directly by camp, causing the remuda to join them and, as they had not been hobbled for the night, came near leaving the cowboys all afoot, the remuda man's horse being the only one staked. And as one of the boys ran to mount him he, catching the contagion of fright, pulled up his stake and went rushing by camp. The Negro cook, taking in the seriousness of the situation, grabbed the rope and went bumping along for about a hundred yards before he could stop him. He then mounted and assisted in trying to stop the herd that had by this time crossed the creek." [15]

By the late seventies and early eighties, trail drivers found some ranches located in the eastern Panhandle and in the Cherokee Strip. Reginald Aldridge, for instance, established a ranch about 165 miles south of Dodge, where he employed a five-man winter crew that included two Mexicans and one Negro.[16] Other ranches appeared in the Cherokee Strip. To one such ranch the foreman brought a new wife, Molly Snow, from a small Kansas town. Unused either to the open range or to its code of hospitality, she gave a curt greeting to a Negro cowboy who rode in one day to ask for a meal. At any other ranch in the Strip he would have been fed without question, but Molly went for a six-shooter. Seeing her expression and her actions, the cowboy ran for his horse and quickly rode away, luckily escaping unharmed from Molly's wild shots.[17]

Once a crew got through the Cherokee Strip, it neared trail's end at Dodge City. Dodge was a shipping point, a market and a jumping-off place for drives to the ranges farther north and west. It provided the beer hall, saloon, whorehouse, outfitter and haberdashery for almost every crew that arrived or passed through. It provided also a new rendezvous for gamblers, thieves and outlaws—a dangerous place for the innocent, the careless or the unlucky.

The first man killed in Dodge City was both innocent and unlucky. He was a tall Negro named Tex, whose only mistake was standing in a crowd on the street during some minor excitement. The crowd milled around, guns were fired, and Tex fell dead. At the time, everybody thought his death was an accident, but years later a gambler named Denver, then many miles from Dodge, boasted that he had shot Tex "just to see him kick." [18]

This kind of disorder and violence led to the formation of the Vigilance Committee. Composed at first only of the

leading merchants of Dodge, for a time it acted effectively
to persuade desperate characters to leave town. But then it
grew, and soon the hard cases and badmen joined it. Then
they controlled it, and the Committee became a rioting
gang of toughs and thieves.

Their rule ended when a group of them murdered still
another Negro. Their victim was a "polite, inoffensive, in-
dustrious" man named Taylor, the servant of the commander of Fort Dodge. Taylor regularly drove a wagon
the five miles between Dodge City and the fort, buying and
hauling supplies. On one of his trips he left his wagon in
front of a store while he made his purchases. A group of
drunks, several of them "vigilantes," seized the wagon and
began to drive it away. When Taylor ran out of the store to
protest, they shot him, watched him fall and then continued
to shoot at his prostrate body.[19]

The commander of Fort Dodge took prompt action. His
troopers occupied the town, and he appealed both to his
superiors and to state officials for authority to punish the
guilty and establish order. Although he did not get the authority he wanted, the leaders of the vigilantes fled town,
and responsible citizens set about establishing order.[20]

Dodge City then hired a series of marshals and deputies,
of whom Wyatt Earp and Bat Masterson were among the
most famous. Lawmen like these soon became known for
their courage, ruthlessness and marksmanship. Most buffalo
hunters and cowboys learned to check their guns and respect the local law, which normally was enforced with un-
romantic but extremely effective shotguns.

Yet wise men still took measures for their own protection, as young George Bolds discovered on his first night in
town. (James P. Horan retells the story in *Across the Cimarron*.) Tired by his journey from Adams County, Indiana,

Bolds took a room at the Dodge House and quickly fell asleep. He was awakened by a loud banging, and went to open the door.

There he found Colonel Draper, an old man wearing two guns and a Prince Albert coat. Behind the Colonel stood the biggest Negro that Bolds had ever seen.

Colonel Draper explained that the hotel was full and that the clerk had suggested that Bolds might be willing to share his room. Bolds invited them in.

The old man took off his coat and guns and hung them on the back of a chair. The Negro spread a blanket on the floor and put a paper parcel down beside it.

"Now you don't mind Zeke," the old man said. "He's my handyman down at the ranch. I brought him along to guard that parcel."

"What's in it?" Bolds asked.

"Five thousand dollars wrapped in that paper. Going to buy a herd of breeders tomorrow when they come in," the Colonel answered.

Zeke lay down on the blanket, took a long knife from inside his shirt and stuck it into the jamb of the door. Then he took out another knife and drove it into the floor, convenient to his hand.

So guarded, Bolds and the Colonel spent a quiet night.[21]

A Bowie knife or a pigsticker could be a terribly effective weapon, particularly in a crowded saloon or a lone encounter. But because it was a limited weapon, of little use against snakes, wolves or Indians, the ordinary cowboy preferred a Colt. The freighters had a weapon peculiarly their own—the bullwhip.

In the hands of an expert fresh from the Santa Fe Trail or the Indian Nations, the bullwhip was a deadly weapon that could blind or maim or kill a man in a few minutes.

It could tear a gun from his hand, the clothing from his body, or the flesh from his bones. With its twelve-foot lash the bullwhacker could reach the ear of a lead ox or mule, and with equal accuracy he could flick a cigar from a man's mouth.

A grudge fight between two bullwhackers could be a cruel and bloody affair. Yet some fights were held simply as contests, in which two gladiators fought for money. One such contest—sometimes called "lapjacket"—between two Negro freighters was held on Front Street in Dodge in 1877. They borrowed heavy new whips from a harness shop, toed their marks and began fighting for fifty cents prize money and "the championship." The snapping of their whips sounded like pistol shots, and every stroke cut deep into the flesh. "Blood flowed and dust flew and the crowd cheered until Policeman Joe Mason came along and suspended the cheerful exercise." [22] It was with this kind of entertainment that Eddie Foy and his theatrical troupe, then playing Dodge City, had to compete.

Violence and even murder were frequently considered entertaining. Dodge was amused when a cattleman named Peppard took a shotgun and went gunning for his trail boss. The trail boss saw him first and ducked behind a saloon icebox, which was riddled by the shotgun blast. Then Peppard, having failed to kill his man, tried to get him convicted of murder.

The trail boss had murdered a Negro cook on the drive to Dodge, and Peppard knew about it. He took another man, rode down the trail and dug up the body. The Negro had been dead for two weeks, and the weather had been warm. So Peppard chopped the head from the body, brought it into Dodge and accused his trail boss of murder.

Now the whole macabre action turned to legal farce. The head was introduced in evidence, and the bullet hole in the skull was admitted to be certain proof of violent death. But the defense argued that only a part of the body had been produced and that if the court assumed jurisdiction, there was no reason why other courts in other counties might not assume jurisdiction over other parts of the body. The court finally granted a continuance until such time as the rest of the body could be produced, and Peppard gave up. He left town, "disgusted with the decision." [23]

Negroes were not always victims. Sometimes they were killers. Henry Hilton, for instance, owned a ranch and ran a small herd of cattle near Dodge. One day as he rode into town with a bunch of white cowboys, they began to torment him. When one of them tried to lasso him, Hilton warned them that he would not stand for any hazing, even "if he was a nigger." When another cowboy persisted, throwing a loop and almost pulling Hilton off his horse, the Negro drew his gun and killed him. About half the cowboys, according to one citizen of Dodge, believed that Hilton "was justifiable in killing his man; it was self defense. . . ."

Hilton was bound over for murder, but he never stood trial. Before his case was called, he got in a late Sunday night saloon brawl with another Negro, Bill Smith, and they "were both found, locked in each other's arms . . . the next morning, lying on the floor in front of the bar, their empty six-shooters lying by the side of each one. The affair must have occurred some time after midnight, but no one was on hand to see the fight, and they died without a witness." [24] This description resembles a scene from a Frederic Remington painting; it also sounds a little strange, for surely even in Dodge City someone would ordinarily have investigated ten or twelve shots heard in the small hours of Monday morning.

Hilton fought and killed for his dignity as a man, refusing to be roughed up merely because he was a Negro. Others found champions in their white friends. Like the cook who was freed from the Abilene jail, they could expect their friends to stand up for them. One walked down a Dodge street with Bill Sparks, a white cowboy who had ridden with him up the trail from Texas. They were stopped by a drunk, "who began to abuse the Negro for no apparent reason other than he appeared to be colored." Not wanting trouble, the Negro did nothing, but Sparks took up the quarrel and fought and won a fight with the drunk. No sooner was that fight finished than Sparks was accosted by a middle-aged cattleman who berated him for siding with "a nigger." When Sparks defended himself and his friend the second time, the cattleman knocked Sparks out with a loaded quirt. After he came to, Sparks got a coupling pin and coldcocked the cowman. Later the two men, having discussed the issue in forthright Dodge City fashion, became friends.[25]

Although Negroes suffered from discrimination and abuse in Dodge City, there were many white cattlemen like Jim Thornhill. One of his friends explained him this way:

"Jim had a code of his own. I knew his affection for his boys, yet I have heard Jim say he would rather see any of his boys dead than ever take a backstep when they knew they were in the right.

"Unlike so many of his kind, Jim held no racial prejudice. Black, white, yellow and red, they were all alike to Jim. Yet he believed that no race as a whole was worth the powder to blow it to hell. To Jim the human race as a whole was a failure. Only the individual counted, no matter what his color or creed—and a friend could do no wrong." [26]

Jim Thornhill was probably fortunate in not numbering Ben Hodges among his friends, for Ben was an expert in cheerful wrongdoing. A superb confidence man, he was also a competent forger and cattle thief. The son of a Negro father and Mexican mother, Ben came up the trail from Texas with one of the first herds to arrive in Dodge City. There he stayed, talking his way into and out of trouble, stealing money and cattle, sometimes worrying and sometimes amusing the townspeople. Cattlemen and cowboys came and went, and Wyatt Earp and Bat Masterson stopped only briefly, but Ben remained until his death in 1929.

When Ben Hodges first arrived in Dodge, he heard a widely discussed rumor that a range being used by several of the bigger cattle companies was part of an old Spanish land grant and that the grant was still valid. Because Ben had always claimed to be descended from an old Spanish family, a cattleman facetiously suggested that Ben should claim title.

To the cattleman the idea was a joke, but to Ben it was an opportunity. Seeing a way to fashion a case for himself, he shrewdly began his campaign. He knew that if his claim was to get anywhere, he would have to contend with two different groups. One included most of the old-timers of Dodge, who knew that he was no more nor less than any other average cowboy. But these old-timers loved a practical joke, and any kind of fun was "a scarce item on Dodge streets at that early time." The other group, which could be fooled, was made up of newcomers and transients, some of whom were lawyers, bankers and businessmen.

Ben made a trip to Texas and returned with a number

of documents showing him to be a legitimate claimant of the grant as well as the representative of other claimants living in San Antonio. Armed with these documents, he found a local lawyer willing to take the case and draw up papers for the claim. The fact that Ben, like any other cowboy, had long since spent the last of his trail pay did not hinder his progress. His seeming sincerity and apparent honesty brought out men who were willing to "buy in" to his claim. He also won support from undeceived old-timers who enjoyed watching the hoax develop; they helped him with money and with fresh affidavits and petitions for his collection. Even other cowboys, many of whom had ridden with Ben, picked up the story and gleefully pushed it. Finally Judge Sterry, of Emporia, Kansas, offered to take Ben's case on a contingency basis and to contribute both time and money.

As prominent lawyers and businessmen showed interest in Ben's claim, even the old-timers began to exchange outright disbelief for questioning doubt. Ben Hodges became a man of prominence—a perfectly understandable phenomenon that would have delighted Mark Twain. Many cattlemen, knowing that almost anything could happen in the West, supported Ben because they thought he might possibly be a winner.

So when Ben asked for credit, he usually got it. His saddle was no ordinary one, but rather a saddle befitting his new position. Many storekeepers who questioned Ben's claims were willing to allow him a fine pistol or a beautiful set of spurs, if only because the show was worth the price.

While his case as claimant to the Spanish land grant moved slowly in the courts, Ben began to capitalize on his newly acquired prestige. Like Mark Twain's Colonel Beriah Sellers, he dreamed other schemes. One of the most ingenious of these was made possible by a disastrous fire at the Wright and Beverly store, a fire which gutted the building and dropped the store's four-ton safe into the basement. The safe fell on its doors, and for a time its contents were securely out of circulation.

Ben acted promptly. He had earlier learned that thirty-two sections of land in Gray County, Kansas, were open for settlement. He had written to the treasurer of Gray County, minutely describing the land by quarter sections and asking for a tax bill. Now, fortified with the tax bill and the knowledge that the Wright and Beverly safe could not be opened immediately, Ben was ready for a new swindle.

He visited the president of the Dodge City National Bank, a newcomer in town. Ben explained that the affidavits of transfer proving his ownership of the land were temporarily locked up in the Wright and Beverly safe, but he produced the tax bill as evidence of his good faith. He talked so persuasively that the bank president wrote him a letter of credit stating that Ben was known to be the owner of thirty-two sections of Kansas land. Then Ben used both the tax bill and the president's letter to get other letters confirming not only his ownership of the land but also his reputation for honesty, sobriety and frugality.

With all this evidence, Ben rode down the trail to the range around the Beaver and Cimarron rivers and contracted for spring delivery of thousands of cattle. Then he returned to Dodge City to try to borrow money from Eastern bankers. If he had been successful, he would have made a large profit, for the price of cattle rose steadily. But he found that all bankers, Eastern and Western, were more careful about lending money than about writing letters of recommendation. He could not raise the money, and his cattle deals fell through.

With smaller swindles he was more successful. Every year he got free passes from the railroads, persuading them that he was a large owner and shipper of cattle. And he could always make a few dollars from a credulous cattleman.

One of his swindles was made possible by the separation of two partners and their agent. The two partners, John Lytle and Major Conklin, drove thirty herds up the trail and encountered spring storms that scattered many of their herds near Dodge City. So the cattlemen separated, Lytle continuing north to deliver cattle, Conklin going to Kansas City to attend to the partners' business there, and an agent, Martin Culver, remaining in Dodge City to receive stray cattle and horses as they were recovered. Culver offered to pay one dollar a head for Lytle and Conklin cattle recovered, and two dollars a head for horses. He paid with receipts which were to be redeemed by Major Conklin.

Ben saw the weakness of this system of doing business. He promptly visited Major Conklin in Kansas City, presenting forged receipts for several hundred Lytle and Conklin cattle and horses. Conklin did not question the receipts, which seemed to be in order, but he decided that he could drive a hard bargain with a poor and ignorant Negro cowboy. So he offered Ben less than the agreed-upon sum, finally settling by paying for Ben's room and board, buying him a complete new outfit and a return to Dodge and giving him about sixty dollars.

When Lytle arrived in Kansas City, Conklin met him in the bar of the St. James Hotel. A number of other cattlemen were with them, drinking and talking, when Conklin boasted of his deal.

"John," he said, producing the forged receipts, "I made a shrewd business deal and got your receipts for several hundred cattle and horses for less than half price, from Ben Hodges."

He got no further. All the other cattlemen knew Ben, and both the laugh and the drinks were on Conklin. Ben had pulled a classic swindle, for Major Conklin was hardly eager to enter a court and describe his "shrewdness" in bargaining with a cowhand. It was better to accept the loss and set up the drinks.

Not all of Ben's victims took their losses so philosophically, however. When the whole herd of a local dairyman was stolen one night, Ben was charged with the crime. The circumstantial evidence was damning, and it seemed certain that he must be convicted. He had only a few real friends, no money and a bad reputation. He had no lawyer.

Ben pleaded his own case. After all the evidence had been presented, he rose to address the jury. He talked for more than two hours, sometimes making them laugh, sometimes becoming serious or indignant.

"What! Me?" he cried at one point, "the descendant of old grandees of Spain, the owner of a land grant in New Mexico embracing millions of acres, the owner of gold mines and villages and towns situated on that grant of whom I am sole owner, to steal a miserable, miserly lot of old cows? Why, the idea is absurd. No, gentlemen; I think too much of the race of men from which I sprang, to disgrace their memory."

At another point, disregarding all consistency, he represented himself as a poor but honest cowboy being persecuted by personal enemies. At all times he was persuasive, bewildering and entertaining. When he finished his pleading, he had won his case. The jury brought in a verdict of not guilty.

A few days later the missing cows came home. Ben had

indeed stolen them and driven them some fifty miles to a hidden canyon. He had left them unguarded, and a storm had started them moving. Fortunately for Ben, they returned after he had been acquitted.[27]

Adventures like these made Ben a notorious figure in Dodge City. But he was unconcerned, and his ambition was limitless. He next decided to seek appointment as livestock inspector at Dodge City. He petitioned the governor for the job, citing his services to the Republican party and supporting his petition with the signatures of local saloon-keepers, cowboys, gamblers and dance-hall girls. They found the idea amusing.

Not so the town's businessmen and cattlemen. They knew that Ben's asking to be a livestock inspector was "like a wolf asking to guard the sheep pen." They promptly informed the governor that Ben was one of the country's most competent cattle thieves, and his petition was rejected. Barred from a political career, Ben continued his life as a private citizen.

He outlived almost all his friends and enemies. By 1929, when Ben died in Dodge City and was buried in the Maple Grove Cemetery, many of the old-time cattlemen had preceded him. His grave was near theirs.

"We buried Ben there for a good reason," one of his pallbearers is reported to have said. "We wanted him where they could keep an eye on him." [28]

Even in death, Ben Hodges was a lucky man. He had lived through Dodge City's most turbulent times, had been a notorious rascal during the days when Wyatt Earp and Bat Masterson had been deacons in the Reverend Wright's church, and had lived on to see Fords and Chevrolets parked thickly on the city streets. And when he died he found a secure resting place among the founding fathers of the town.

More violent rascals were less lucky. Those who fought and died during the roaring seventies were buried on Boot Hill. Their lives were short, and even their graves were temporary. When the cattle trade shifted farther west and farther north, their bodies were exhumed and moved to make way for progress. In 1880 the city leaders dedicated a new schoolhouse—one built on the site of the old Boot Hill graveyard.[29]

❦[6]❧

On to Ogallala and
Deadwood City

North of Dodge City lay Nebraska and the Dakota Territory—great plains grazed by buffalo, roamed by Indians
and coveted by whites. Even before the Civil War the
forty-niners had driven through Nebraska, following the
Valley of the Platte. After the war the Union Pacific Railroad followed the same route, and by 1867 its rails had
crossed Nebraska and pushed into Wyoming.

In 1867, too, Nebraska became the thirty-seventh state.
Unlike Colorado, it early accepted the principle of equal
suffrage for white and Negro, and a bill for its admission
to the Union as a state was passed by both houses of Congress over President Andrew Johnson's veto. On March 1,
1867, the President was forced to sign the proclamation
granting statehood to Nebraska.[1]

The new state had fewer than a thousand Negro residents. Many of them, like most of the rest of the population, lived in the Omaha area. But some were on the
frontier, pioneering in difficult country, doing many kinds

of work. Some, indeed, broke the law, as is shown by the April 20, 1869, diary entry of Major Frank J. North, organizer and commander of the famous Pawnee Scouts: "This morn," he wrote, "[I] went to Omaha with Joe Baker Yost & Negro Henry. the Negro under arrest for selling whiskey to Indians had the trial and put the Negro to Jail." [2] Major North was stationed at Fort Kearney, near Columbus, Nebraska.

Still farther west was Ogallala, a new Nebraska shipping center for Texas cattle. Located on the South Platte, a few miles west of the merging of the North and South Platte rivers, Ogallala held a key position in the West. From there, Texas cattle could be shipped east or west on the Union Pacific: east to Omaha or west to the open ranges of Wyoming. Or they could be driven still farther north to new ranges in the Dakota Territory. By 1870, Ogallala was becoming the "cowboy capital" of Nebraska, quite properly equipped with "the most substantial jail west of Omaha." [3] To Ogallala came literally thousands of cowboys—a number of them Negro. And the Negroes, like all the others, were of many kinds—some quiet, some noisy, some dangerous.

One was an ex-slave known only as Snowball. After serving as a general roustabout in the company of General Custer's troops during the Civil War, Snowball went to work for James Cowan, who had been a soldier in the same company. Together they located a desirable piece of land on the Trinity River in Texas, and Cowan began to build up a ranch.

In the spring of 1866, Cowan left Texas and returned to Illinois. He sold his farm there, married his old sweetheart, bought four horses and a wagon, and drove back to Texas. "Snowball had not been idle. He had put in a good crop, taken care of the cattle, and developed into a real cowboy. He had branded all the calves and quite a few mavericks." [4]

During the next six years the ranch prospered as Cowan and Snowball guarded their cattle and joined with the Texans in hunting and branding mavericks. They sold cattle, sending them north with various trail drivers. Then Cowan made his own drive to Abilene in 1873 and heard stories of the wonderful grass country up north. He immediately decided to gather his herds and move to the new range. He hired a crew, rounded up all his cattle and headed north. Cowan's wife and three children drove one wagon loaded with bedding and water barrels, while Snowball and his wife drove the chuck wagon. Cowan himself drove a third wagon behind the herd and tried to save some of the newborn calves. All three wagons were drawn by oxen.

Their drive was like many others, including a long, dry run from Oasis Springs to the Red River: "A nightmare," Cowan's son later wrote, "that I can never erase from memory—the bawling of cattle, the groaning of men and horses, and the rattle of chains in the ox-yoke rings." [5] As the herd neared the river, both the oxen and the cattle smelled water and started to run. Cowan's wife stopped her wagon by shooting the near ox of her team, and the cowboys stopped Snowball's chuck wagon by roping his oxen. The herd stampeded—catching, trampling and killing one cowboy—and ran till it was widely scattered up and down the bank of the Red River.

Cowan was delayed by the stampede, and he was further delayed by minor Indian trouble after he crossed the Red. Consequently it was turning cold by the time he and his crew reached Ogallala. They made camp and wintered the herd there, holding it together near the South Platte, waiting for spring. Enduring the Nebraska winter, protecting their Texas longhorns through the bitter cold and raging blizzards of the unfamiliar northern range, Cowan and his wife and children experienced some of the worst hardships of the Western pioneers. So did Snowball and his wife, who stayed with their employer and drove on west with him after the spring thaw. Eventually they reached the present site of Meeker, Colorado, where Cowan established his new ranch.

Snowball and Cowan had wintered at Ogallala because they were forced to halt their drive. Most other cowboys stayed there for only a few days before returning to their home ranges or driving on to the North or West. So the town was built to accommodate a transient population. It had one good hotel, a railroad depot, a small store and four saloons. "All the saloons," one cowboy remembered, "were on the south side of the Union Pacific railroad and were two stories high, with rooms above, and were good looking buildings." [6] In this town the permanent population was small, and resident Negroes were few.

For one of these, an elderly Negro, an invasion of Ogallala by cowboys was torture. On a hot July day in 1879 he found himself on the street surrounded by four or five drunken cowboys who had finished the long drive from Texas. They had spent too many hours in Ogallala's four saloons and had burst out looking for sport. They amused themselves by drawing their guns and making the old Negro dance. They kept shooting near him, reported the Cheyenne *Daily Leader,* "just to see how near they could come to him without inflicting a wound." When one of their shots went through the railroad station and narrowly missed the wife of the station agent, they angered the whole community. The sheriff gathered a posse, chased them out of town and killed two of them before the others surrendered.[7]

An elderly Negro, dancing in the streets, pursued and frightened by the shooting of drunken Texans, seems like an archetypal figure in the folklore of the West. He—and Snowball, for that matter—fit perfectly into the stereotype of the humble Negro who always runs out of the livery stable to hold the hero's horse.

But what of Kelly, Print Olive's cowboy, who was a villain? E. C. Abbott rode with him and the tough Olive crew into Nebraska. Kelly, he wrote later, "was quite a character. They called him Olive's bad nigger, because he was a gunman and fighter himself. The Olives used to send him ahead to talk turkey to the settlers; where one of these fellows had taken up a homestead on good water, not to work it you understand, but just so he could charge the trail herds a big fee. . . . They would send Kelly, and that big black boy with his gun would sure tell them punkin rollers where to head in at. He'd roll up his eyes like a duck in a thunderstorm and grit his teeth—Lord, he could play a tune with his teeth. Most of the settlers were poor Northern folks that had never seen many niggers and was scared of them anyway, and when they saw Kelly they would come down quick enough from twenty dollars to five dollars as the price for watering the herd." [8]

The Olive outfit was tough, too tough, and it came to Nebraska only after it had killed so many men in Texas that it had to flee from frontier justice. In Nebraska, too, the outfit overreached itself as it fought to take over a large range. The Olive brothers, sided by their tough Mexican hands and their "gun niggers," terrorized the Nebraska settlers. When they shot up the Mitchell and Ketchum families—Mitchell was first hanged, then shot, and then doused with coal oil and burned—a local paper ran the story under this headline: "Nebraska Settlers Victims of Heinous Crime Out of Inquisition." Headlines, however, did not bother the Olives. Print Olive moved from bar to bar, wearing his gun loosely in his worn holster and boasting "that there weren't enough men in the whole goddam state of Nebraska to take him." [9] But they did take him, and the Olives and their gunhands died or ran before vigilante justice.

As a tough Olive gunman, the big Negro Kelly frightened settlers in western Nebraska; at almost the same time some quite different settlers in eastern Nebraska were debating "the Negro question." In the Rock Creek community, about sixteen miles northeast of Lincoln, the local Mutual Improvement Society held a series of debates in 1880 and 1881, and in these debates the proper status of Negroes was a recurring question. The decisions of the judges, though undoubtedly influenced by the forensic skill of the debating teams, seem also to have reflected the community sentiment. Thus the judges agreed that Guiteau should be hanged for shooting President Garfield and that Chinese immigration should be prohibited, but they did not believe that enfranchisement of Negroes should be gradual nor that Negroes should be colonized in Africa.[10] They believed that American Negroes were citizens of the United States and should be recognized as such.

While the Rock Creek community debated the treatment of Negroes (a question almost as academic in their part of eastern Nebraska as the question of Chinese immigration) hundreds of Negroes continued to ride to or through Ogallala on the northern extension of the Western Trail from Dodge City. Many have remained nameless, and many were never described as Negroes unless they were remembered for some particularly unusual performance, like that of an old trail cook who distinguished himself on an 1879 drive from Texas to Ogallala. Years later he was remembered by Samuel Dunn Houston because he had driven off thirty Indians who surrounded his chuck wagon. He began "to get crazy," Houston wrote, and the Indians "got on their horses and left." As Houston explained, "An Indian won't stay where there is a crazy person. They say he is the devil." [11]

Certainly the Indians were having a hard time staying anywhere in the West. White hunters systematically exterminated the buffalo, and the U. S. Army conducted an unremitting campaign against the Indians, who faced inevitable defeat. They fought bravely, but even as they won battles, they lost the war. By 1876, as Sitting Bull rode among his warriors before the Battle of the Little Bighorn, he could predict the end. "Be brave, my children," he said. "Your wives and little ones are like birds without a nest." [12] Only a year later, after having been betrayed by a mixed-blood (Sioux and Negro) scout, the young chief Crazy Horse was bayoneted at Fort Robinson, Nebraska. With his death, the "real tall-tale man of the Plains, their very essence, died." [13]

Soon almost all of the Dakota Territory was open to exploitation and settlement. Although it had been made a territory in 1861, the creation of the great Sioux Reservation in 1868 had closed a large part of its western extension to white settlement. Even after the discovery of gold in the Black Hills in 1874, the government tried for a short time to keep white (and black) men out of the reservation. But by 1876, when the Indians won the Battle of the Little Bighorn, they had lost the territory. Miners came first, closely followed by cattlemen and cowboys.

Negroes were among the miners, and some of them dug great quantities of gold from their claims. In Lawrence County, on the border of Dakota and Wyoming, "Nigger Hill" took its name from a group who arrived at the mines in 1875 and staked a claim on a hill some distance from a creek. White prospectors sent them there as a joke, and the innocent tenderfeet began to work a dry claim. Carrying all their water, they began placer mining and soon hit a rich pocket that yielded thousands of dollars.[14] Farther south, in Pennington County, both "Nigger Creek" and "Nigger Gulch" took their names from a miner named Jackson, who worked, died and was buried in the area. Hundreds of other Negroes came to work on the claims or in the mines, but they were not celebrated in place names.

By 1879 Deadwood City was a famous town. Wyatt Earp had visited it, and Wild Bill Hickok had died in it. Great numbers of miners moved through it, as did white and Negro Army regiments. At intervals it was "hoorahed" by Negro troops from Fort Meade, and at least one gambling house and dance hall was run by a Negro.[15] Among the permanent residents, moreover, were several Negro families.[16]

There were also Negro entertainers—some genuine, some "Negro" only by virtue of burnt cork and greasepaint. Through Kansas, Nebraska and Dakota rode medicine shows and fast-talking, fast-selling confidence men who were frequently accompanied by Negro dancers or musicians.[17] There also were minstrel shows, some of which employed Negroes, but most of which featured "burnt cork artists" like Jim Crow Rice. There were all-Negro groups like Blind Sam and His Brothers, entertainers "who brought cheer and amusement to the lonely inhabitants of the little towns." [18]

Entertainers who came to Deadwood City found cowboys as well as miners in their audiences. The miners had been followed by cowboys bringing herds of Texas cattle to the mines and to the rapidly opening Dakota ranges. Immediately after the first discovery of gold in the Black Hills, cattlemen found that beef brought premium prices in the mining towns of Deadwood, Lead and Spearfish. In these towns a grown steer that cost only a few dollars in Texas was worth about a hundred dollars as a butchered beef.[19] Cattlemen promptly saw the possibility of building new ranches on the Dakota plains. By 1875 it was abundantly clear that the value of the Texas longhorn increased with each mile he was driven northward. A steer worth $7.20 in Texas was valued at $13.30 in New Mexico, $18.40 in Colorado and $20.20 in Montana.[20] The cost of getting a steer north varied with the distance, but he could be driven to the northern range for approximately two dollars. After a few weeks or months on free grass, the once rangy Texas steer tripled in value. By the early 1880's, thousands of cattle were coming up the trail; in the summer of 1882, for instance, 27,000 were driven from Texas to the Black Hills.[21]

Wherever Texas cattle went, Negro cowboys pushed them. Like most other cowboys who rode the trails north, they were transients: they rode with a herd to South Dakota or eastern Montana, collected their pay, had a few drinks and headed back south. They did the same work and shared the same pleasures as all other cowboys. This circumstance, accepted as a matter of fact on the trail, surprised some observers. When Galliot François Edmond, Baron de Mandat-Grancey, visited the Black Hills in 1883, he observed a group amusing themselves on the street in front of a saloon. They were practicing roping and doing some wrestling. "One of these cowboys," the baron wrote, "is a negro; for all that he plays and wrestles with the others on a footing of perfect equality. It is very curious that a sentiment so rooted should have disappeared so quickly in a country where, only twenty-five years ago, a negro was admitted neither into a theatre nor an omnibus in New York."[22]

Yet the baron's surprise led him to overstatement. Even the Negro cowboy rarely enjoyed "perfect equality." The imperfections of that equality are illustrated by the story of a man now known only as Negro John.

He was hired in Dodge City by a large outfit driving 4,800 steers north from Texas in 1879. The old cook had left the drive, and John was hired to replace him. As the drive moved north toward Ogallala, John proved himself an excellent cowboy but a miserable cook. He was the best roper in the outfit, but his cooking left everybody hungry and unhappy. "With [him]," one wrote, "we got nothing to eat."

In Ogallala the crew delivered all the big steers and then pushed on with a thousand head of yearling steers for delivery to Warren and Guiterman on Warbonnet Creek (now Hat Creek) in South Dakota. By the time the crew finished that trip, their food supplies were exhausted and John was cooking nothing but coffee. They were reduced to begging cornmeal and bacon from other outfits.

Early in September they reached the Warbonnet, made delivery and helped with the branding of the herd. Although John was acknowledged to be the best roper, he was forced to give place to a white man who refused to work on foot—wrestling and branding cattle in the dust of the corral—while a Negro sat above him on a horse. The branding took two days.

The job finally done, the crew took baths in the creek, put on clean clothes and started for home. For the first time in months they were "off herd," free of responsibility for cattle. At noon they stopped to rest their horses, ate a meal of bread and bacon and lay down for a nap. When they woke, John was gone. He had taken what he wanted —not only food but also a dictionary and a Bible from the pack of the man who had taken his place as roper. Perhaps he wanted the books—though he could not read—or perhaps he chose this way of expressing resentment. In any event, the crew never saw him again.[23]

Unlike John, some Negro cowboys stayed in the Dakota Territory. But they were few, and some of them undoubtedly met discrimination more unfair than that of being forced to wrestle steers while a less skillful man roped. As late as 1903, for instance, one who was working in South Dakota had some difficulty. His boss was a small rancher, Bill Benoist, who was feuding with the enormous Matador Land and Cattle Company over a piece of disputed range. Whenever Benoist's cattle came near Matador herds, the Matador wagon boss, Con McMurry, cut them out and drove them back to Benoist's home range. He drove them hard and sometimes mistreated them.

One of the Matador's cowboys described Benoist's reaction: "To offset the long, turbulent drives—sometimes twenty miles or so, which chousing and disturbance were bad for his stock—Benoist sent his cowboy, a colored man named Bunk White, to rep with us. White was to represent the W B Bar brand, and Bill intended him to stay right with the Matador wagon. . . .

"White was a very good cowboy and rider. There could have been no real aversion toward him among the men. I know I did not dislike or refuse to work with him, but for some reason, Con would not allow Bunk to work with the wagon. One morning, he told him to get his horses out of the *remuda* and go home, which Bunk did." [24]

It is difficult to judge Con McMurry's motives in turning Bunk White away from the wagon. Perhaps he resented White because he was Negro, but perhaps he was merely carrying on the feud between the Matador and Benoist. Certainly Benoist refused to be beaten; he continued to turn his cattle loose on the Matador range, and he continued to feud with the Matador outfit as well as with the Indian Agency, which wanted to collect grazing fees for his use of reservation land. His feuds ended seven years later when his roping horse fell, pinning him and killing him instantly. As for Bunk White, nothing more is known: perhaps he continued to work in South Dakota, perhaps he rode south, or perhaps—the cowboy life being what it was— he died before his boss.[25]

One Negro cowboy who stayed in South Dakota was more fortunate than many. He worked as a horsebreaker, and his methods were admired by Theodore Roosevelt, who first came into a little town in the Bad Lands in 1883. Roosevelt built himself a place on the Little Missouri River, served as a deputy sheriff and became a cattleman.

The Negro cowboy was named Williams, and he worked for the Langs, near-neighbors of Roosevelt. Williams's specialty was horsebreaking, according to Lincoln A. Lang, who later wrote a book, *Ranching with Roosevelt*. Williams did not "bust" horses or break their spirits; he broke them to saddle by winning their friendship and confidence. In Lang's account Williams was a "past-master of the art— cool, collected, apparently fearless—if there was anything he did not know about handling horses, we never found it out. Moreover, if there was a horse in the range country that could throw him, nobody ever produced one." According to Lang, "Williams was the first to introduce sane horse breaking in our section of the country."

Roosevelt became "an interested and sympathetic observer" of Williams's methods. He watched the Negro handling horses in the corral—getting them used to mounting and dismounting, accustoming them to saddle and harness—and then the rancher adopted the same methods, as far as possible, on his own ranch.

Roosevelt also became a close friend of the Langs.[26] Once he complimented the senior Lang on naming his son after Abraham Lincoln, and this led to a discussion of the "race question." Listening to that discussion, the son learned much: "it became impressed upon me," he later wrote, "that the color of a man's skin is no voucher for the qualifications lying beneath. That the devil is just as likely to be found masquerading beneath a white as a dark one: so it would seem just as well to go slow in drawing conclusions." [27]

These truths were impressed upon Lincoln Lang by a conversation that his father and Theodore Roosevelt held in South Dakota in the early 1890's. But they were truths known not only to Northerners and admirers of Abraham Lincoln. More than twenty-five years earlier they had been known by an ex-Confederate soldier, a fine cattleman and pioneer, a man who opened the way for great cattle drives to New Mexico and Colorado—Colonel Charles Goodnight.

·◄[7]►·

To Lincoln County and
Tombstone

Charles Goodnight, one of the pioneers of the cattle industry, died in 1929. He was born in 1836, the year Texas declared its independence from Mexico. Thirty years later, in 1866, he joined with Oliver Loving to blaze a new trail for Texas longhorns. While others opened the Chisholm Trail to Abilene and other Kansas towns, Goodnight led the way out of Texas into New Mexico, driving first to Fort Sumner, and then later pushing into Colorado and on to Wyoming.

But he did not do it alone. Riding with him were many good cowboys. One of them, who lived almost as long as Goodnight, also died in Texas in 1929. Saddened by the old cowboy's death, Goodnight—a short time before his own death—erected a marker: [1]

Bose Ikard

Served with me four years on the Goodnight-Loving Trail, never shirked a duty or disobeyed an order, rode with me

in many stampedes, participated in three engagements
with Comanches, splendid behavior.

C. Goodnight

Bose Ikard was a Negro cowboy, one of those who rode
with cattlemen like Charles Goodnight, Oliver Loving,
John Chisum and John Slaughter as they broke out of
Texas and drove thousands of cattle over deserts, past alkali
holes, through Apache, Sioux and Comanche territory, on
toward the New Mexican reservations and Army posts, the
Arizona and Colorado mines, and the Wyoming ranges.
Negroes wrangled horses, drove chuck wagons, rode point
and drag, and fought Indians. Some were like Bose Ikard,
who returned to Texas and lived out his life there. Others
stayed in the new territories to grow up with the country.

Bose was born a slave in Mississippi in 1847 and was
brought to Texas by his master's family, the Ikards, when
he was five years old. Growing up on the frontier near
Weatherford, Texas, he learned to ride, rope and fight,
skills that were to make him a valuable hand later. After
the end of the war, he was hired by Oliver Loving, who
was rounding up cattle and hoping to find a market for
them.[2] Loving was an older man, a veteran of prewar cattle
drives toward Colorado, and a frontiersman with an intimate knowledge of the Southwestern plains. He knew well
the hazards of trying to drive straight toward Colorado,
for he had met and fought the Comanches and Kiowas who
held the Texas Panhandle. So he joined forces with Charles
Goodnight, who had gathered his own cattle and proposed
to drive southwest down the route of the old Butterfield
Overland Stage as far as the Pecos River before turning
north toward New Mexico.

Loving and Goodnight agreed to throw their two herds
together—two thousand in all—and begin their drive, start-

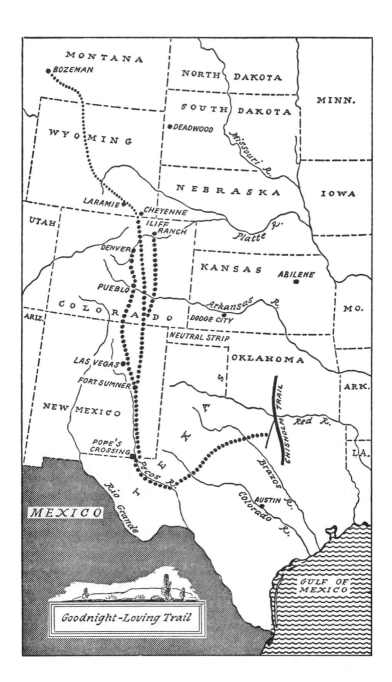

Goodnight-Loving Trail

ing from twenty-five miles south of Belknap, Texas, not far from Weatherford. Their herd was mixed, containing both steers and cows, and they faced all the special problems that such a herd presented. The steers normally traveled faster than the cows, and the cows were further delayed by calving on the way. The calves could not keep up at all.

Goodnight and Loving were planning too long a drive and too hard a trip to permit them even to think of trying to run a calf wagon. All they could do was kill the calves and drive the bawling mothers along the trail with the herd.

The worst job fell to a Negro cowboy, Jim Fowler. Every morning Goodnight gave the cowboy a six-shooter and told him to shoot the calves dropped during the night. Then the other hands drove the cows off the bed-ground. At the end of a day's drive the cows had to be hobbled to prevent their going back to look for their calves.

Fowler did his job, but he did not like it. Killing calves every morning was far worse than drowning kittens. Finally he asked Goodnight to get someone else to do the shooting.

But everyone else was busy, and Fowler had to go on acting as an unwilling butcher. Goodnight was understanding, but he had too many worries to spend much time lamenting the fate of the calves or sympathizing with their executioner.[3]

Goodnight and Loving knew that the way would be hard. They drove as far as the headwaters of the Middle Concho without difficulty, and there they paused to let the herd drink its fill of fresh water and prepare for the long dry stretch ahead. Then they began a drive through eighty miles of desolate wasteland to the Pecos River. At first they tried to pace the restless herd, driving them in the late afternoon and early morning, hoping to save the strength of the cattle. The thirsty animals would not bed, but merely milled around, so that the cowboys found it easier to drive continuously. Goodnight led the way, guiding the point riders, and Loving stayed with the drag, saving every animal he could. They lost some cattle on the drive and even more at the river, where about five hundred head stampeded after smelling the water of the Pecos. And they lost a few more to the poisoned alkali water of potholes that lined the trail.[4]

At the Pecos they turned north, following the river. At Pope's Crossing they forded the river and entered New Mexico. Still driving north, they crossed the Black River, recrossed the Pecos and drove by Comanche Spring and Bosque Grande to Fort Sumner. There they found a market for their steers, selling them to the general contractor of the fort for eight cents a pound on the hoof. They were able to sell all the steers, for the government was desperate for beef to feed the nearly starving Navajos it had crowded into a newly established reservation.

Loving continued the drive, taking the remaining stock cattle on to Colorado, where he sold them to John Iliff at Denver. Goodnight took the twelve thousand dollars they received for the steers and rode back to Texas to assemble another herd. Both men were probably accompanied by at least one Negro; Bose Ikard rode back with Goodnight, and Jim Fowler apparently went on with Loving's cows and calves. And it seems probable that others in the trail crew were Negroes not identified in surviving accounts of the opening of the Goodnight-Loving Trail.[5]

Certainly Goodnight and Bose Ikard soon became nearly inseparable. When Oliver Loving died the next year, having been weakened by wounds, loss of blood, and exposure during a long fight with Comanches, Bose became Goodnight's man exclusively. From then until 1869 they rode together.

Bose, said Goodnight, "surpassed any man I had in endurance and stamina. There was a dignity, a cleanliness, and a reliability about him that was wonderful. He paid no attention to women. His behavior was very good in a fight, and he was probably the most devoted man to me that I ever had. I have trusted him farther than any living man. He was my detective, banker, and everything else in Colorado, New Mexico, and the other wild country I was in. The nearest and only bank was at Denver, and when we carried money I gave it to Bose, for a thief would never think of robbing him—never think of looking in a Negro's bed for money.

"We went through some terrible trials during those four years on the trail. While I had a good constitution and endurance, after being in the saddle for several days and nights at a time, on various occasions, and finding that I could stand it no longer, I would ask Bose if he would take my place, and he never failed to answer me in the most cheerful and willing manner, and was the most skilled and trustworthy man I had." [6]

It would take many pages to describe all the trails that Bose Ikard and Goodnight rode together. The story has already been masterfully told by J. Evetts Haley in *Charles Goodnight: Cowman and Plainsman*. According to Haley, Bose Ikard "added life, friendship, and color to the Goodnight Trail." He wrote that "to the end of his long days Goodnight subscribed his greatest debt to man still due this negro who saved his life several times, this superb rider, remarkable trail hand, and devoted servant." [7]

Haley quoted Goodnight's description of a stampede in 1867 that came at the end of a quiet night, just before the dawn. Goodnight had left Bose alone with the herd and had ridden in to the wagon to wake the cook and get the crew moving. Suddenly something startled the cattle, which came stampeding down toward the camp.

Goodnight grabbed a blanket and ran out waving it and making as much noise as he could. In this way he was able to split the herd, which poured around the chuck wagon and the men sleeping on the ground. Then he found his horse, which was still tethered to the wagon wheel, mounted and raced up the side of the stampeding cattle.

By now dawn was near, and Goodnight could see. Near the front flank of the herd he saw Bose, and in a few minutes Bose looked back and saw him. Then Bose immediately moved in to turn the leaders. Working together, Bose and Goodnight soon had the herd circled and the stampede stopped.

After things quieted down, Goodnight asked Bose why he had not tried to turn the herd earlier. Bose's explanation was simple: he had ridden flank near the front until he could see, for he had been afraid that Indians might be riding at the rear. This fear was realistic, for stampeding trail herds was a favorite Comanche trick.[8]

Bose had a wary respect for Indians because he had fought them, had pulled arrows from the bodies of friends and had lost his first employer, Oliver Loving, as the result of a Comanche attack. But he was no coward. When Goodnight was injured in northern New Mexico in 1868 and lay helpless in the shade of the wagon, Bose rode out to stop a local outlaw leader from cutting the herd.[9] At the end of the 1868 drive, when Goodnight drove from Colorado to Texas carrying all the profits of the year's drives with him, Bose was in the driver's seat, armed and alert. They were following "the usual trail down the bitter Pecos," a trail menaced by outlaws, Indians and lawless Mexicans.[10]

Bose was only one of the Negro cowboys Goodnight employed. Most of the others are now nameless, as are most of the white cowboys who rode with Goodnight on the early trails up the Pecos River into New Mexico, but their existence is shown by a strange bit of folklore and by an occasional anecdote.

The folklore is preserved by J. Evetts Haley. Describing Goodnight and his trail crews, he writes, "Often in the rush of work, in disregard of clock and calendar, they were uncertain of the date, but their arguments were finally settled by appeal to Bose Ikard, or any other negro hand that happened to be along, for negroes alone never lost count of time." [11]

A typical anecdote, also told by Haley, is that of the theft of Goodnight's favorite saddle horse. Jim Loving, a son of old Oliver, had left his mercantile business in Weatherford to conduct a drive. Goodnight's saddle horse was in a herd of trail horses guarded by Frank Mayes, Loving's Negro cook. Shortly before the start of the Loving drive to Dodge City, the horses were stolen by Comanche Indians. Later, when Loving's cattle drive reached the Arkansas River, the camp was surrounded by more than six hundred Indians, and Loving began parleying with Big Black Beaver, the Indian chief.

Just as Loving, who knew the Comanche hatred of Texans, had nearly convinced Big Black Beaver that his was a drive from the Cherokee nation on government contract, Mayes interrupted. He recognized Goodnight's stolen horse in the Indian band, pointed to it and yelled, "Yonder is Mr. Goodnight's horse!"

"Shut your mouth!" yelled Jim Loving. "The Indians will have your scalp on a pole."

"And I hushed," Mayes later admitted.[12]

No cowboy talked out of turn on a Goodnight drive. As his memorial to Bose Ikard shows, Goodnight was an almost feudal figure, backing his men all the way and demanding complete obedience and loyalty from them. At the start of every drive he ordinarily drew up a contract stating each man's responsibilities, forbidding gambling, drinking or cursing, and providing that any man committing a crime would be tried on the trail and punished on the spot.

He enforced this contract even with men not in his own crew. When he was receiving cattle from John Chisum in New Mexico and one of Chisum's men shot another, Goodnight demanded justice. Curly Tex, the murderer, had shot an unarmed man without provocation, and Goodnight refused to let him go unpunished. Chisum objected that taking Curly Tex and all the witnesses to the distant county seat would destroy the roundup and delay delivery of the cattle.

Goodnight countered by ordering a trial on the spot. One of his men arrested Curly Tex, a jury of cowboys was selected, and a trial was held. After the jury had heard all the evidence, including that of "Nigger" Frank—Chisum's horse wrangler, who had witnessed the shooting—it found the defendant guilty. Then the two crews propped up a wagon tongue and hanged the murderer.[13]

Although John Chisum was reluctant to interrupt his roundup to punish a crime, he was never indecisive or soft.

He had been one of the first to follow Goodnight and
Loving up the trail from Texas to New Mexico. For several
years after Oliver Loving's death, Chisum contracted to
deliver Texas cattle to Goodnight at Bosque Grande on
the Pecos River in New Mexico. Goodnight then trailed
the herds on into Colorado and Wyoming. But this partnership was ended when Goodnight refused to take delivery of eleven hundred head of obviously stolen cattle.[14]

Chisum took his profits from the Goodnight partnership
and built a great ranch on the Pecos River near Roswell,
New Mexico. There, at one time, he ran as many as sixty
thousand cattle. Many of these he acquired by obtaining
power of attorney to market various Texas brands: presumably he was to pay for these after his return to Texas.
Other cattle he acquired by giving notes for them. Neither
all of his contracts nor many of his notes were honored,
and he soon developed a reputation as an unscrupulous
operator.[15]

He pioneered a rough country. As his cattle increased
and his range spread, he hired larger numbers of tough
hands, both white and Negro, to defend his herds against
Indians and Mexican cattle thieves. Even so, he continued
to suffer from Indian raids in the 1870's. Finally, in 1877,
he "sent a band of armed men to the Mescalero Indian
reservation, where they got the government's agents suf-
ficiently drunk to put them out of action and then murdered a large number of Indians within a mile of the
central post. Thereafter the Indians hesitated to molest
Chisum's cattle." [16]

Chisum's cowboys were tough, but the country was even
tougher. In this now legendary land west of the Pecos, the
"prevalent lawlessness was more a matter of disorder than
of immorality." Into this "moral vacuum," according to

one writer, "came bad men of all kinds—bad Mexicans, bad Negroes, bad white men—and the bad white men were the worst of them." [17] Chisum's ranch lay in an area that was to become infamous in the history of the West, and Chisum himself was engaged in business with a number of men soon to die violent deaths. His ranch was in Lincoln County, New Mexico, and the Lincoln County War was about to begin.

It is difficult to tell the story of the Lincoln County War in a few paragraphs or a few pages, for even the books that have been written about it are necessarily full of conflicting and confusing testimony. A number of personal and business feuds got knotted into a bloody tangle, and violence became so wanton and so general that any story of the war loses almost all shape and continuity.

One thing is clear. In this bloody feud both whites and Negroes died. Negroes fought on both sides, and Billy the Kid rode with Negroes. When the Kid and his faction were trapped in a burning building, Negroes were with them, while outside Negro troops surrounded the house. When Territorial Governor Lew Wallace searched for witnesses, trying to learn the truth about the madness in Lincoln County, he sent a Negro rider to find Billy the Kid and offer him safe conduct.

The center of the Lincoln County War was Lincoln, a small cowtown halfway between the Pecos River and the Rio Grande, approximately one hundred miles north of the Texas border. Eight miles from the town was Fort Stanton, a military post used to control the Indians on the Mescalero Apache Reservation. And from the fort, which was used for some years after the Civil War as a mustering-out point for volunteer troops, rode some of the more important fighters in the Lincoln County War.

One was Major Lawrence G. Murphy, who left the Army and started a business in Lincoln. He also started the new war. Another was Major William Brady, who left the Army and became the sheriff of Lincoln County. He was a casualty of the war. A third was Colonel Nathan A. M. Dudley, who stayed in the Army and eventually commanded the fort; under his command were several companies of Negro troops. He became involved in the Lincoln County War and moved his cannon and his soldiers into the middle of the fight.[18]

Even in the early seventies Sheriff Brady and the military had to face sporadic outbreaks of senseless violence—murders growing out of prejudice and Reconstruction bitterness. Thus one Frank Freeman, who admitted leaving Alabama only after killing several Negroes, shot and killed a Negro sergeant who sat down at his table in a Lincoln restaurant. Freeman was arrested, but later escaped from a squad of Negro soldiers who were guarding him. He claimed that he had been forced to escape because he had heard the soldiers talking about hanging him to a nearby tree without the formality of a trial.[19]

Another infamous killer was Clay Allison, "a clean-strain Southern fighter" who shot a Negro sergeant and four Negro soldiers merely because they entered a bar where he was drinking.[20] For a time, at least, Negro soldiers on the New Mexican frontier had more to fear from trigger-happy Southerners than from the Apaches.

There were many tough hands near Lincoln. J. C. Chisum employed cowboys who were also Indian fighters and gunmen. Major Murphy ran a general store, saloon and gambling house, but he also had outlying ranches with tough crews. Soon Murphy and Chisum were riding on each other's ranges, and the first arguments started. Finally Chisum accused some of Murphy's cowboys of rustling.

Murphy then turned to his lawyer, Alexander McSween, who had come to Lincoln in 1875. McSween refused to defend Murphy's cowboys, perhaps because he thought them guilty, or perhaps because he was reluctant to cross Chisum. "At this point," wrote a biographer of Billy the Kid, "the business relationship of Murphy and McSween was terminated, and the first fuel was fed to the flame that was to engulf all of Lincoln County." [21]

McSween did more than refuse to represent Murphy's men: he helped Chisum to prosecute and convict them. He also helped and represented a young Englishman, John Tunstall, who arrived in Lincoln in 1876, bought a ranch and established a store and a bank. Thus Murphy's profitable monopoly was challenged, and he came increasingly to blame McSween for Tunstall's unwelcome competition.

Both sides sought allies. Murphy was sided by two small ranchers, James Dolan and John Riley, as well as by the sheriff, Major William Brady. McSween, on the other side, was supported by Tunstall and by his business connections with Chisum. Both sides employed large numbers of cowboys and gunhands.

The Lincoln County War began in the courts with charges that McSween had embezzled money owed to Murphy. It became more serious when the Murphy men tried unsuccessfully to drive off Tunstall cattle. It exploded when Murphy's men ambushed and killed Tunstall on February 18, 1878.

One of Tunstall's cowboys was William Bonney, better known as Billy the Kid. After Tunstall's death, Billy rode with the deputy's posse to arrest Tunstall's killers; at the

end of the chase he shot two of them. Then he and a group
of his men ambushed Sheriff Brady and his men, killing
both the sheriff and Deputy Sheriff Hindman. All this violence caused excitement throughout the New Mexico Territory, and visitors came into Lincoln from as far away as
Las Vegas, three days by horse. One visitor, Calvin Simpson, reported to the Las Vegas *Gazette:* "Killing people in
Lincoln is the leading industry at the present time. They
kill anybody, native or stranger, with or without cause,
according to circumstances and inclination." [22]

With the deaths of Sheriff Brady and Deputy Hindman,
the Lincoln County War grew more intense. Only Mc-
Sween, who had once studied for the Presbyterian ministry
and who carried a Bible instead of a gun, still hoped for a
peaceful solution. With a lawyer's faith in the law, he
planned to defend his case in the courts. But he was both
opposed and aided by violent men, and the final solution
was violent.

One of Murphy's men, Deputy Dad Peppin, immediately assumed the title of acting sheriff. On the evening of
April 1, only hours after Brady's death, Peppin entered
and searched McSween's home, acting without a search
warrant. Then, having failed to find Billy the Kid or any
of the others who had been shooting that morning, Peppin
arrested McSween and four of his men, charging them
with "implication" in the deaths of Brady and Hindman.
Two of the men he arrested, George Robinson and George
Washington, were Negroes. [23]

While Peppin badgered McSween, "Buckshot" Rogers
succeeded in finding the Kid. Rogers was a Murphy man,
suspected by the McSween forces of being one of the killers
of Tunstall. He was also a superbly competent and self-
confident gunman. When he learned that the county com-

missioners had posted a two-hundred-dollar reward for the capture, dead or alive, of Billy and several of his companions, Rogers went after them.

On April 4 he found them at Blazer's Mill, a sawmill on the edge of the Mescalero Apache Reservation. But he blundered into a gun battle and ended up fatally wounded, lying on the floor of an outbuilding nearly surrounded by McSween men. Before he died, however, he wounded two of them and killed Richard Brewer, who had been Tunstall's foreman and the leader of McSween's forces.

With the death of Brewer, Billy the Kid became the new leader. He provided medical treatment for his wounded men and waited for the results of McSween's legal fights. They were not long in coming.

McSween was cleared of all criminal charges by a grand jury, but in all else he was worsted. At this time the command at Fort Stanton was changed, and Colonel Nathan Dudley took over. The new commander, if not actually a Murphy man, had no sympathy for McSween. Only a few weeks later, the territorial governor appointed Peppin sheriff. Now the officers of the law were all Murphy men, and McSween began to fear for his life and property.

Billy the Kid and his men rode into town and joined McSween. With them were at least three Negroes—George Washington, George Robinson and Sabrien (Zebrien) Bates. On the other side, riding with the Murphy forces, was the Negro John Clark. And now the Lincoln County War reached its bloody climax.[24]

More than eighty men were gathered on opposite sides of the town to fight it out, the Murphy group on the west and the McSween faction in the buildings on the east. Murphy men, once they had secured the support of the Army, surrounded the McSween house. Colonel Dudley rode into town with a squad of artillery and a detachment of Negro cavalry. He set up a twelve-pounder and trained it on the McSween house, and he ordered his cavalry to take positions in town and cover the surrounding hills. Then the Murphy men set fire to the McSween house.[25]

Mrs. McSween escaped—or was permitted to escape—from the burning building, as did Sabrien Bates and George Washington. But McSween himself, still carrying only his Bible, was killed, as were four others of his party. Billy the Kid and five of his companions escaped, breaking for the river and finding cover in the brush. Then the Murphy faction, in order to celebrate their victory, "drank, sang, and danced the gruesome hours away." They made McSween's Negro hands, Washington and Bates, both of whom were good musicians, sit on an adobe wall "and play their violins through the long hours of that sad night" while their employer's body lay nearly at their feet.[26]

The next morning it was George Washington who helped Dr. T. F. Ealy clean up the mess and bury the dead. Dr. Ealy, a minister as well as a physician, conducted funeral services for both sides. It was said that during a five-month period he conducted thirty-eight services, but only one of the deaths had resulted from natural causes.[27]

Billy the Kid was now a fugitive charged with five murders and wanted by the law. He wandered the territory, working for small ranchers and changing jobs frequently. He did not work for John Chisum, for they had quarreled; some said the quarrel was caused by Chisum's failure to provide the support he had promised the McSween faction during the fighting. Chisum soon began to blame the Kid whenever any of his cattle were stolen, and he ended by offering a reward for the Kid's arrest.[28]

In the fall of 1878 President Hayes appointed Lew Wallace territorial governor, and Wallace soon visited the Fort Stanton–Lincoln area to investigate the war. When he learned of Mrs. McSween's efforts to prove the guilt of her husband's killers, he called on her for evidence. Her story was credible, as well as damning to both Colonel Dudley and Murphy, but her witnesses, among them Billy the Kid, were all fugitives. So Wallace offered safe conduct to Billy if he could be found.

George Washington was chosen to find and bring Billy in. He succeeded, and Billy finally appeared for a conference with Wallace. After at least one other conference and several exchanges of correspondence, Billy agreed to being arrested so he could testify before a grand jury. He went peacefully to jail, and Governor Wallace went back to routine duties and extraordinary unofficial ones.

Lew Wallace was busy writing *Ben Hur,* the novel which was to become a best seller in 1880. While Billy waited in jail and Mrs. McSween and George Washington searched for other witnesses, Wallace kept writing, seemingly without caring about the aftermath of the Lincoln County War. Only after several months had passed was the Kid brought from jail to testify against Dudley, whom Susan McSween believed to have been chiefly responsible for her husband's death. Billy's testimony was forthright and, with Mrs. McSween's, damning to Dudley.

But Billy the Kid was already infamous, and rumor had successfully blackened Susan McSween's reputation. Their testimony was discounted as that of a killer and a notorious woman, and Colonel Dudley was exonerated. When the Kid rode away from Lincoln, having been released as Governor Wallace had promised, he was again an outlaw and a wanted man. Less than two years later he was dead.

George Washington was more fortunate. He was enlisted

as one of Governor Wallace's Lincoln County Riflemen, organized in 1879 to "assist the civil authorities in repressing violence and restoring order." Like the other Negro civilians directly concerned with the Lincoln County War, he went through violence without being killed, wounded or convicted of crime.[29]

Not all Negroes in New Mexico were so lucky. Long after the Lincoln County War had ended, the territory remained dangerous. Quarrels were still frequently settled with guns, and Negro cowboys were among those who fought. In Raton in 1881 two cowboys, one white and one Negro, had a set-to in which pistols were drawn but no shooting done. The white cowboy seems to have remained quarrelsome, however, for he got himself killed the same evening in a match with another white man.[30] Two years later, when two cowboys from the Canaditos Cattle Ranch in San Miguel County disagreed, one "George Withers wantonly and without provocation shot and killed George Jones (colored)." The Denver *Tribune* reported that if Withers were captured, "Judge Lynch [would] doubtless have a job." [31] In 1887, *Field and Farm* reported the death of still another Negro cowboy and accompanied its report with a little moralizing: "A colored cowboy named Lawson Fretwell, employed by the Home Land and Cattle company, a bad man from the Indian nation, was shot and killed by an officer at Trinidad on Monday night. Fretwell was in a gambling institution and got up a gun play in which he himself was killed. The cowboy seems to be keeping up his reputation this year as well as ever, and the mortuary reports are as entertaining as usual. It's generally the cowboy that gets the worst of the racket and he is not such a successful bad man as he has been pictured." [32]

The most successful cowboys were those who stuck to the cattle business, staying out of saloon brawls and range wars. One of these was "Nigger Frank," who spent a lifetime wrangling horses for John Chisum. One year he was Chisum's only cowboy after the others had left. Chisum had maintained a crew of about thirty cowboys through the winter, but in the spring all of them except Frank quit their jobs to hire on with a trail herder at double pay. Chisum was so enraged by this desertion that he vowed never to hire another Texan. "Mistah Chisum hired Mexicans," Frank later recalled, "—wouldn't take on no white men for a year." But Chisum's Mexican hands were inexperienced: unlike the vaqueros of southern Texas, they took half a day to get started, and then they couldn't stay on their horses. Finally Chisum gave up and went back to hiring Texas cowboys. And Frank continued to handle their horses.[33]

Other Negro cowboys worked on New Mexico ranges throughout the seventies and eighties, never getting in the newspapers, but getting known by everyone in the cattle business. "Nigger Add," for instance, was a range boss of the LFD outfit, usually heading a crew of south Texas Negroes. According to Howard Thorp, himself a cowboy, songwriter and ballad collector, Add was one of the best cowhands on the Pecos River: "Cowmen from Tozah, Texas, to Las Vegas, New Mexico, knew Add, and many of them at different times had worked on roundups with him." [34]

Experience as a range boss made Add an expert. His expertise became famous and eventually became the subject of a cowboy song. According to Howard Thorp, the song "concerns a critter found in one roundup and claimed by no one. Nigger Add was a dictionary on earmarks and brands, but this one was a puzzler even to him. He read the tally of the brands:

> She's got O Block an' Lightnin' Rod,
> Nine Forty-Six an' A Bar Eleven,
> Rafter Cross an' de double prod,
> Terrapin an' Ninety-Seven;
> Half Circle A an' Diamond D,
> Four-Cross L an' Three PZ;
> BWL, Bar XVV
> Bar N Cross an' ALC

"Since none of the punchers claimed the critter, Old Nigger Add just added his own brand—'For one more brand or less won't do no harm.' "[35]

Though not above appropriating a poor cow whose flanks were already mostly scar tissue, Add was known and respected all over the Pecos area of New Mexico. Consequently the news of his plans spread rapidly when he told a few friends one fall that he intended to be married on Christmas day. Widely separated ranchers, all of whom knew and liked him, decided to send presents. Most of them, prompted by their practical wives, decided on the same present. So when Add and his bride rode on their wedding day to the Roswell freight depot, they found nineteen cookstoves waiting for them.[36]

When Howard Thorp was riding for the Bar W brand in the spring of 1889, he found Add still at work bossing a roundup crew. Thorp rode in at night, guided by the campfire and by the sound of a song. Add's crew gave him coffee and stew, and then they pointed out the singer, a Negro cowboy known as 'Lasses. Thorp got 'Lasses to repeat the song, as much as he knew of it, and his two verses of "Dodgin' Joe" inspired the beginning of Thorp's career as a cowboy song collector.[37]

Add and his men were working cowboys, not gunhands. Although certainly they were among the New Mexicans whom Caroline Davis described as "of a rare breed, rough, adaptable, and totally self-sufficient," [38] they were respected for their skill with cattle, not with Colts, and they are remembered because of their songs, not their killings. By the time Thorp rode into their camp in 1889, the lawless days were nearly over. Billy the Kid was dead, and the Lincoln County War was only a bitter memory. New Mexico was becoming civilized.

So, for that matter, was Arizona. By 1889 the Apache wars were over, and the Indians had been pacified. Even the miners and cowboys had become fairly peaceful. But the Arizona Territory could remember its recent violent history, and many of its place names recalled memories of range wars and gunfights: Galeyville in the southeast corner of Cochise County, the favorite rendezvous of cattle rustlers; Pleasant Valley in the Tonto Basin, where the Graham-Tewksbury feud went on for years; and Tombstone, the town where Doc Holliday, the Earps and the Clantons met and fought at the O. K. Corral.

Negroes had a part in the early history of the Arizona cattle industry. There were fewer of them in Arizona than on the trails to Kansas and New Mexico, but some who came to the new territory were big, tough and colorful. They took their chances, and they fought hard.

One was a near giant named Jim, who rode for John H. Slaughter. He came with Slaughter's herds from Maverick, Texas, through New Mexico to Slaughter's San Bernardino ranch. Slaughter was one of Arizona's shrewdest and most enterprising cattlemen, known and respected for his courage and integrity. Living near Tombstone, he knew gamblers and outlaws (his testimony put Doc Holliday near the scene of an 1881 stage robbery), and he was near at hand when Holliday, the Earps, the McLowerys and the Clantons fought. Some time later he was elected sheriff and "cleaned up the district." [39]

Slaughter's cowboy, Jim, shared his employer's courage. A "magnificent" man, with "strength in proportion to his giant's frame," he was afraid of nothing. When Frank Leslie, notorious as one of Tombstone's killers, tried to jump a mining claim that Jim had staked, Jim ran him off. Jim always had strength and "the nerve to back it up." [40]

On another occasion, however, his strength and nerve merely earned him a beating. John L. Sullivan came to Tombstone in 1884 and offered five hundred dollars to any man who would face him for two rounds. Jim volunteered, and the match was set.

When the two men stepped out on the stage of Schiefflin Hall, Jim towered over his opponent, making "Sullivan look like a runt by comparison." The audience, mostly miners, cheered their champion, and the fight began. Jim began with a looping roundhouse swing that caught Sullivan high on the head and threw him off balance. The miners cheered again.

But that was their last cheer. Jim had strength, but no science, and the Great John L. had no more patience. It took him only a few seconds to end Jim's ring career, and then Jim was "carried out feet first like a ton of coal." When he was interviewed the next day by the Tombstone

Epitaph he said that he must have been doped, for he was still "feeling dopey."

Nobody else in Tombstone agreed with him. Having seen what John L.'s famous right hand could do, all the local citizens were impressed. When John L. offered to fight the four biggest men in Tombstone in one ring, nobody volunteered. When the world champion offered to knock out a mule with one punch, nobody offered an expensive mule for the sacrifice. Tombstone had already offered its best in Jim.[41]

Jim remained in Tombstone, settling down and occasionally reminiscing about early days in the territory, telling of eighty-mile cattle drives without water, remembering some of the more exciting adventures of John Slaughter's move into the Arizona Territory. He remembered, too, that he had been only one of Slaughter's Negro cowboys. Another was known as Bat, and it was Bat who accompanied Slaughter and his foreman into Mexico on a dangerous cattle-buying expedition. When the three of them were attacked by a "good-sized bunch of Mexican bandits" near Montezuma, Bat helped to fight them off. Slaughter always hired good men.[42]

The good men and the bad men—indeed most of the population of Arizona—were concentrated in the southern part of the state. It is no accident that Cochise County and the town of Tombstone are among the most famous Arizona names in early Western history. The northern counties were more thinly populated and less wealthy; consequently much of their history was less eventful.

Yet their pastoral peace could be disturbed. In the Tonto Basin, for instance, the Grahams and the Tewksburys began a bloody sheep and cattle war that did not end until the last of the Grahams had been shot by the last of the Tewksburys. More than twenty-five men died in this Tonto Basin War, a prolonged guerilla action in an area known ironically as Pleasant Valley.[43]

East of the Tonto Basin was the town of St. Johns, first settled in 1873 by Solomon Barth, who took a Mexican wife and soon became a leader of the sheep-raising Mexican-American community. He and his brothers constructed a dam and irrigation ditches and prospered as the town grew.[44]

Their peace was disturbed by the arrival in 1877 from Texas of the Greer family, who established a large cattle and horse ranch near Concho. Almost immediately conflict broke out between the Greers and the Mexican sheepmen. First the Greers' cattle were stampeded and scattered, and then the Greer crews rode against the sheep camps, shooting and scattering flocks. The Mexicans got reinforcements from New Mexico, and the Greers hired additional cowboys, both white and Negro, from Texas.

By 1883 the conflict had settled down to an uneasy truce. The Mexicans controlled the town of St. Johns, seat of Apache County, but the Greers were favored by an American territorial government and judiciary. The fight was at a temporary standoff.

On June 24, the day of St. John the Baptist, patron saint of St. Johns, the Mexican community planned a fiesta complete with feasting and a bullfight. They sent a special invitation to Dick Greer, inviting him to bring his cowboys and telling him that cattle would be for sale cheap.

Greer came with his cowboys, but soon found that the fiesta program included not only a bullfight but also an ambush. Seeing that he was slowly being surrounded by armed Mexicans, he and his cowboys began to edge back toward their horses. The Mexicans moved to cut them off. Only three cowboys reached their horses. One was Hi Hatch, who was wounded in the first shooting and had to be helped out of town by a second cowboy. The third cowboy, "Nigger Jeff," protected their rear. Jeff was himself wounded before they finally escaped into Dry Lakes Country after a long running fight.

Dick Greer, his brothers and the other cowboys found shelter in an adobe house and held off the crowd. Only after a prolonged siege, the deaths of two of the cowboys and a parley with Solomon Barth did they surrender. Thrown into the county jail, charged with the murder of Mexicans killed during the fight, they were saved from lynching by the intercession of friendly Mormons. Later freed by a cowboy jury and a sympathetic judge, the Greer brothers returned to their ranch and home range. But they returned only to organize and resume the fight. Now the range war was again in the open.

Accompanied by Jeff and Joe Woods, Dick Greer soon killed another Mexican sheepherder. Then the three of them rode to Holbrook, a friendly cattle town, where Greer surrendered to the judge. While he was being examined, sixteen Mexican deputies rode in, arrested Jeff and Joe Woods, and prepared to return them to St. Johns for trial. The situation of the two cowboys was desperate. Both they and Greer were certain that if the Mexican posse took them out of Holbrook they would never reach St. Johns alive. They believed that they would be shot on the trail and that their captors would swear that they had tried to escape.

At this point Greer appealed to Commodore Perry Owens, who had a horse ranch at Navajo Springs. Owens, an old long-haired Indian fighter, came into town carrying two six-shooters, a single-shot Sharps rifle sighted "to shoot a mile" and a light magazine rifle for closer work. Carrying all of his weapons, Owens picked four or five other Texans and "surrounded" the hotel where the Mexicans held Jeff and Joe prisoners. Then he walked in, bluffed the posse and ordered the prisoners out.[45] With this jail delivery, "Nigger Jeff's" name disappears from the stories of the range war. He may have left the range, or he may have left Arizona.

Or he may have continued to ride and fight. His story illustrates the difficulties faced by any modern reader who tries to discover the role of Negro cowboys in the West. Jeff might never have been remembered as a Negro if his nickname had not included an offensive epithet or if he had not posed for his picture with a group of his friends in a local photographic studio. He might never have been remembered at all, for that matter, had he not ridden through a large crowd of hostile Mexicans, fighting a rear guard action against nearly hopeless odds, helping to save the life of another cowboy.

Most of the thousands of cowboys who rode through the West are now nameless. They drove cattle, crossed rivers, got sick on alkali water or bad whiskey, and retired young. But they never made the papers, never fought in bloody range wars and never were named or described in memoirs of old cattlemen.

It is no accident, then, that in Arizona the existing records show only a few Negro cowboys—such as Jim, who fought John L. Sullivan; Bat, who fought off Mexican

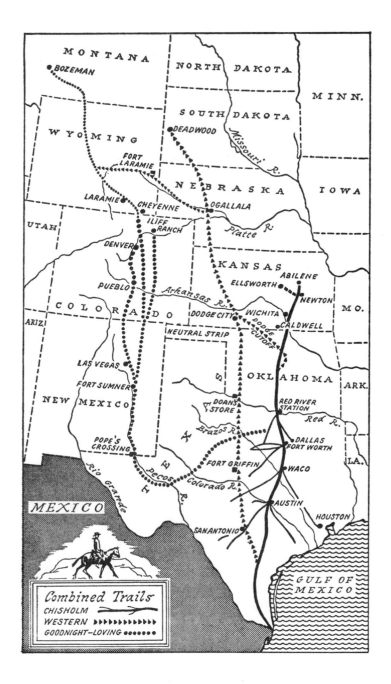

MONTANA
BOZEMAN

NORTH DAKOTA

MINN.

WYOMING

SOUTH DAKOTA

DEADWOOD

FORT LARAMIE

LARAMIE

CHEYENNE

NEBRASKA

IOWA

OGALLALA

ILIFF RANCH

Platte R.

UTAH

DENVER

PUEBLO

Arkansas R.

KANSAS

ELLSWORTH

ABILENE

NEWTON

MO.

COLORADO

DODGE CITY

WICHITA

CALDWELL

ARIZ.

NEUTRAL STRIP

DODGE CUTOFF

LAS VEGAS

FORT SUMNER

OKLAHOMA

ARK.

NEW MEXICO

DOANS STORE

RED RIVER STATION

Red R.

Brazos R.

POPE'S CROSSING

Rio Grande

Pecos R.

FORT GRIFFIN

Colorado R.

DALLAS
FORT WORTH

LA.

WACO

MEXICO

AUSTIN

HOUSTON

SAN ANTONIO

GULF OF MEXICO

Combined Trails
CHISHOLM
WESTERN ▶▶▶▶▶▶▶▶▶
GOODNIGHT–LOVING ●●●●●●

bandits; and Jeff, who rode in a range war. For the same reason, too, the story of Negroes in Colorado, Wyoming and the northern ranges is out of focus. It concentrates on blood and booze and booty. Not because all Negro cowboys were peculiarly fierce, drunken or criminal, but because only murder, theft and riot made news.

·⊰[8]⊱·

Driving to the Open Range

In Colorado, Wyoming, Montana and Idaho the cattle business began with the misfortunes of travelers, the hostility of Mormons and the hunger of miners. During the two decades before the Civil War, traders and mountain men established road ranches and posts along the Oregon Trail, selling supplies and equipment to the pilgrims bound for Oregon and California. From this trade, selling flour for as much as a dollar a pound and potatoes for five cents apiece, they made large profits, but they soon found an equally profitable sideline. Their own beef and work cattle grew strong and fat on the rich bunch grass of the high plains at the same time that the covered wagon trains found that long weeks on the trail wore down, lamed and gaunted their traveling stock. Consequently a trader made profitable deals: one of his own steers for two of the traveler's, or a few pounds of pork and a scant measure of flour for an exhausted milk cow. A trader's herd grew rapidly as emigrant trains moved west.[1]

Some traders were abruptly ordered out of Mormon territory in 1857. In that year, when the Mormon church ex-

pelled all Gentiles, storekeepers traded their goods for
cattle, making the best deals they could, and drove west
toward California mining camps or north toward the Oregon Trail and on to the isolated valleys of western Montana, where they could hold and winter their stock in com-
parative safety.

Discovery of gold in the Rocky Mountains opened a
market for all these cattle and many more. By 1859 thousands of miners were pouring into Colorado for the Pike's
Peak gold rush. Only a few years later gold was discovered
in Montana, and soon new towns like Helena and Virginia
City were full of hungry men. Beef prices soared: "Even
a poor worn-down ox might bring one hundred dollars in
gold when its owner auctioned it off to the Sunday crowd
of miners in the street of Virginia City." [2]

The Colorado mines were the first to create a demand
greater than the local supply. Soon the Colorado towns
bought beef cattle from northern New Mexico; and John
Iliff, who had arrived in the Colorado Territory in 1859,
began building what was to become one of the largest of
the Western cattle empires. By 1861 he supplied Colorado
mining towns from herds that ranged over seventy-five
miles of the South Platte. In 1866, after Goodnight and
Loving had pioneered their trail out of Texas, Iliff took
delivery of the last of their herd.

By 1867 other beef markets opened. The Union Pacific
Railroad tracks reached Cheyenne, Wyoming, and at its
end of track more than ten thousand hungry people waited.
Even more significantly, it offered an outlet to Eastern
markets and so a reason for stocking the northern ranges.
With the coming of the railroad the stage was set for the
great Beef Bonanza, the two decades of boom and bust that
accounted for the cattle industry of the northern plains.

During those years the rails continued to push west as well as north and south, linking Denver with Cheyenne and Kansas City by 1879, and entering Montana a decade later.

Up to the northern ranges came hundreds of thousands of Texas cattle, first to Colorado, then to Wyoming and finally to Montana and Idaho. This was the direction and sequence of the great drives, although there were always early pioneers and maverick Texas drovers who entered distant ranges years and even decades before others followed. Thus in 1866, the same year that Goodnight and Loving started their drive to New Mexico and Colorado, Nelson Story left Texas and drove more than six hundred longhorns from Dallas to Montana. He followed the Bozeman Trail—a route pioneered by prospecting John M. Bozeman in 1862—along the old Oregon Trail to a turnoff at Fort Fetterman, near the North Platte River, and thence north to Montana at about the place where the Little Bighorn River crossed the territorial line. Then he drove northwest to Virginia City, where he sold most of his cattle and turned the rest out to fatten on the grasses of the Gallatin Valley.[3]

Story's drive was the exception, not the rule. Few cattlemen wanted to follow his example, for they knew the Bozeman Trail was long and dangerous. It was menaced by the Sioux, tribes so fierce and so capably led by chiefs like Red Cloud that they soon forced the federal government to abandon three forts built along the trail in 1866 for the protection of travelers.[4] Montana hardly seemed attractive to Texas cattlemen and cowboys, most of whom turned instead to nearer markets.

When the Union Pacific reached Cheyenne in 1867, Texas cattle had already headed that way; and when the Kansas Pacific arrived in the Colorado Territory in 1869, the longhorns were there waiting. By 1870 Colorado ranges were being cleared of buffalo by an annual kill of 1,000,000, and more than 271,000 head of stock grazed in the territory. Ever increasing numbers of Texas cattle and Texas cowboys began moving to and through the state.

As always, the name of a single cowboy emerged from sweaty, dusty anonymity only if he made news. Thus Dan Diamond, one of the "worst" Negro cowboys ever to come to Denver, made headlines in the early 1870's by participating in a break from the county jail, a group escape which "resulted in one of the most exciting scenes ever witnessed in a prison." He broke out of the jail, stole a horse and rode more than twenty-four miles down the South Platte before being recaptured by a posse.[5]

Throughout the seventies Colorado continued to develop its cattle industry, and in 1876 it took the lead in the incorporation of new cattle companies, some small, some large. In 1878 when John Iliff died, he was acknowledged the "great cattle king of the Western Plains," owning thousands of cattle on rangeland that stretched along the South Platte River through Logan and Morgan counties and into the Lone Tree Creek and Crow Creek areas of Weld County.[6] By 1881, Denver had become a major stock center, with stockyards built near the center of town and many more constructed along the South Platte. "In the next seventy years," one historian reported, "thirty-three and a half million cattle, nearly four million calves and more than a hundred and one million sheep would pass through the Denver stock yards."[7]

Many Negroes, not all of whom were cowboys, worked in the stockyards. Others worked in mines like the Robert E. Lee at Leadville, where $118,500 in silver was mined in one day. Still others worked in saloons: when the little town of Robinson, near Leadville, opened its first school, one of its students was a ten-year-old Negro girl named Pearl, who went to school during the day and sang in a dance hall at night.[8] At least one Negro was hired as a detective—"and he proved quite a capable detective"—to track down a murderer. He stationed himself in the Pueblo, Colorado, cattleyards, being pretty sure that Schamle, the murderer, would eventually turn up there. The Negro was right, and Schamle was soon caught.[9] A few Negroes worked outside the law until they ended up inside some of the new jails of the Centennial State. In 1884, for instance, when a disguised detective was mistakenly arrested and thrown into the bullpen of the Denver jail, he remarked that "it contained about twenty of the worst specimens of humanity, both black and white, that it was ever my misfortune to be housed with in one small room." [10] Two years later Andy Green, "a negro tough" who had been convicted of the murder of a horse car driver, was the last man to be hanged publicly in Denver.[11]

But many Negroes rode into or through the state as members of Texas trail crews. As new ranges opened up, some Negroes remained to become permanent settlers. Even in the remote fastnesses of Brown's Hole in the northwestern corner of Colorado—a notorious resort of train robbers, rustlers and horse thieves because of its nearness to the borders of the three separate territories of Utah, Colorado and Wyoming—Negroes found permanent places in the cattle business. Brown's Hole, a valley thirty to thirty-five miles long and about six miles wide, had been used as a winter range as early as 1871; but not until the early eighties did it contain permanent, established ranches engaged in year-round operation. Then it showed "in microcosm everything that had characterized the vast range-cattle industry." [12]

The cowboys came from everywhere. "We had men from Texas, California, Idaho, Nevada, Oregon, Montana, and a few from New York, and other Eastern states," Charley Neiman reported. "Occasionally a Mexican puncher would drift in with one of the Texas trail outfits. I know of several Negro cowboys . . . [who] made extra good cowhands." [13]

One Mexican, possibly the most notorious in Brown's Hole, was Juan José Herrera, known as Mexican Joe. When his reputation in Wyoming became too unsavory and his unpopularity too great, he fled south. His flight was hastened by a last gunfight with a Negro badman who had contracted to kill him. In that fight the Negro failed; indeed the Negro "departed this life," and Mexican Joe fled to the Hole.[14] How he then made his living is not clear, and it is doubtful that many men asked.

Even less is known about Albert Welhouse, a Negro who operated a ferry across the Green River in the western end of the Hole. He seems to have been remembered by old-timers only because of his nickname (he was "known more familiarly as the 'Speckled Nigger'") and because he had the misfortune to fall foul of a vicious rancher named Charlie Crouse, who cut "the guts out of the Speckled Nigger in a drunken fury." [15]

In Brown's Hole, as in other parts of the West, Negroes made news by killing or being killed. But some slowly made their reputations by proving their superiority in the day-to-day work of trail and range. One such was Thornton Biggs, who worked for Ora Haley's Two Bar brand.

The Two Bar brand became a symbol of success on the

Colorado and Wyoming ranges. Ora Haley made a fortune by hiring and trusting good men. According to one report, "Haley's phenomenal success in the cattle business [was] said to be due, in part at least, to the contribution made by a long-time employee, a colored man named Thornton ('Thornt') Biggs, who during an eventful life won the reputation of being the best top hand ever to fork a bronc or doctor a sick cow on the Laramie Plains. Although he never became a range manager or even a foreman, it is said that . . . Biggs taught a whole generation of future range managers, wagon bosses, and all-around cowpunchers the finer points of the range cattle business.

"Thornt was no angel. He shot craps with consummate skill, hit the bottle occasionally, and, when he felt the urge, visited the girls in Susie Parker's house on Laramie's Front Street. Eventually he quit cowpunching, married a woman of his own race, and settled down in Laramie to a life of abject domestic misery. That is neither here nor there, the point being that Thornt Biggs was one of a small group of dedicated men without whose loyal support and technical know-how Ora Haley never would have amassed the fortune that he did amass." [16]

Like Thornt Biggs, many another cowboy moved with the center of the cattle business north into Wyoming. Colorado always remained an important stock-raising territory, but its grazing lands were limited by comparison with those of Wyoming, where nearly fifty million acres of unfenced land awaited exploitation. As early as 1879 most of the Colorado range was overstocked with both sheep and cattle, and many Colorado cattlemen joined Texans in trailing cattle north. Both they and the first settlers of Wyoming were prompt to appreciate the potentialities of lush open ranges lying along the Platte, Laramie, Sweetwater and Popo Agie rivers.[17]

Cattle moved toward Wyoming ranges, and by 1870 it was estimated that there were seventy-one thousand head in the territory.[18] During the next year, perhaps a hundred thousand cattle were added to ranges of Wyoming and western Nebraska; the Snyder brothers alone brought fifteen thousand head to Wyoming in ten herds.[19] Summing up the experience of 1871, the Cheyenne *Leader* commented: "The season of 1871 has been a memorable one in the stock business on the plains. Its success was doubted by many newcomers, but the year has closed with their unlimited confidence in the complete practicability and profits of stock growing and winter grazing. The number of cattle is now double, if not four times larger than in 1869." [20]

Cheyenne was the first capital of the Wyoming cattle country primarily because it was Wyoming's first town. Like all of the early cities of the territory, it was created or made possible by General Grenville Dodge and the Union Pacific Railroad. It was the first site in the territory of the "moving metropolis" of five to ten thousand men who made the final resurveys of the road, prepared the roadbed and laid the track. While Cheyenne was at end of track it held the boarding train, commissary and office cars, freighting depots, restaurants, saloons and whorehouses required by the construction crews. Overnight it became a city of ten thousand people in 1867, and after the railroad pushed farther west in 1868, it survived as a town of fifteen hundred.

The moving Union Pacific city, with its thousands of laborers—most Irish, but at least three hundred Negroes—pushed on across Wyoming toward Utah, leaving behind some ghost towns like Benton and Bear River ("a few barrel hoops and 100 nameless graves") but also giving lasting life to towns like Laramie, Rawlins, Green River and Evanston. By the time the Union Pacific met the Central Pacific at Promontory Point in Utah on May 10, 1869, it had changed the face of southern Wyoming. When the railroad had first approached the territory, the total permanent population had been only a few hundred people; after the railroad was completed, Wyoming had a population of about ten thousand.[21]

Many of the new population were employees of the railroad, and of these some were Negro. The manager of The Mountain Trout House (later renamed the Union Pacific Hotel) in Evanston, Wyoming, was Jo Cossley, a Negro who supervised a number of white, Negro and Chinese employees. When Woods Kocker Manley stopped at The Mountain Trout House with her father in 1873, Cossley learned that her father was a doctor and asked for help for one of the maids. The train was about to leave, but Cossley had the authority to hold it until Dr. Kocker had treated his patient.[22]

Another Negro, not an employee of the railroad, owned perhaps the finest hotel in Cheyenne. His name was B. M. Ford (some references say B. L. Ford), and he must have built his Ford House almost immediately after the arrival of Union Pacific track, for by 1868 he was turning guests away. When John W. Meldrum—many years later known as the Grand Old Man of Yellowstone National Park— came from New York to Cheyenne in April, 1868, with his new bride and a small wedding party, he found the hotel full. For a while he pled and argued in vain. Then, as he later remembered, "The landlord finally said he could give us one room, that was the best he could do. I told him to give the girls the room and we would go out and rustle. He told us that he had lots of floor space in the office, lots of rugs and buffalo robes, but no beds. We spent the night in the office and were packed in like sardines. When you wanted to turn over you had to holler 'spoon.' That was how I spent my first night in Cheyenne." [23]

The old Ford House stood for nearly two more years until January 11, 1870, when it burned in a great fire that razed several blocks in Cheyenne. Then Ford made plans for a new hotel, "a fine modern three-story structure," which he completed in 1875 or 1876. Said to be "one of the finest in the far West," Ford's Inter Ocean Hotel was "in style and magnificence fully equal to the Grand Central in Omaha." But by 1876, it had a competitor in the Railroad House, and the two hotels vied for patronage by sending runners and criers to the depot whenever a train pulled in. Joe of the Railroad House was famous for his "ten pound Websterian words," while Bernard, "with the persuasive eloquence of a Calhoun drew patrons to Ford's Inter-Ocean."

Ford's Inter Ocean Hotel housed a variety of guests during colorful times. One was a bridegroom who wore a high silk hat, but who was persuaded to abandon it when he was told it would surely be shot off his head if he tried to wear it on the main streets of Cheyenne. Another was Chief Spotted Tail of the Brules, who only three weeks before Custer was killed at the battle of the Little Big Horn was a guest at the Inter Ocean Hotel and warned a disbelieving audience that hostile Indians were gathering near the Powder River. One was Captain Pollock of the 9th Infantry, who met his death by falling down the hotel stairs. Other guests, like those who stayed in the hotel during a five-day blizzard in March, 1878, were grateful for its three-story magnificence, for they "walked out of second story windows on top of the drifts." [24]

B. M. Ford was obviously a successful and prominent businessman in Cheyenne's earliest days, and his hotel was the center of much of the city's life. There seems, indeed, to have been comparatively little anti-Negro prejudice in Wyoming; Cheyenne's first school, for instance, was built at the same time as the Ford House and was dedicated on January 5, 1868. The "best citizens" who gathered there for the dedication, crowding together while the thermometer outside dropped to twenty-three degrees below zero, were proud of having established a school that would be open to "all rich or poor, black or white." [25] Only ten years later, Cheyenne continued to show the same disregard for most racial and religious differences: "The Catholics held fairs and festivals to raise money for church work; the Ladies Sewing society of the Congregational church sewed for the needy and helped to raise money for the 'yellow fever' sufferers of the south. Jewish residents celebrated Yom Kippur with much ceremony. Colored voters organized a political club and nominated one of their members, W. J. Hardin, a popular barber, to the territorial legislature. Hardin was elected and served with credit." [26] Even today, as students of the University of Wyoming sing their alma mater, they boast:

> . . . the college throws its portals
> Open wide to all men free.[27]

All through the seventies and eighties, as cattle poured up the trail to Wyoming, Cheyenne was host to crews arriving with new stock. So, to a lesser extent, was Laramie. The inevitable brawls and shootings usually occurred in saloons or on the streets, for few working cowboys could afford to frequent hotels like the Ford House or the Railroad House. Sometimes bloody fights were briefly reported, as was a killing of December 12, 1870, in the Laramie *Weekly Sentinel:* "Pressly Wall shot and killed in the Bullard Saloon by Littleton Lawrence. Both colored." [28] Sometimes they were more fully described, as in this newspaper report of a Cheyenne argument: "A shooting scrape occurred last night about 12 o'clock in a house of prostitution . . . kept by some colored women. A colored man named Dozier was shot three times by a cowboy from Walsenburg who was in town, but who escaped and whose name cannot be learned. Only one of the bullets struck the negro, and that passed through the left arm and tore away the left nipple. The man bled copiously, but he boarded a train and left town last night." [29]

Some arguments were less sanguinary. When there was much excitement in Cheyenne in 1874 over the reported discovery of rich gold mines in the Dakota Black Hills, there was brief talk of mounting an expedition through hostile Indian country. Two Cheyenne Negroes, both somewhat eccentric, were persuaded to hold a public debate in the old courthouse. One was "General" Sam Fields, who spoke first and urged immediate action. The other was Henry Watson, who urged caution and explained that "the only way to get into the Black Hills was to get together an army of 10,000 men with 600 pieces of artillery." Though the "debate" seems to have been arranged as entertainment rather than as a serious deliberation, Watson may have been the winner, for no rash expeditions were mounted that year.[30] For several years more, certainly, the citizens of Wyoming had reason to respect and fear the Plains Indians. The foolhardy or unlucky learned hard lessons. In 1876, for instance, Charles Metz and his wife, accompanied only by Rachel Briggs, a Negro woman, were killed, scalped and mutilated by Indians as they traveled on the road to Laramie. Rachel Briggs was taken prisoner, but her body was later found some distance away, full of arrows. She seemed to have made a fight of it.[31] And in the same year Custer and his men died at the Little Big Horn.

Yet Texas cowboys driving great herds continued to arrive on the Wyoming ranges. Ab Blocker brought in a herd of 3,700 in 1877, using both white and Negro cowboys on the drive. His chuck wagon was drawn by oxen, and some extra work cattle were included in the drive. One of the oxen, a "most individualized" animal named Bully, soon made himself conspicuous by refusing to leave the wagon. When he was not pulling it, he was following it, with his head right at the tailboard.

One of Blocker's Negro hands exploited old Bully's love of the chuck wagon. When the outfit reached the Platte River, ice cold and running high, Blocker decided that he had no alternative but to drive the herd in and across. But the Negro cowboy proposed a different plan. He suggested that they drive the herd up the river a few miles to an old government bridge: there start the chuck wagon across the bridge but hold Bully with the lead steers on the near side; before the wagon reached the far side, let Bully loose and hope that he would bolt for the wagon, taking the lead steers and the rest of the herd with him.

Blocker tried the plan, and it worked. "The great herd strung across the bridge like a remuda of horses—the first bridge any steer in it had ever put foot upon." [32]

Other large herds came to and through Wyoming in the seventies and eighties as the plains were cleared of Indians and the open range cattle business boomed. Attracted by stories of fabulous profits, foreign investors helped to build and stock cattle companies controlling thousands of acres of rangeland. As the boom gathered momentum, Cheyenne became a financial and social center of the cattle business.

At one time Cheyenne was said to be the richest city per capita in the world. The Cheyenne Club, incorporated in 1880, became a center of power and wealth, serving imported wines and fresh oysters to men and women in formal dress. Cowboys, after watching their bosses parading by in starched white shirts and black coats, called them "Herefords" (after the white-faced range cattle).[33] Other cowboys watched—and occasionally served—great hunting parties like those of Moreton Frewen, a founder of the $1,500,000 Powder River Land and Cattle Company. One typical excursion is briefly noted in Frewen's guest book: "The party left the Big Horn Ranche the beginning of September and returned in about six weeks, the weather being beautiful. Attendants included five camp hustlers, one black cook, and Pauline (French maid). All satisfactory."[34]

For the cowboy himself, pleasures were necessarily cheaper and simpler. "His weakness," Bill Walker remembered, "ran to cards, ladies, and booze. He learned young that there wasn't much profit in any of them, but that didn't teach him sense. Any kind of gamble took his mind off everything else, and, if you wanted to see a circus, all you had to do was just dare a cowpoke to put one on."

Walker claimed that the best circus he ever saw took place in Cheyenne, where he arrived with a crew that was trailing a large herd of steers. Finding sweet water and good grazing in a coulee south of Cheyenne, the crew halted the slow drive to give the cattle a rest and to give themselves a chance to ride into town and spend their money.

"Cheyenne had only one real street then, about three blocks long, but it was sure a great street of its size," Walker remembered. "It had a clothing store with a plate-glass front, and that store front was the only mirror that a lot of those cowboys had ever looked into. That burg had plenty of ladies, too, as well as saloons and poker joints, and they all got plumb fat and prosperous as soon as our bunch hit town."

Three days later Walker's outfit was back with the herd, nearly broke, still a little drunk, probably a little hung over, and somewhat resentful of the bartenders, gamblers and "ladies" who had so efficiently emptied their pockets. So they planned one last fling, something to make Cheyenne remember them.

One of the cowboys was Bronco Sam—perhaps the same Bronco Sam who became a part of the folklore of the Chisholm and Western trails, perhaps another with the same name. In any event, he was known as a "genuine black buckaroo" who "wasn't afraid of anything and [who] could ride them all." So the crew decided to rope the biggest longhorn in the herd, saddle it, and have the Negro bronc buster ride it through Cheyenne's main street. Bronco Sam, who was no more sober than the rest, liked the idea.

They roped and saddled the steer and Sam mounted it. Then they rode toward Cheyenne, whooping and hollering and swinging knotted ropes to drive the bucking steer. By the time the show got into town, Sam's mount was frantic and maddened, and when it saw itself reflected in the plate glass window of the clothing store it was ready for a charge. Charge it did, through the window, down the aisles, over the counters, around the shelves—with the clerks diving into corners for protection. Then it charged back out through the empty frame.

According to Walker, "Sam was still in the saddle, the steer's horns decorated with pants, coats, underwear, and other odds and ends of gearin'." The steer was still jumping as the cowboys closed in to drive him back toward the herd, and Sam was shouting that he had brought out a suit of clothes for everybody in the crew.

Sam and all the others had sobered up by the time they tied the steer, unsaddled it and turned it back into the herd. Sam roped his horse, and they all rode back to town to face the music. When they got there, the storekeepers gave them a cold reception. But "Sam was wise enough to act right, all smiles, good manners, and apologies, and asked terrible polite what the damage might be. That was different. The store men got their books and tallied up, and when they told him the price—three hundred and fifty dollars—old Sam never even batted an eye; he just peeled it off in good old greenbacks and passed it over like he was donating." Then he and his crew drove out of Cheyenne.[35]

Most of the Negro cowboys who came to Wyoming in the seventies and eighties were like Sam: they rode through, staying a few days on the way or celebrating after they delivered a herd. Then they rode back to New Mexico or Texas. But some of them stayed. Sometimes they were welcome, sometimes not.

One who was unwelcome came to the Brown ranch in the middle eighties. The ranch was preparing for a roundup, and the cowboys brought in a "Negro bronc buster" who was unacceptable to the Irish cook. Forbidden to sleep in the bunkhouse, the bronc buster "slept under the stars. But he was a nice quiet man, and before long they all liked and respected him." [36]

One who was welcome was big Jim Simpson, who first came up the trail from Texas with a white and Negro crew driving a herd of longhorns. Instead of returning to Texas after the herd was delivered, Jim Simpson and Joe Proctor, another Negro cowboy, stayed in Wyoming and worked for the Flying E Ranch. Both were good hands, but Jim Simpson was more: soon he became known as "about the best roper on the range." When he became older and heavier he turned to driving a chuck wagon and cooking.

As a ranch and roundup cook he earned a reputation as one who really "knew how to wrastle Dutch ovens, pots and pans." He also knew the range and its ways, and he became a friend, philosopher and adviser for younger cowboys. When one of them became sick from drinking alkali water, Jim would send him off the next morning with a can of tomatoes and instructions to drink nothing but tomato juice. When a young cowboy on a roundup was puzzled by the disappearance of all the married cowboys—every one of them had gone home "for a clean shirt"—Jim explained: "You know them fellers are not foolin' nobody. They's just goin' home to sleep in a warm bed and cuddle up close to their wimmin folks."

On roundups, Jim was a respected member of the crew, whether he hired on as a cowboy or, in later years, as a cook. When the weather was bad, the crew all slept in a big tent, and when the weather was good, they slept outside. When Jim was a cook, everybody helped to drag in his wood, and when he yelled, "Come and get her," the crew took care to keep from raising dust or messing up his camp.

Although Jim knew his trade, building cooking fires that were steady and even, rarely blackening up his pots and pans, he had the inevitable problems of any cook on the high Wyoming ranges. Floyd Bard, a cowboy who rode with Simpson, remembered one morning during a late-season roundup. A heavy snow fell during the night, and everybody was cold. "It didn't take us long," Bard said, "to get dressed and to start running foot races to warm up a bit. Simpson over under the fly of his wagon was having a lot of trouble trying to cook some breakfast. The wind was blowing out the fire just about as fast as he could build it. It was about ten o'clock before we had breakfast."

During the winter, Jim played his fiddle for "kitchen dances," so called because frequently the kitchen of a small ranch house was the only room available. "Only four couples were allowed on the floor. Most always there were four times as many men as there were women. The men didn't get enough dancing even with daylight just around the corner. With the women folks it was different. They were ready to drop in their tracks, but they wouldn't own up to it. Jim Simpson, the roundup cook, was usually the fiddler and a good one." During the winter, too, Jim was welcomed at the homes and ranches of his many friends. He spent at least two winters at the George Harper ranch, assisting Mrs. Harper, who had lost a hand from blood poisoning but had still to care for her four small children. Jim, who "was neat and clean about everything he did," took over, "helping with all kinds of work." [37]

A few years later Jim Simpson appeared in a situation like a scene in an old Western movie in which shy cowboys kiss only their horses. Although women and children were becoming an increasingly important part of Wyoming society, the Flying E Ranch remained "a bachelor stronghold." As a result, when a newly married schoolteacher arrived at the ranch, all its cowboys scattered. According to the account in *Annals of Wyoming*, "when the new bride stopped in one day to get warm while on the way to Buffalo, the assembled cowboys gave one glance and disappeared like magic, leaving Jim Simpson, a colored round-up cook, fiddler and expert roper, to entertain her." [38]

Many cowboys may have been shy when they met "respectable" women, but they might better have been afraid. In a very real way the arrival of grangers, their wives, their children and their schoolteachers doomed the continued existence of the open range. Even before the cattle barons of Wyoming and Montana were staggered by the great freeze and "die-up" of 1886–1887, they felt the pressure of new settlers who took up homesteads along the rivers, claimed much of the best bottomland and began to threaten the cattlemen's control of county and territorial governments. Owners of large ranches and big cattle companies charged that the settlers rustled and butchered their cattle, and they tried vainly to outlaw or intimidate men who settled on their ranges. They complained, and apparently with some justice, that law officers (elected by settlers) would not arrest rustlers, and they found that juries (made up of settlers) would not convict the few rustlers who were arrested. Some cattlemen, at least, so despaired of legal remedies that they resorted to intimidation and murder in an attempt to maintain their control of the range and to protect their herds.

The settlers and small ranchers, in their turn, complained that the big cattle companies arrogantly persecuted all the little outfits—cutting their fences, trampling their crops, branding their stock, refusing them membership in stockmen's associations, denying them representation in roundups and threatening their lives and those of their families. Settlers grew so bitter that some of them justified or condoned the rustling or butchering of cattle company stock.

In the Wyoming Territory this conflict between cattlemen and settlers erupted finally in the famous Johnson
County War. In 1892 a group of wealthy cattlemen, claiming that their herds were being raided by rustlers who
masqueraded as grangers, organized a vigilante party, hired
a group of toughs and professional gunmen, and planned to
rid Johnson County of "rustlers." They secretly moved
their small army from Cheyenne to Casper, Wyoming, and
from there set out to strike at their enemies in Johnson
County.

They struck first at the KC Ranch, killing two homesteaders. Then they moved on toward Buffalo, the county
seat. But they soon found that news of their invasion had
preceded them and that they were about to meet a much
larger force led by Sheriff Angus of Buffalo. Quickly they
retreated to the deserted TA Ranch, where they barricaded
themselves and prepared to withstand a siege.

Now their situation had become desperate. Instead of
being man hunters, they were the hunted, surrounded by a
large and angry force of armed men. They raised rough
fortifications, and they were adequately supplied with
water, but they were trapped. As hours and days wore on,
their situation grew nearly hopeless.

News of their plight finally reached Cheyenne, and Acting Governor Barber tardily learned that some of the "best
citizens" of Wyoming were in danger. He wired the President immediately, declaring that a revolt was in progress
and requesting intervention by federal troops.

Meanwhile the situation of the cattlemen and their hired
gunmen worsened rapidly. The sheriff and his men re-
modeled a hay wagon into a fortified movable platform,
loaded it with dynamite and prepared to push this "go-

devil" against the ranch house where the cattlemen were trapped. If the sheriff had been able to carry out his plan, all the cattlemen would have been doomed, for nothing could have kept them from being blasted, burned, shot or hanged.

But the cavalry—three companies of Negro troopers— rode on the scene just in time. (Though some historians report that their commanding officer, who had little sympathy for the cattlemen and their actions, "regretted that his command had arrived quite as soon as it did.") The cattlemen and their gunmen surrendered to the federal troops, who took them into custody. So they were saved from the vengeance of the settlers they had sought to kill or terrify. The settlers could only watch as the cavalry led the cattlemen away.[39]

Among the watchers was Floyd Bard, then a boy of fourteen. "I got to see all of them," he said, "as they were being marched from the TA [Ranch] to Fort McKinney, two miles south of Buffalo. All told there were fifty of them. They rode horseback in pairs, with a Negro soldier riding on either side. First in this parade were the cowmen. Then came about ten of their seasoned killers. Bringing up the rear were the hired Texans. They were a sorry-looking lot with their stubble beards, and eyes that looked like burned holes in a blanket. They hadn't shaved for a week, had had very little sleep and nothing much to eat while bottled up in the TA ranch house." [40]

With the inglorious end of the Johnson County War, cattlemen in Wyoming began to realize that the old days of open range were over. A few diehards fought on, some hiring killers and "regulators" like Tom Horn in an effort to terrorize settlers, but as the century ended, it became increasingly obvious that barbed wire and the disappearance or regulation of the public domain made the maintenance of great cattle empires nearly impossible.

Cattlemen in Idaho and Montana learned much the same lesson at about the same time, but for them the shock was somewhat less. They had never completely controlled their territorial governments and economies, having usually been less numerous and less powerful than mining and agricultural interests. Herds in Idaho and western Montana had always been limited by mountainous country to smaller areas of land, to more clearly defined pastures, so that the transition to ranching on privately owned land was less painful. And the range cattle industry in central and eastern Montana started later than that in Wyoming, having been delayed by Indian wars, exclusion from Indian reservations and distance from markets and railheads.[41]

Central and eastern Montana did share in the great open-range boom of the eighties. As early as 1879, the editor of the *Rocky Mountain Husbandman* could write, "Eastern Montana is booming. The shackles that have bound it in years past have suddenly burst asunder and its latent resources are beginning to be aroused. . . . Stock is pouring in from every hand . . ." [42] A year later the first railroad track entered the territory.

There were probably fewer Negro cowboys in Idaho and Montana than in any other part of the cattleman's West. One reason was race hatred and bitterness: early steamboat traffic up the Missouri had resulted in the immigration into Montana of many "unreconstructed" Southerners and the simultaneous arrival of a number of transient Negro steamboat crewmen and river front roustabouts. According to one writer, "Many frontier towns in the Far West suffered from anti-Chinese sentiment and riots, but [Fort] Benton was one of the few which also bore the burden of anti-Negro racism. By 1882 this hostility reached such heights that the town's leading citizens petitioned the local school board to establish a separate school for its colored children." [43] This petition was in order because the territorial legislature had early passed a law requiring separate schools for Negroes. That law, however, was repealed a year later: the legislature found that no such schools had been established, and "colored children had been deprived of education." [44]

Some bitterness led to murder. John Beidler, for instance, was a deputy marshal in Helena, Montana, when an unarmed Negro was shot down on election day. According to his story, "There was bitter feeling. The territorial legislature had passed an act prohibiting colored people from exercising the right of franchise conferred upon them by the Constitutional amendment. Marshal Pinney received orders from Washington to see that the colored vote offered should be cast.

"In the morning, about nine A.M., before the polls opened, I was riding a good horse. About the head of Main Street I heard a shot fired down the street. I went there in a few jumps and found a Negro, lying dead on the sidewalk. Got off my horse, handing the lines to a boy. There was a man in the middle of the street, six-shooter in hand, still smoking."

Deputy Beidler investigated and found that the killer, a white mule skinner named Leech, had been going to the polls when he had met the Negro and said, "You nigger son of a bitch! Are you going to vote today?" The Negro said, "I don't know, boss." With this provocation, Leech drew his gun and fired. He was later arrested and jailed, but he soon broke out. No reward was offered for his recapture, and he was not seen in Helena again.[45]

This kind of violence, sometimes provoked, sometimes unprovoked, seems even to have spread to the ranches and roundup camps. Here, for instance, is one cowhand's story of a killing in the middle nineties:

"Long Henry (Henry Thompson) was repping with our outfit in 1896 for the M—N. He had come up the trail with that outfit, and was supposed to have killed four men at different times. He was considered a bad man. But I knew Henry very well and I can't recall a more good natured fellow. He was always laughing, and would give you his shirt. The only killing that I know he done was a Negro cook that was working for the same outfit as Henry was. The cook started for Henry with a big butcher knife, and Henry didn't argue with him but shot him through the heart.

"I have always had a curiosity to know how a person felt that had killed somebody, and one time when Henry and I were alone I asked him about the killing of the negro. It didn't seem to bother him one bit. He laughed all the time he was telling me about it. He said that when the negro started for him he just picked out a button on his shirt and throwed the old forty-five down on it and hit it dead center. That seemed to tickle him that he had made such a good shot. He was tried in the court at Miles City and was cleared on the grounds of self-defense." [46]

Montana had no monopoly of cheerful killers, but it seems clear that its citizens, school boards and legislatures did little to make the territory or state particularly attractive to Negroes. The late opening of its eastern ranges also acted to reduce the number of Texas trail crews entering the territory. Consequently few Texas Negro cowboys entered or remained in Montana. Negro cowboys drove longhorn cattle, which were no longer in great demand. By the early eighties the range cattle industry was beginning to develop interest in improving the breed of its herds. Cattlemen imported Shorthorn, Durham, Angus and Hereford stock from the East and Middle West to supplant the rangy longhorns. Train shipments began to replace many of the old trail drives.

So the census figures, though never very accurate indicators of the drifting cowboy population, show comparatively few Negroes. The census counted 183 Negroes in the Montana Territory in 1870, and 346 in 1880. A census of Billings County in 1885 showed 737 inhabitants, "nine of them Negroes, one Indian." [47] Consequently the memoirs and tales of Montana cowboys mention few Negroes.

Scattered references, however, show that even the Montana range was never so lily-white as it seems to be in Western fiction and on motion picture and television screens. The bullwhacker who drove the lead team of a Murphy, Neel and Company thirty-wagon train carrying silver bullion was a Negro.[48] A number of ranch and roundup cooks, too, were Negro, though the names of few are recorded. One of them was George of the RL Ranch, who was long fondly remembered for his skill with pies and cakes and for his kindnesses to drifting cowhands.[49] Other Negroes lived in towns and served cattlemen and cowboys at livery stables, saloons and hotels.

Typical of those associated with the cattle business, though not a part of it, was the Negro woman who ran a laundry in the little town of Maiden. Assisted by her sixteen-year-old daughter Laura, the laundress conducted her business efficiently and earned the respect of the commu-

nity. She also retained the respect of cowboys from the surrounding range, who used to gather in the warm laundry
on winter evenings. They joked with her, and they enjoyed
her retorts, for she was, as one of them remembered, "some
fighter, and we all knew it." They learned, too, that one
house rule was rigidly enforced: "If any of the boys said the
least thing out of the way to Laura he had to get out and
not come back again either." [50]

Another Negro woman known as a fighter was "Black
Mary," onetime nurse and servant to the Ursuline Sisters
at St. Peter's Mission. She later became a restaurant owner,
a freighter, a stagecoach driver and finally, when she was
about seventy, a laundress in Cascade, Montana. During
her long life, Mary Fields learned to use a revolver and a
shotgun, fought at least one gun duel and developed a taste
for hard liquor and black cigars. Even in her seventies,
when a defaulting customer passed the saloon in which she
was downing a straight shot, Mary took direct action. She
followed him down the street, grabbed him by the collar
and knocked him down with her fist. Then she marched
back to the saloon.

"His laundry bill is paid," she said.[51]

Mary Fields and the other Negro men and women living
in Montana were isolated and their numbers were few.
And clearly they were not cowboys. Most of the few Negro
cowboys who worked in the territory seem to have come
from Texas, delivered their herds and ridden back down
the trail. They came to Montana, but they were never a
part of it.

Among them, for instance, were cowboys from the XIT
Ranch in the Texas Panhandle. They shipped and drove
cattle from a three-million-acre ranch in Texas to a two-
million-acre range in Montana. They began this movement

of cattle in 1890 and continued it until the turn of the century, bringing young steers from Texas to the finishing range in Montana. Characteristically, the crew of the first drive included not only six white cowboys but also "a colored man by name of Charlie who lived at Tascosa and Channing. He was the horse wrangler." Other drives followed, and "before the Montana summer range closed down, many an XIT cowboy had learned the route north from Buffalo Springs, the XIT collection spot in Texas. Some became Montanans for life; to others it was always a foreign land, curious and likable but no place to live." [52] Presumably most of the numerous Negro XIT hands were in the second group.

The manner of their going and coming signaled the approaching end of the heroic days in the cattle industry. By 1890 the cattleman's West was changing rapidly. No longer did trail bosses drive north from Texas through Indian territory. Instead, like the XIT bosses, they loaded their cattle and cowboys on trains. For the XIT the trip from Channing, Texas, to Wendover, Wyoming, was a direct run on the Chicago, Burlington and Quincy Railroad. Then the XIT crews drove their herds only the comparatively short distance from Wendover to Custer County, Montana. After the herds had been released on the new range, the cowboys rode horseback to Wendover and took the train to Texas.[53]

When most of a "drive" from Texas could be made in cattle cars and coaches, the old trails were abandoned. In describing the cattle drives of 1890, Maurice Frink wrote, "What had been a flood, fifteen years earlier, was now a trickle that would soon run dry. Rail transport was being used. Ranges along the old trails were so fully stocked and so well managed that passing of the northbound herds was a loss and inconvenience to ranchmen along the way adjoining the trails." [54]

The day had come when most cowboys rode fence, not trails.

···❧ 9 ❧···

The End of the Trails

The trail drives and the open range cattle industry had to be short-lived. The cattle kings, with their large crews of cowboys and their great herds of cattle, helped to open up the West, but in doing so they helped to doom their own way of life.

First of all, because pioneering cattlemen made fortunes, their success quickly attracted others. Beginning in the middle seventies, the incorporation of cattle companies gathered momentum each year until the early eighties, when the cattle business entered a time of boom and speculation, drawing capital not only from the East but also from Scotland and England, with investors buying and selling unseen herds on "book count," expecting 10, 15 or 20 per cent profits, and throwing ever larger numbers of cattle on seemingly unlimited ranges. By the summer of 1886 most of the best rangelands of New Mexico, Colorado, Wyoming and Montana were overcrowded and overgrazed.

Partly as a defense against other cattlemen or sheepmen and partly in an attempt to bar homesteaders from access to the public domain, cattle barons began to string thousands of miles of fence, frequently enclosing not only land that they owned but also federal lands. They used the new barbed wire—two strands so twisted that they held barbs rigid—that had been developed by Joseph Glidden and Isaac Elwood and put into large-scale manufacture in 1874. By 1880 more than 80,000,000 pounds of wire had been sold, and spiny barriers began to cross and recross the Western ranges. In time barbed wire threatened to cross and block the established trails.[1]

By overgrazing and fencing their ranges, the cattlemen contributed to the great debacle of 1886–1887. They held hundreds of thousands of marketable cattle on already overcrowded ranges during 1885 and 1886 because of what they believed to be temporarily low beef prices. Then the summer of 1886 in Dakota, Montana and Wyoming was the hottest and dustiest on record, drying up water holes and parching the grass. As the drought continued through July, streams ran low and stopped, and fires roared through the dry grasses. By the end of the summer the best of the winter forage had been destroyed.[2]

Then followed the worst winter ever to strike the northern ranges. It began in November with an early storm in which temperatures dropped to zero and it continued with colder weather in December. By January, when sixteen inches of snow fell on the level and the temperature in Montana dropped to forty-five degrees below zero, some animals froze to death standing. Herds were "drifting helplessly, unable to find food or water. On top of the snow an icy crust formed which lacerated the animals' noses and cut their legs. They died singly and in huddled masses."[3] Many that might have saved themselves by drifting with the wind were stopped by barbed wire and died.

The next spring, when cowboys rode the devastated range, they found piles of dead cattle all along the fences.[4]

Estimates of losses varied widely. One Montana historian, describing the destruction on the northern ranges, claimed that the "most fortunate lost half of their stock, but many of the losses exceeded 75 percent." [5] This kind of catastrophe was dramatized by Charles Russell, a cowboy artist who was working with a crew in the Judith Basin. When his boss wrote in the spring of 1887 to ask about his cattle, Russell made a famous answer. On a postcard he drew a poor gaunt cow standing on shaky legs, and underneath the picture he wrote, "The Last of 5000."

The winter in Wyoming was less severe, though crippling. T. A. Larson estimated that "while some herds suffered losses of eighty and ninety percent, the loss for all Wyoming Territory was not much above fifteen percent." [6] Losses in Colorado were smaller still, and New Mexico and Texas were almost untouched. Yet all cattlemen suffered in 1887 as the boom ended and thousands of cattle were dumped on the market to satisfy creditors. Cattle prices in Chicago dropped so low that Western steers brought little more than freight charges.

Throughout the West the cattle industry was in crisis. The blizzards and die-up of 1886–1887 dramatized the hazards of the open range at the same time that much of the range itself was disappearing. Land along the water courses, in the lush valleys where the grass grew tall and cattle could find shelter, was being settled by homesteaders. When these "nesters" fenced their places, they shut off access to water, and as their number increased, their fences made exploitation of thousands of acres of adjoining rangeland difficult or impossible.

In Wyoming alone, by 1888, small farmers were coming

in at the rate of fifteen families a day. Maurice Frink described the situation in neighboring states: "In Dakota the population had more than doubled in the early 1880's; by 1885 there were 415,600 persons living in an area where five years before there were 135,177. By 1890 there would be half a million. In Montana, between 1880 and 1890, the population increased 365 per cent. One rancher moaned that he had been ruined 'by the three G's—God, Government and Granger.'" [7]

All of the "three G's" accelerated the transition from open range to ranch operation. Although some diehards tried to continue as before, some like those who organized their own little army and launched the Johnson County War in Wyoming, most cattlemen realized that the old days of great herds, great drives and great roundups were over. Increasingly they turned to growing hay and other supplemental feeds, to reducing the sizes of their herds and improving the quality of their stock and to giving better care to smaller herds. Necessarily they withdrew to lands that they owned or leased. As the size of cattle companies and ranches was reduced, the number of cowboys they employed was also reduced.

Certainly the rough winters of the northern ranges encouraged this change, but so did the facts of the marketplace. Even in New Mexico, where the climate was kinder than in Montana, the trend was to smaller ranches. Writing in 1890, the governor of New Mexico reported: "After years of experience, the owners of cattle have demonstrated that the business of cattle-ranging on the open ranges is not profitable, and there is a disposition to smaller holdings and to confine the cattle in inclosed pastures. Prominent ranchmen express the opinion that 500 cows confined in pasture will produce more profit than 5,000 on the open ranges." [8]

Even in Texas, where land was most plentiful, many large operations were finally abandoned. Perhaps the story of the XIT Ranch best illustrates the changing nature of the cattle business at the end of the nineteenth century.

The genesis of the XIT Ranch was an act of the Texas legislature in 1875 which authorized the sale of state lands to finance the construction of a new state capitol. That authorization was implemented in 1879 by the appropriation of 3,050,000 acres to underwrite construction. Then the legislature sold 50,000 acres to pay for the cost of surveying the rest, and it advertised that 3,000,000 acres would be allotted to whoever would build the new statehouse.

Although the contract was first let to Matthias Schell of Rock Island, Illinois, it was soon assigned to the Chicago syndicate of Taylor, Babcock and Company. In return for the 3,000,000 acres in ten counties of the Texas Panhandle, the syndicate built the $3,334,593.45 structure which is still the capitol of Texas. Then the syndicate prepared to start a ranch three times as large as the present-day King Ranch.[9]

It organized the Capitol Freehold Land and Investment Company, Limited, in England in 1885, and used the land as security for the issuance of bonds. Next the syndicate leased back the land and began to build its herds. By 1886 it had purchased more than 110,000 cattle for one and a third million dollars, had strung more than 700 miles of fence, and was preparing to trail cattle to Northern buyers in Kansas. In later years it ran as many as 150,000 head of cattle, and its cowboys rode along 6,000 miles of fence.[10]

This incredibly large ranch, split into seven divisions, sprawling over an area larger than some Eastern states, employed both white and Negro cowboys. Together they fought fires and storms, broke horses and strung fence, and drove cattle and raised hell. One white cowboy, L. L. Derrick, later remembered working with Jo Johnson, a Negro hand, to put out a prairie fire. Derrick's account is typical of the style of many cowboy reminiscences: "We finely put it out on the east and north and went to the west side. Perry Cox and Felix Castelo, that was camped at Black Water, came to us, and Yearwood sent them to watch the north side and the fire didn't break out again, as that was clost to XIT fence. The wind was from southwest, and about midnight it changed to northeast. I told the boys the wind changed; so some of them didn't think so; so pretty soon it commenced showerin'; so the fire went out." [11]

At another time, when Derrick and Jo Johnson and their crew were lost in a snowstorm, Derrick and the Negro argued that their camp was northeast, but their boss and the other hands said it was southwest. Derrick and Johnson later proved to be right.[12]

Other white XIT hands remembered adventures shared with Negro cowboys. J. W. Standifer, for instance, recalled driving one hundred miles in two days in a four-mule wagon. "Frank Owens and a man named Jones," he wrote, "are the only names of the men I can recall now, except the Negro Hal." [13] He also remembered bunkhouse "shindigs" during which Negroes sometimes danced while other cowboys watched and applauded. "Their particular favorite was an old Negro named Big Joe, whose real fame came neither from his cowpunching nor his sideline of banjo-picking, but from a pair of the most enormous feet any of the other cowhands had ever laid eyes on. Big Joe's feet got that way from going barefoot all summer. He even rode barefoot." [14]

At least two of the XIT's cooks were Negroes; one of them was Jim Perry, remembered by many men as the best cook they had ever known. Both were top hands and good riders. One white cowboy, W. T. Brown, frequently tried to ride mean, unbroken horses, but he acknowledged Jim Perry's superiority: "If they throwed me," he said, "he would ride them for me." Another white cowboy, J. A. Smiley, remembered a day on roundup when it rained so hard that the men stayed in camp with nothing to do but ride broncs. The one ride he recollected best was that of Old Bob, a Negro cook in Division 6 of the XIT. "It kept us guessing," he said, "who would win, old Bob or the bronc. Finally the bronc lost. Old Bob had just about give it up when the bronc gives out." [15]

The XIT crew grew to more than 150 men while the ranch itself moved slowly toward the twentieth century. Even before 1890 it began to replace or improve Texas longhorn stock by introducing Hereford, Shorthorn and Angus cattle. As it improved the breed, it necessarily abandoned open range practices; a cattle breeder has no desire to have someone else's scrub bulls roving through his pureblood herds. "By 1900," according to Cordia Sloan Duke and Joe B. Frantz, "the XIT consisted of seven divisions with ninety-four separate pastures, each with its particular purpose." [16]

But not even the excellent management of the XIT could show an adequate profit. The day of the corporation ranch was nearly over, and the future of the cattle business lay with individual stockmen or family ranches. In 1901, when the syndicate faced receivership because of failure to redeem English-held bonds, it began to liquidate its empire. Starting with the sale of 253,858 acres, it broke up the ranch, selling both land and cattle. By 1912, the XIT was no longer in the cattle business. After that, until nearly 1950, it sold land.

The valedictory for the XIT and its tens of thousands of cattle has been written by its historians, Cordia Duke and Joe Frantz: "In the nearly seven decades of its existence before 1950 the XIT had seen the vision of the original partners of the Capitol Syndicate realized. The nine counties, plus the thin slice of Cochran County into which the XIT lapped over, that composed the ranch had become fine agricultural acreage, with good yields of wheat, cotton, and sorghums. The area still had spaciousness, but 100,000 people now lived where formerly 150 cowboys and a handful of foremen, women, and children had been the total population. Railroads and highways crisscrossed the ranch area; women met in Wednesday study clubs and men in Chambers of Commerce; and law and respect for order had replaced a morality sometimes enforced by strong-arm methods. Civilization, whatever that is, had marched on." [17]

It is true that civilization spared a few giant ranches; and of these, the greatest is the King Ranch, with headquarters in Texas. But perhaps it is better to say that the astute family management of the King Ranch anticipated the changes that civilization would bring. The ranch was among the first to abandon long trail drives, for after 1885 it shipped all its cattle by train. The ranch never incurred a large bonded indebtedness that could force liquidation of its holdings, and it pioneered in cattle breeding as well as in scientific range management. As early as 1886 it began systematic efforts to improve the beef qualities of its stock, efforts that culminated in the development of the Santa Gertrudis breed. This cross between Indian Brahma stock and pure-blood Shorthorn cattle was admirably suited to the subtropical summers of the Texas coastal ranges and helped to make the King Ranch far more profitable than it might otherwise have been. The King Ranch management was also especially farsighted in pioneering the clearing, seeding and watering of its range and in being prompt to adopt mechanical advances to ranch operation. And finally, of course, after more than eighty years of success as a cattle ranch, it was aided by the drilling of its first productive oil well in 1939. Other wells producing substantial revenues followed in rapid succession.[18]

Today a visitor to the King Ranch can spend a week and "never see a cowboy." Now the foreman drives a Buick sedan, and most of his crew drive or ride in trucks. The talk on the ranch is about artificial insemination of cattle, about entomological experiments for control of the screwworm fly, and about the evils of government subsidies and acreage controls. The ranch does have eighty men who sometimes ride horses, but their work is far different from that of the old cowboys who rode the original cattle trails. If the foreman is asked how many cowboys he has, he replies, "Well we don't use the word cowboy." [19]

Other people do use the word, but its meaning has changed. Except on a few ranches on isolated marginal lands, a cowboy is now more a farmer and mechanic than he is a horseman and roper. When he rides, it is usually in a jeep or pickup truck. If a job does require the use of a horse, frequently both man and horse ride to work, with the man in the cab of the truck and his mount in a horse trailer. Some horses learn to enjoy the rides and jump in their trailers without being driven or led.[20]

One of the best descriptions of the modern cattle business has been written by C. L. Sonnichsen in *Cowboys and Cattle Kings: Life on the Range Today*. In 1948 Sonnichsen, already known as a versatile scholar whose wide-ranging interests embrace both seventeenth-century English literature and nineteenth-century Texas gun battles, accepted a commission from the Rockefeller Committee at the University of Oklahoma and traveled from end to end of the cattle country studying the way of life of modern cattlemen and cowboys. His book was his report.

He found what he had probably suspected: that the old frontiers have vanished and that the old cowboy has disappeared from almost every range except the newsstand, the bandstand, the motion picture theater and the television screen. There, of course, the cowboy still fights and sings either in a timeless past or in an unreal present. "The stories and songs," Sonnichsen concluded, "never even hint that the old cowhand from the Rio Grande does most of his business in a pickup truck these days and spends the best part of summer in the hayfield, though such are the facts." [21]

To illustrate the change from trail herding to scientific beef building, Sonnichsen quotes the *1948 Annual Report of Texas A. and M. College:* "What happens when good crossbred cattle are put on improved, fertilized pasture, given mineral supplement, sprayed with DDT for flies, treated with rotenone, phenothiazine, BHC and hexachloroethene, and rotated from pasture to pasture with the seasons?" [22] The report answers its own question enthusiastically, predicting bigger and better calves and steers. But for lovers of romance, for readers of *The Virginian* and viewers of *Gunsmoke,* the question itself is depressing—almost as appetite-killing as the list of chemical additives, restoratives, fresheners and preservatives on a box of dry breakfast cereal.

The modern steer is an aristocratic behemoth, an expensively developed machine for making tender beef from grass, grain and special feeding mixtures. He is a comparatively docile beast, not even a distant relative of the rangy old longhorn. He is best worked by men on foot, slow moving and gentle, for if he is disturbed by noisy horsemen playing cowboy, he loses weight and his owner loses money. As a consequence, many ranch hands wear muddy workshoes and save their polished high-heeled boots for wear on Saturday night in town.

"We may regret the passing of the cowboy," Sonnichsen says, "but we need not be surprised at it. He belonged to a peculiar breed of men who were produced by the peculiar characteristics of the early-day cattle business. The industry has gone through revolutionary changes, and there just isn't any place for the old-time ranch hand. He would be about as much at home on a slicked-up modern ranch as Daniel Boone at a debutante party." [23]

Explaining the changes in the cattle industry, Sonnichsen continues: ". . . the all-round cowpunchers of the past are becoming victims of specialization. In their places you find tractor men, windmill men, herdsmen, and so on; and even the riders have a good many jobs to do besides riding. Milking, gardening, trucking, haymaking, cultivating, barn cleaning, and even egg gathering are taken in stride nowadays. Chores that the cowboy would once have scorned as degrading to his cavalier status he now performs without a quiver. As the farm has merged with the ranch, the cowboy has merged with the hired man." [24]

But the hired man, ironically enough, still thinks of himself as a cowboy, dressing in cowboy costume when he is not working and trying almost pathetically to identify himself with a vanished West or with the romance of a time that never existed at all. Western pictures are nowhere more popular than in Western towns, and modern ranch workers flock to see every horse opera.

Professor Leslie Fiedler watched Montana cowhands sitting at the Saturday night show. "In their run-over-at-the-heels boots and dirty jeans, they were apparently willing to invest a good part of their day off watching Gene and Roy, in carefully tailored togs, get the rustlers, save the ranch and secure the Right; meanwhile making their own jobs, their everyday work into a symbol of the Natural Gentleman at home.

"They *believed it all*—not only that the Good triumphs in the end, but that the authentic hero is the man who herds cattle. Unlike, for instance, the soldier at the War Picture, they never snickered, but cheered at all the right places; and yet going out from contemplating their idealized selves to get drunk or laid, they must somehow have felt the discrepancy, as failure or irony or God knows what. Certainly for the bystander watching the cowboy, a comic-book under his arm, lounging beneath the bright poster of the latest Roy Rogers' film, there is the sense of a joke on someone—and no one to laugh." [25]

Sometimes the joke is cynical, and a Western town laughs at itself while visitors join in the laughter. On "Roundup Day" or in "Stampede Week" the whole town plays cowboy. Gas pump attendants, drugstore clerks and real estate men wear boots and paper Stetsons, while waitresses and cashiers masquerade as cowgirls. A few old-timers may complain that the "taint of cheap and gaudy commercialism grows stronger when the Chamber of Commerce induces bald and paunchy business men to go tottering around on a pair of spiked heels to advertise rodeos or to entertain tourists," but the businessmen keep tottering around.[26]

In all these games and rites, of course, the Negro has little part. When the West became myth or a game of "let's pretend," the Negro became the invisible man, or at best, an Uncle Tom. There was no place for him in these community theatricals. He had been a real cowboy, but he could not easily pretend to be one.

The real Negro cowboys rode out of Texas after the Civil War, and most of them rode back after they had delivered their herds. A few of them stayed in Wyoming or Colorado or Arizona, but even fewer married and reared families there. They were among the pioneers, but few of their children are among the sons of the pioneers.

Some Negroes still ride on Southern ranges, herding Florida cattle or working in Texas pastures, particularly along the Gulf Coast.[27] In the 1940's, for instance, "a Negro top hand" worked for Henry Blackwell of Cuero, Texas; Jake "a real ranch cook," worked for the Lamb's Head Ranch near Albany, Texas; and all the hands on Miller Ainsworth's 10,000 acre ranch near Luling, Texas, were Negroes.[28]

One Negro cowboy will be remembered primarily by historians of science, not by historians of the cattle business. He was George McJunkin, who in his youth rode on several drives out of Texas and worked in the 1920's on the old Shoemaker ranch near Folsom, New Mexico. A good bronc buster and a top hand, he was also a collector of Indian arrowheads. On a spring day in the middle 1920's, McJunkin followed the trail of some straying cattle up a deep arroyo known as Dead Horse Gulch. Glancing across the arroyo at the other side, he noticed some bones sticking out of the bank. They looked a little like cow bones, but they were buried many feet below the surface. This strange circumstance made him curious, and so he got off his horse, slid down the side of the arroyo and began to investigate. Prying with his knife, he soon loosened a chipped flint point different from any arrowhead he had ever seen or collected. He took it with him, and eventually carried both his story and his unusual flint point back to Raton, New Mexico. From there the story was relayed to Dr. J. D. Figgins, a Colorado paleontologist.

Dr. Figgins was interested in the bones, not the flint points. But when he identified the bones as those of an Ice Age bison, the archaeological significance of the strange flint became apparent. George McJunkin, a twentieth-century Negro cowboy and bronc buster, had discovered the debris left by an Ice Age hunting party, and by doing so had rolled back the history of early America a hundred centuries.[29]

·☙ 10 ❧··

Negro Mustangers

It is not surprising that the first running of the Kentucky Derby—at famous Churchill Downs in 1875—should have been won by a Negro jockey. Not surprising because of the fourteen horses entered, thirteen were ridden by Negroes.

From the first running until 1902, Negroes won eleven of the Derbies: Jockey Lewis in 1875, Willie Walker in 1877, Isaac Murphy in 1884, 1890, 1891, Clayton in 1892, "Soup" Perkins in 1895, Willie Sims in 1896, and Jimmie Winkfield in 1901 and again in 1902. Isaac Murphy was America's finest rider during the last two decades of the century, and he was the first rider to win three Derbies. It was forty years before Earl Sande tied the record.[1]

It is also not surprising that Negroes were good horsemen. In the South they were traditionally associated with horses, working as stableboys, trainers and jockeys. And they did far more riding than most men in the North. Because the sticky clay of the South, until modern times, prevented the building of good roads, all men rode horseback. During the Civil War, white Southerners proved their horsemanship in the cavalry; after the Civil War both white Southerners and Negroes showed their skill in the cavalry and on race tracks and open ranges.[2]

When Texans began driving their longhorns to market they needed good horses—forty, fifty or even a hundred for each drive. When they went out to the open range to round up wild longhorns, they also searched for wild mustangs. The drives to market required more horses than were ordinarily available. And horses, during the first years of the cattle drives, were more valuable than cattle.

"The mustangs or mesteños," according to George Gaylord Simpson, "were originally the feral horses, the 'wild herds,' the horses that belonged to nobody, and in their original form they were probably almost pure Spanish. Some of these were caught and broken and 'mustang' came to mean also a cowpony of what had become the native western stock, with little or no infusion of more cultured strains. The years of fending for themselves in the wilds had changed the offspring of the proud Andalusian type, and the mustang lacked much in size, grace, and finish. It was, however, a horse of almost incredible stamina and endurance and was also exceptionally alert and intelligent." [3]

Once caught, a wild mustang had to be broken, and here again the Negro cowboys acquired a reputation as bronco busters. Emerson Hough, one of the first to write on the American cowboy, reported, "Some of the early Southern busters were Negroes, and very good breakers they made." [4] Clifford Westermeier also wrote of the Negroes' ability as horsebreakers.[5] Several writers, in their reminiscences of life on the range, recalled men like "Nigger George," a "most competent bronc-stomper," who worked on various Texas ranches.[6] Another horsebreaker was Joe McCloud, a Negro cowboy who worked west of the Nueces. When Joe found a really wild mustang, he tamed him gradually, and thereafter that bronc "likely became a one-man horse." [7] Yet another was Broncho Sam, "who rode anything led out to him." [8] For the good Negro horsebreaker, a bronc with a belly full of bedsprings was only a challenge.

Men like these were common in Texas, but a Negro bronc buster and horse trader in Corning, Iowa, was a conspicuous and romantic figure. For the small white boys of the community, he provided excitement and thrills. And to one of them he offered a chance to go West and become a cowboy.

The boy was Hubert Collins, the younger son of the local Methodist minister. His older brother had already gone to the cattle country, where he was a part owner of the Red Fork Ranch on the Cimarron River. Hubert plagued his parents to let him join his brother, and they finally gave in to his insistence. But they stipulated that he must be accompanied by an older person.

The man who agreed to take him was Jim Owsley, whom Hubert Collins later remembered as a tall, handsome, broad-shouldered Negro. "Jim's business," Collins wrote, "was that of a horse trader, dealing in half-wild mustangs from the prairies of Texas. Each season he traveled by rail to Caldwell, Kansas, took the Chisholm Trail there and rode into the Lone Star State for his stock in trade. Driving them up the trail to Caldwell he would ship them from there by rail into Corning. My playmates of those days must recall Jim and his herds. They combined to make excitement for us as they tore along our streets to the railroad cattle corrals, with a roar of hoofs mingled with yells of men and squeals of frightened beasts, all hidden in a cloud of dust. I knew Jim, and had him enshrined as one of my heroes, and was therefore pleased when father asked him to take me on his next trip down the trail and leave me at Red Fork. He consented, and I lost no time in acquainting all my chums of my good fortune. I became the hero of the day within my circle. This was in the month of May, 1883." [9]

Also in the year 1883 Theodore Roosevelt first went into the Bad Lands of the Dakotas, where he eventually established a ranch, and where he became interested in the Negro bronc buster Williams, described by Lincoln Lang as the first one to introduce sane horsebreaking in that section of the country.[10]

Not all Negro bronco busters were as successful as Joe McCloud, George, Broncho Sam or Williams. One who was not was reported by a man named Cole in a story told to J. Frank Dobie. When the ranch owner acquired two new horses, he turned them over for breaking to Cole and a Negro cowboy. "I roped one," said Cole, "he was a big sorrel. A Negro he roped the other, a barrel-built dun. When we saddled up, my sorrel didn't do a thing but stand as if he had been saddled every day for a year. The dun he pitched all over the pen with the saddle. The Negro was afraid to ride him and so we swapped. Well, sir, the sorrel horse nearly killed the Negro, and the dun never even humped his back after I got on him." [11]

Breaking horses was dangerous, but catching wild mustangs was more difficult. A traditional term used by horse hunters was "walking"—arising, apparently, from the theory that Indians were supposed to trail wild horses on foot, and from the story of the forty-niners who, having lost their horses, set out on foot to capture wild mustangs.[12] Walter Prescott Webb told of a team of two men capturing wild horses while on foot,[13] but J. Frank Dobie wrote that "it is doubtful if any cowboy or American mustanger ever footed it after wild horses." [14]

According to Dobie, the "social unit among mustangs, the *manada*—a bunch of mares under the command of a stallion—was as well defined as a tribal unit among the Indians." [15] A herd traveled within a limited area, rarely more than twenty-five miles across, but within that area they were fast and elusive.

The method generally used for capturing wild mustangs was for two men on horseback to walk down the herd. The two mustangers, riding alternately and on fresh mounts, pursued the herd until it was worn out from lack of rest.

The herd's success in outwitting the mustangers depended on the stallion. Normally he led his mares, taking them via devious routes, especially at night. At times, however, he got behind his herd, nipping chunks from the rumps of the slow mares. On occasion he fought another stallion—to the death if necessary—who attempted to move in on his domain.

Once the stallion was captured, preferably alive—although it was sometimes necessary to shoot him—it was not so difficult to round up the mares. But for as long as two weeks the stallion could be a devil, and frequently the mustangers gave up before the mustangs gave out.

John Young told J. Frank Dobie a story of the summer during which he decided to walk down a *manada* of mustangs which traveled between the Nueces and the Frio. The stallion, a beautiful sorrel, had thirty-five mares in his herd. Helping Young was a Negro named Bill Nunn. Young and Nunn alternated walking the mustangs for several days, until the herd appeared to be near the exhaustion point and ready for capture. But at the crucial moment for Young, when he was miles from relief, his own horse dropped dead, and he found himself alone and on foot. After many painful hours and dozens of blisters, he finally made his way back to the temporary camp. Thereupon he presented his interest in all the mustangs in Texas to Bill Nunn. "I offered to lend him saddle horses to ride while he caught them," Young said. "I had never set myself up as a mustanger; I was through with mustangs forever." Bill Nunn got a Mexican mustanger to help him and soon brought in the *manada*, which he sold for a good price.[16]

One of the most unusual of all the mustangers (Dobie called him the "most original") was a Negro named Bob Lemmons. One of Lemmons's unusual qualities was that he mustanged alone. Another mark of distinction was, in his words, "I acted like I was a mustang. I made the mustangs think I was one of them."

Unlike most mustangers, who had to keep the herd in sight, Lemmons followed tracks. He knew the tracks of his herd so well that although it might mingle with another, or cross the tracks of still another, he was always close behind. He could, in fact, distinguish the droppings from the herd he was following from the droppings of any other group. He once trailed a group of mustangs for five days without actually seeing it.

When this unusual cowboy began to follow a *manada*, he disassociated himself from all human contact. (Both J. Frank Dobie and Florence Fenley tell Lemmons's story under the same title: "The Mustanger Who Turned Mustang.")[17] He changed neither clothing nor horse. His food was placed in a tree, and he picked it up only after it had been there long enough to have lost its man-smell.

For a few days Lemmons followed his mustangs at a distance, gradually closing in. Finally, as he trailed them at close range, they began to accept him as part of the group. By the second week Bob Lemmons had moved into the group, supplanted the stallion, and was leading the mares. He had not only become a mustang, he had become the stallion.

After this transformation, Lemmons began to win the confidence of the herd. He took them to water, or he kept them from going to water. He smelled for danger in a way they could understand. If a stallion came too close it would be driven off. He led them in a flight, from fear; and he led them in a stampede. Gradually he took them onto new ranges, where he tested their confidence in him. In every way Bob Lemmons became a mustang, "except in not eating grass and in having the long, long thoughts that only a human can have."

When the band of mustangs was completely under control, Lemmons slowly led them homeward. Anticipating his arrival, other cowboys waited. The gates of a temporary corral were opened, and Lemmons suddenly broke into a dead run, leading his herd into the pen. Now that a single man, turned horse, had captured an entire herd of mustangs, it was up to the cowboys to take over and do the breaking. Bob Lemmons "actually became the leader of a band of wild horses that followed him into a pen as fresh as they had been when he first sighted them."

J. Frank Dobie was unable to account for Lemmons's unusual talents. He knew, he said, only two such men: "one was a Mexican and one a Negro—primitives with primitive instincts not worn slick by the machinery of society." [18]

Another Negro with the "primitive" qualities attributed to Bob Lemmons was a cattleman named Willis Peoples. But instead of walking down mustangs, Peoples used his talents to track down a killer wolf. The story is told by Harry Chrisman in his *Lost Trails of the Cimarron*.

Down "Crooked Creek to the Cimarron was a wild country invested with loafer wolves, 'catamounts,' coyotes, and other predators that gave cattlemen much trouble." All of these animals preyed on the stock, but the big lobos were the most destructive because they could pull down a full-grown cow and severely cut up a range bull. The cattlemen most feared a wolf known as "Old Two Toes," so called because he had once lost part of a front paw in a trap. The loss did not make him any less vicious, but made him easier to track.

The cattlemen were determined to catch Old Two Toes, whose trail of mangled cattle tripled when he took to mate "a large, black, and fierce bitch wolf." The cattlemen offered a reward, and then raised the reward, but even the professional wolfers who were brought in were unsuccessful.

One day Willis Peoples, who had a small ranch south of Meade, Kansas, near the Neutral Strip, came to town when the ranchers were discussing what to do about Old Two Toes's destructiveness. Peoples offered a proposition: if the ranchers would leave the wolves alone for one month and promise to help him in his campaign, he would guarantee to bring in the killer wolf. How, the cattlemen wanted to know, did Peoples propose to do this? He answered that he would camp on the trail of Old Two Toes day and night and would live with the wolf and his mate until the two wolves had their paws in the air while they begged forgiveness. Some of the people in the town laughed, but the ranchers who knew Willis Peoples believed him.

Peoples got a Negro friend to keep him supplied with

food, water and fresh horses, the supplies to come from the ranch nearest to where he was each day. For two weeks he stayed on the trail of Old Two Toes and his mate, never allowing either of them an unmolested rest. By this time the bitch had had enough and deserted her mate. A few days later Peoples began to detect a weakening in the lobo, and he sensed an increasing advantage. The tired wolf was now less careful in hiding its tracks and in doubling back, and late one day it finally crawled up an arroyo and lay down under a bank of clay. There Peoples came upon it and shot it in the head, from a distance of fifty feet.

The next evening he drove into Meade and dropped Old Two Toes from his wagon into the street—a wolf which measured seven feet in length. The ranchers gathered to thank and to congratulate Willis Peoples. How, one asked, did he know from the outset that he could capture the wolf, especially when he knew that so many others had failed?

His answer was simple: the wolf represented "bad," at least it was "bad" for the community. Only "good" could kill the wolf. Peoples was not sure that he was good enough, but he knew, he said, that any man with "his mind made up is a majority." His mind, he added, was made up, and that was "how it was." [19]

Peoples was a cattleman—one of the few Negro ranch owners in the West—rather than a professional wolfer, and so his story is properly told here. He was truly a cowboy. But stories of other Negroes in the West—no matter how successful their careers or exciting their adventures—are more properly told in another book. A man is not necessarily a cowboy merely because he hunts wild animals or even because he rides fast horses.

In horse racing, for example, Negroes were found not

only at Churchill Downs. Throughout the West, whenever the Indians were subdued and settlements secured, someone proposed a horse race. And when the race was run, frequently Negroes were participants. Whether they were owners, riders or trainers, they were at the starting post or the finish line.

Up in Idaho in the early 1870's, there were race tracks in many of the towns. One of the best tracks was at Boise, a half-mile course just north of town, and one of the best-known racers was a Negro named Walker—usually called "Silver" Walker, because when he was not racing he was a barber in Silver City. He owned a string of race horses which he took from track to track, throughout Idaho, and "many a dollar did he win." Not only was he a barber and a horseman, but he also took a place in state-wide activities. "The sports, most of them Southerners, never drew the color line against Walker; they dubbed him 'Silver' and admitted him without objection to the sporting fraternity. Walker was a Republican and always occupied a front seat at all the political meetings in Silver." [20]

Like most other Westerners, Walker raced his horses at little tracks, usually in small towns. But Negroes were also prominent in the development of big-time racing in the West. They were rarely owners, it is true, but they made important contributions to the sport. That contribution is illustrated by the story of one man—John (Jack) Fisher.

Fisher spent his earliest years as a slave, working as a houseboy and stablehand. After the war he worked for Edward Butler, a St. Louis politician and livery stableman. Soon he developed a great reputation among men who knew racing: they praised "this skinny Negro horseshoer whose hands could curve a horseshoe for race horses like those of no other human being."

E. J. ("Lucky") Baldwin heard of Fisher's exceptional abilities and set out to hire him. But even the persuasive Baldwin, who operated large stables in San Francisco, had initial difficulties in getting Fisher to leave St. Louis. Fisher was bound to his old employer by loyalty and affection growing out of long years of service. And he was also afraid, Baldwin discovered, of the Indians in the wild West.[21]

Lucky Baldwin's persistence and generosity eventually overcame Fisher's doubts. Fisher came to Baldwin's establishment in San Francisco, and when Baldwin later moved to the great Rancho Santa Anita in Southern California, Fisher accompanied him. There he "bred, trained, shod, and cared for" Baldwin's Derby winners, and there, too, he became the foreman of a ranch employing more than four hundred men. Today the ranch has been broken up, and most of the old oak groves have been cut down to make way for freeways, subdivisions, electronics plants and towns like Arcadia and Monrovia. But each year, even now, on the day after Christmas and until the middle of March, as many as fifty thousand people go daily to the beautiful Santa Anita track to watch the horses run over ground where John Fisher "did much to help give California a place in racing history." [22]

Fisher achieved a kind of fame, but other Negroes became infamous. The real West was like all Western stories in having a number of bad guys. They wore no uniforms; unlike the villains of old silent movies, few of them wore black masks and rode black horses. But some of them—and at least one of them among the most desperate men in the West—had black faces.

·⊰[11]⊱·

Some Were Badmen

A famous picture of Billy the Kid shows a nondescript, popeyed, bucktoothed youth staring vacantly into the camera lens. Yet Billy has become the epitome of the Western badman, the subject of many books, the hero of stories, ballads and even ballets. The slow growth of legend has made a kind of American Robin Hood out of a tough, ugly kid.

Far more handsome, though just as tough and twice as vicious, was the cowboy who rode into the Red Fork Ranch in the Indian Territory (Oklahoma) about ten years after Billy's death. He was tall and graceful, a copper-skinned man whose long wavy black hair fell to his shoulders. His clothing and Stetson were expensive, his bridle silver mounted and his rope made of black and white horse hair. He was cheerful and charming and gracious.

The young ranch owner assumed, quite correctly, that his guest was part Indian, part Negro, but welcomed him willingly. "No matter what his parentage," wrote an observer, "Red Fork Ranch was entertaining a young man who was as full of life and the joy of living as ever passed that way. He let go all holds, unbuckled his reticence, and gave himself over to the full enjoyment of unfettered talk. His life's history (his own version), stories and anecdotes came in a constant flow. He sang ditties, danced jigs and indulged in good-natured banter at the expense of the ranchman, to while away the afternoon and evening." [1]

Next morning the lively guest made preparations for a trip to the Panhandle. He donned a heavy coat and buckskin gloves, buckled on his gun belt and stowed his Winchester in its saddle holster. Then he leaped onto his horse.

"For two or three minutes he reined in the beast with one hand and allowed it to buck-jump from pure fullness of spirits. With every jump of the animal, the man let out a whoop of the same joy that animated the broncho. Then giving the horse the rein with a final yell, he tore away, turning in the saddle to doff his hat in graceful adieu, and waving it to and fro till he had passed from sight." [2]

The charming guest was Cherokee Bill, an outlaw who fascinated women, murdered countless men for fun and profit, and died on the gallows only a month after his twentieth birthday. Born Crawford Goldsby at Fort Concho, Texas, in 1876, of parents who were part Negro, white Anglo, Indian and Mexican, Bill began his inglorious career at fourteen by shooting and killing his brother-in-law. After that, he killed professionally, adding railroad agents, Indian police, express agents and storekeepers to the list of his victims. He rode with a gang specializing in the armed robbery of stores, trains and express offices, but he killed wantonly and gleefully, inspiring fear and horror throughout the Indian Territory. According to Glenn Shirley, Cherokee Bill made desperadoes like John Wesley Hardin and Sam Bass look like "small potatoes" at a time when "there was no Sunday west of St. Louis, and no God west of Fort Smith." [3]

For women he seems to have had irresistible charm. He was said to have "a sweetheart in nearly every section of the country," and for several years he traveled freely through the Indian Territory without being challenged. At least one town, according to Glenn Shirley's account, "in the interest of preserving the lives of its citizens, passed an ordinance making it a misdemeanor for anyone to molest him when he was abroad within its limits." [4] So Cherokee Bill could ride gaily from crime to crime and from woman to woman.

His very success led to his destruction. As the number of his crimes increased, so did the amount of the reward money posted for his capture. As he became more self-confident and careless he also became a more valuable prize for man hunters. When finally he visited his favorite sweetheart, Maggie Glass, the cousin of Ike Rogers, a former deputy United States marshal, he laughed at her warnings and sneered at her cousin. For a night and a day he visited Maggie while Rogers waited patiently. Then finally on the second night Bill relaxed his guard and was felled by a blow with a poker.

Handcuffed and chained, he was turned over to deputy United States marshals and carried to Fort Smith, Arkansas, to be tried before Judge Parker, a man famous throughout the West for quick trials and summary executions. Though Cherokee Bill stood accused of many crimes, he was tried and convicted for the murder of one unarmed man in a post office robbery and was sentenced to death. Then he was lodged in jail to await execution.

He did not wait quietly. He arranged to have a gun smuggled in to him and tried to stage a mass prison break of 250 federal prisoners. He sent for Lawrence Keating, the head jailer, covered him with the gun and demanded that he unlock the cell doors. When Keating refused, Bill killed him. Then, even after all hope of escape was lost, he continued a gun battle with the other guards.

This was his last battle. Forced to surrender, he was once more tried before Judge Parker, who again sentenced him to hang. This time the judge expressed regret that the law provided no harsher penalty. Glenn Shirley quotes a part of the judge's denunciation:

"You are," the judge said, "undoubtedly the most ferocious monster, and your record more atrocious than all the criminals who have hitherto stood before this bar. To effect your capture brave men risked their lives and it was only by the keenest strategy that it was effected. Even after you had been placed within the prison walls your ferocity prevented docility, and your only thought was to break away that you might return to the scenes of bloodshed from which an outraged law had estranged you. In order to make your escape you would have trampled under foot the will of the people, and releasing hundreds of your ilk, fled to your mountain and forest haunts, there to gather around you a larger and more bloodthirsty band; there to defy all power under heaven while you indulged your passion for crime; there to burn and pillage and destroy the lives of whoever stood for a moment in the way of your campaign of destruction. . . ."

The judge had even more to say, for he was a master of rolling nineteenth-century rhetoric. Not so Cherokee Bill, who walked quietly to the gallows on March 17, 1896. Asked if he had anything to say to the crowd, he answered, "No. I came here to die—not to make a speech." [5] And he died quickly.

For Judge Parker, Cherokee Bill was the worst, but certainly not the first of the bad whites, Indians and Negroes appearing before the bench of his Fort Smith court. From the very beginning, from the time the judge first picked up his gavel on May 10, 1875, he saw a long procession of criminals, and to all he meted out a kind of even, inexorable justice.

During his first two months on the Fort Smith bench, the judge tried ninety-one criminal cases. Of the eighteen men tried for murder, fifteen were convicted and eight were sentenced to be hanged. One of the eight was killed while trying to escape, and one had his sentence commuted to life imprisonment because of his youth. Six were left on September 3, the day set for their execution.

According to Wayne Gard, "The six who played stellar roles on that day were three white men, two Indians, and a Negro. One of the whites, Daniel Evans, twenty years old, had killed a Texas youth to get his boots. John Whittington, thirty, had clubbed an elderly neighbor and slit his throat to take the money from his pocket. James Moore, twenty-eight, had stolen two horses from a crippled farmer and had killed one of his pursuers—his eighth victim. One of the Indians, Samuel Fooy, twenty-six, a half-white Cherokee, had shot a barefoot white schoolteacher to rob him. Smoker Man-killer, twenty-six, another Cherokee, had borrowed a neighbor's gun, used it to kill him, and boasted of his deed. The Negro, Edmund Campbell, had killed a Negro neighbor and a young Negro woman." [6] An estimated crowd of five thousand—townspeople, farmers, women, children and newspapermen from as far away as St. Louis—was on hand when the six killers were simultaneously hanged.[7]

Like Edmund Campbell, many of the Negroes who appeared before Judge Parker were neither cowboys nor cattlemen. But they were a part of the pattern of violence on the Western frontier, a part of the violent land through which cowboys drove their herds north. Among these killers was Aaron Wilson, a Negro who in 1875 accepted the hospitality of James Harris and Harris's small boy. Wilson ate their food and spent most of the night with them; then he killed them both and stole their team. Judge Parker sentenced him to hang.[8]

Another killer was William H. Finch, a Negro who was the post tailor at Fort Sill. His story began as bedroom farce when he seduced the daughter of the post barber, also a Negro. When Finch was discovered crawling out of the girl's bedroom window, the irate father shot at him and missed. Hearing of the affair, the post commander ordered Finch off the post, and Finch left; but he took with him two military pistols, a fine pony, a saddle and a bridle—all stolen.

Now comedy turned to melodrama. Two detachments of cavalry pursued the thief and once sighted him and fired at him before he escaped into thick timber. The soldiers then turned back, and Finch's description was wired to law officers throughout the Indian Territory and Texas. Two weeks later he was arrested at Red River Station. Three soldiers were detailed to take him back to Fort Sill, but on the second night of the three-day trip he got away after killing two of his guards and stealing their guns and horses. The third guard escaped death by hiding in the brush by the river bank.

Finch again headed for Texas, once more pursued by a detachment of cavalry. And again he was captured. But this time he was securely guarded, delivered to Judge Parker's court, and there tried and hanged.[9]

Other crimes brought before Judge Parker were some-times grotesque and frequently sordid. Two men were haled before the judge for shooting a Creek Negro they had never met. They had seen a stirring in the brush, they said, and they had mistaken the Negro for a turkey. Grue-some crimes on the frontier were little different from those of today. Thus John Stephens, a Negro who resented the testimony of a widow and her sixteen-year-old son in a larceny case, entered their house at night and chopped off their heads. Judge Parker hanged him.[10]

These were the accidental and the universal, the crimes that might have taken place in Michigan, Ohio or New York. But some were peculiarly crimes of the cattle indus-try, of rustler against rancher. George Moss, for instance, was a Negro in Red River County, Choctaw nation, a settler with a taste for another man's beef. With three other men he shot a fine fat steer, prepared to butcher it and then shot the owner of the animal, who suddenly appeared on the scene. Tracked down by a searching party, Moss surren-dered and confessed. Judge Parker hanged him.[11]

Set on the western border of Arkansas, dealing with crim-inals from the Indian Nations, Judge Parker's court dealt with large numbers of Negro badmen. But other criminals were scattered throughout the West, riding ranges where the law was slower and the federal marshals fewer. Charlie Siringo, arriving in New Orleans in the early 1870's, "hunted up Babe Fisher, a yellow Negro . . . who after-wards became a noted outlaw." [12] Frank Eaton (Pistol Pete) wrote that "upholding the law was a dangerous business"— especially in 1879, when he helped to bring in two mur-derers, one of whom was Dick Van, a Negro.[13] Many states and territories were like the New Mexico of the 1880's, which "contained its full quota of bad men, both white and black. . . ." [14] Even as late as the 1890's, when Tom Smith, the captain of the Texas gunmen who had been hired for the Johnson County War, was saved from death by the timely intervention of Negro cavalry, he was saved only to be killed a few months later "by a Negro desperado on the cars between Gainesville, Texas, and Guthrie, Oklahoma." [15]

The routine crimes of violence were many, but accounts of them soon lose all interest. A catalog of shootings and stabbings, of occasional thefts and family murders, can quickly become as dull as a hardware store inventory. Only when they are parts of a story, crises in the life of a known man, do they take on coherence and meaning.

One such man, Ned Huddleston, was born a slave on a hill farm in Arkansas. When the Civil War began, his master took him and several other slaves and moved farther south. Ned, who was just entering his teens, soon was serving a group of Confederate officers as orderly, cook, nurse and forager—stealing fruit, chickens or any other food that could be used in the officers' mess. According to John Rolfe Burroughs, who has written the fullest account of the life of Ned Huddleston, young Ned "loved thieving." [16]

At war's end, Ned was free but unemployed, and so he began to drift down through Texas and into old Mexico. He worked at a variety of jobs, and at one time he became a clown performing with a rodeo in Mexico. There he met a Mexican lad his own age named Terresa, and the two became partners in stealing horses south of the border, swimming them across the Rio Grande and selling them to Texas cattlemen.

Like all sensible horse thieves, Ned and Terresa soon changed their area of operations. They moved north and west, eventually making their way into the northwest corner of Colorado, where the borders of Wyoming, Utah and Colorado meet near the secluded valley of Brown's Hole.[17] There they spent most of the rest of their lives, and there both died violent deaths.

For a time they separated, Terresa drifting into a loose connection with some local horse thieves and Ned trying life as a miner. Ned became a partner—actually, though he did not know it, only one of a long succession of "partners" —of Jesse Ewing, who was working a copper claim at the upper end of Red Creek Canyon. For a time Ned worked hard and hoped to prosper. But he had met more than his match in Ewing, a powerful man described as a "brown-baked, moody, odd freak of humanity, who cared but little for his own life, and less for the lives of others." [18] Just as he had done with his other partners, Ewing exploited Ned's young strength and strong back, spent all Ned's money on food and blasting powder, and then picked a quarrel and drove the young Negro off the claim.

Angry, bitter and penniless, Ned looked for another job. Soon he ended up working for a Chinese cook, a man who played a formidable game of poker. Later after both were in a crooked card game in which Ned lost heavily, the cook disappeared, and Ned was arrested on suspicion of murder. He was thrown into the Green River jail, where he found that his cellmate was his old partner, Jesse Ewing. Again the two clashed, and again Ned lost. During the middle of the night, he was beaten into submission with his own boot, which Ewing used as a club. Ned was a bruised and humbled man when he was released the next day after his Chinese employer turned up unharmed.

Having failed at mining and cooking, Ned turned to wild horse hunting. Joining with a number of other men, he helped to construct a log corral at Charcoal Bottom on the

Green River. Then he captured and broke wild horses. "No man in the country," Burroughs wrote, "understood horses better than [he] did." [19] Dane Coolidge added that Ned "was considered the best bronco rider that ever threw a leg over a horse." [20] If Ned had stuck to wild horses, he might have led a peaceful and successful life.

But he soon met an Indian far wilder than any of his broncos. Into his camp rode a Shoshone Indian, a woman named Tickup, who was accompanied by her nine-year-old daughter Mincy. She was fleeing the alcoholic brutalities of Pony Beater, her Indian husband, who abused both his wife and daughter. Tickup took one look at Ned, who stood six feet two inches tall—"a magnificent specimen of manhood"—and exercised all her charm. Soon they were sharing the same wickiup.

For Ned this was a happy time. Tickup was entertaining, but Mincy was fascinating. Ned was the first decent father she had ever known, and the two adored each other.

Then Pony Beater appeared, and Ned and his new family fled to the hills, covering their tracks as well as they could. Pony Beater, a Ute Indian and a skillful tracker, followed unerringly and surprised them. He forced Ned to surrender, made Tickup tie her lover with buckskin thongs, and took off with wife, child and all of Ned's belongings.

Pony Beater celebrated his victory by getting drunk, whipping his wife and child and going to sleep. The aroused Tickup went into action and widowed herself by cutting her husband's throat with a butcher knife. Then she took her daughter and the belongings of both her Negro lover and her Indian husband and returned to her own people in Idaho.

Ned, after he had been untied by his friends, found that

he could stand the loss of Tickup, but he desperately missed little Mincy. So he followed them to Idaho, only to find that there the new widow had taken another lover. Ned charged into a fight, nearly killing his rival, but being stopped by Tickup, who intervened with a stone axe. He was forced to retreat with one ear nearly severed from his head. His love affair was over.[21]

Once back in Brown's Hole, Ned again became a horse thief. It was a role suited to his talents, and it was no more nor less dangerous than being Tickup's lover. In the summer of 1875 he joined the Tip Gault gang, made up of Gault, Jack Leath, Joe Pease and Ned's old friend Terresa. It was a wild bunch, but not vicious: it stole horses and occasional cattle, but it was not a group of killers. According to Burroughs, it "was in the game not so much for profit as for kicks, thrills, the sheer hell of the thing." [22]

The kicks and thrills led to the death of all the gang except Ned Huddleston. Their luck ran out when they spotted a big herd of California horses being driven east toward Wyoming cattle country. They scouted the herd for several days and decided to stampede and scatter it so that they could steal some of the horses without risking a head-on fight with the herd's owner and his crew. When one of the horses spooked and ran out of the herd, they roped it and prepared to use it.

Their plan was simple: they would tie sagebrush to its tail and drive the frightened animal back toward the herd. With luck one spooked horse could start a stampede. So while Terresa held a tight rein on the horse's head, Pease brought up the sagebrush. But just as Pease leaned out of the saddle, the horse kicked out with both feet and knocked him to the ground. He lay there unconscious, his jaw broken and his chest crushed.

Two of the gang took the injured man back toward their hidden camp while the other two chased the frantic horse over the hill and into the California herd. All the horses stampeded and scattered, and soon the two thieves were rounding up numbers of them. As they did, they foolishly included some of the horses of a local rancher in their roundup.

Late that night the four thieves were reunited, and Ned learned that the badly wounded Pease had been unable to make it back to camp. He had been left under some trees about a half mile away. Ned agreed to act as nurse, for he had gained experience tending wounded men during the Civil War. He left the camp to watch over the dying Pease and keep him supplied with water and whiskey.

The next morning the gang found that the California herd had moved on, its drivers having feared to linger in country infested with thieves and Indians. So Gault and his men scoured the country for scattered horses, not realizing that a grimly angry local rancher was already tracking his missing saddle stock.

Ned stayed with Pease for a day and a night and most of another day before his patient died. Then he walked the half mile to camp, got a spade and returned to dig a grave. As he dug, the afternoon wore away and darkness came. His three friends rode back to camp, turned out their horses and began to make supper. They were unaware that they had ridden into an ambush prepared by the rancher and a crew of heavily armed cowboys.

Still digging a grave, Ned heard the shots that killed his partners. He was unarmed, except for a clasp knife, but he had food, water and whiskey. His only hope was that his existence was unknown and unsuspected. So he spent the long night crouching in the new grave with the body of his dead friend.

The next morning he cautiously made his way back to the campsite. The camp was deserted and the corral was empty. The rancher and his men had shot down the three rustlers, recovered the stolen horses and ridden away. The bodies of Gault, Leath and Terresa lay where they had fallen, for neither they nor the camp had been touched by the attackers. Ned ransacked the camp, taking money belts from the bodies. Then he made a hasty breakfast and began walking.

Weeks later, after he had walked for miles, stolen a horse, been wounded by its owner, collapsed from exhaustion and loss of blood, and recovered in a secluded hill camp, Ned made his way to Green River City. There, according to Burroughs, Ned "resolved to go straight. He'd leave the country, change his name, and make a fresh start." [23] He boarded a westbound train, taking with him not only his new resolves but also all the money the gang had possessed.

When he got off the train, he called himself Isom Dart. (Dane Coolidge writes this name as Isham Dart.) [24] He wandered for a time, soon making his way back to Oklahoma, where he spent several years raising cotton on rented land. During those years, he re-established contact with Tickup and Mincy, arranged to bring them to Oklahoma and paid Mincy's tuition in a boarding school.

Then Tickup died, Mincy ran off with a man, and Ned (now Isom Dart) found life dull and lonely. Again he rode west, eventually returning to the Brown's Hole country. As Isom Dart, he signed on as a horse wrangler with the Middlesex Land and Cattle Company. He still had all his old skill with horses, and he still had his old love of adventure, whether inside or outside the law.

He became a devoted follower of Elizabeth Bassett, a stouthearted neighbor who had five children, a sick husband and a small ranch. Along with a number of other cowboys, Isom Dart made her place a kind of second home. They soon came to be called the Bassett gang, partly because they never hesitated to "borrow" a steer if the ranch needed food.

As the years passed, their "borrowing" became rustling on a larger scale. The big neighboring Hoy and Scribner ranches began to lose more cattle than they could afford. They had shrewd suspicions, but they could get little proof—at least they could rarely get enough proof for an indictment, let alone a conviction. The one time that they did get a Wyoming magistrate to issue a warrant for Isom's arrest for "larceny of livestock," it was only with difficulty that the Wyoming sheriff could find a deputy to make an arrest. Finally he appointed the toughest of the local citizens, one Joe Philbrick, a deputy sheriff. He promised Philbrick a substantial reward if he would make the trip to Brown's Hole, arrest Isom Dart and bring him in.

Philbrick made the trip in a buckboard. He found Isom and served the warrant without difficulty. Then he and his prisoner began the journey back to Wyoming, driving through rough country. Just as they reached the crest of a grade, a wheel slipped off the road, the horses started to bolt, and the buckboard fell down into a small canyon, taking the men and animals with it.

Philbrick was knocked unconscious, but Isom was unhurt. He tended the deputy's injuries, got the horses and buckboard back on the road, and drove on to Rock Springs,

Wyoming. There he put Philbrick in the hospital and turned himself in at the jail. His action was much praised in the community, and when he came to trial the deputy appeared as his character witness. After Philbrick had finished his testimony, "the jury, completely ignoring the cause for which the colored man was being tried, unanimously agreed that no man who had done what Isom had done was a menace to society, and forthwith turned him loose." [25] Isom returned to Brown's Hole.

Among the best of his friends were a number of children. Just as his first great attachment had been to the nine-year-old Indian girl Mincy, so he spent the last years of his life making friends with other children. After Mrs. Bassett's daughter Josephine married Jim McKnight and had two boys, Isom spent long hours amusing and caring for them. He sang them old songs remembered from his youth in slavery, and he even staged performances based on his memories of days with the Mexican rodeo. Little Chick McKnight boasted to his mother, "Mamma, I'll never have to go to a circus, 'cause I got a circus all my own." [26]

Isom settled down and returned to his old work of catching and breaking wild horses. According to Dean Krakel, in his *The Saga of Tom Horn,* "Dart was a negro, and some say, one of the best cowboys ever to mount a horse in the high mesa country." [27] Krakel quotes George Erhard, a Brown's Hole pioneer, who wrote, "I have seen all the great riders, but for all-around skill as a cowman, Isom Dart was unexcelled and I never saw his peer." [28] With this skill, Isom slowly built up a ranch of his own, trading horses for cattle, and perhaps continuing to throw a long loop over mavericks.

One of Isom's associates was Matt Rash, a Texan who had come to Brown's Hole in the early 1880's. When the

Laramie *Daily Boomerang* reported Rash's death in 1900, it described him as a "Well Known Cattleman" and reported that he "was generally well respected." This report seems to be substantiated by the fact that Rash was president of the Brown's Park Cattle Association at the time of his death.[29]

Yet later writers disagreed. Burroughs said that Rash was a thief and an untrustworthy ladies' man. Dane Coolidge described Rash as a rustler who "ran off thousands of cattle from all the neighboring ranges." [30] Whatever his character, he was Isom Dart's friend, and both men died at the hands of the same assassin.

Their killer was Tom Horn, long famous in the West as a range detective, Indian fighter, "regulator" and murderer. Hired by one or more Wyoming cattlemen, Horn assumed the name of Hicks and rode down into Brown's Hole looking for rustlers. A competent cowboy and a companionable man, he found it easy to win the confidence of his intended victims. Soon he was working and riding with them, and perhaps he joined them in rustling cattle.

He seems even to have liked them. Certainly he first tried to frighten them away. He left each an anonymous note—taking care to leave one for himself—warning them to leave the country or expect to be killed. Some of them took the warning and left, but Rash and Isom Dart remained. Rash had built a large ranch and was looking forward to marrying a local girl. Isom was about fifty, too old to abandon his ranch, his cattle and his friends.

Matt Rash died first. Horn crept up to his door on July 10, 1900, and shot him as he ate breakfast. Then Horn rode off, leaving Rash to crawl to his bed and take off one shoe before he died. Rash's body was found by a friend the next day.

Now Isom Dart was really frightened, but still obstinate. He stayed on his ranch, but made certain that he was never alone, for he hoped to find safety in numbers. But even a crowd is no protection from a sharpshooter with a new 30-30 Winchester rifle. About three months after the murder of Rash, Isom Dart was shot and killed as he walked out of his cabin accompanied by two friends. While the friends dropped and crawled for cover, the assassin escaped unseen.

Ned Huddleston, alias Isom Dart, alias The Black Fox, alias the Calico Cowboy, was buried in a shallow grave on Cold Spring Mountain. He was mourned by good friends and by at least two children who had lost a playmate, a guardian and a circus.

Three years later in Laramie, Tom Horn was hanged for the cold-blooded murder of a fourteen-year-old boy. One of the pieces of evidence against him was a letter he had written in an attempt to get another "regulator" job. Speaking of Montana rustlers, he had written, "I can handle them. They can scarcely be any worse than the Brown's Hole Gang and I stopped cow stealing there in one summer." [31]

·•୬[12]ʕ੭·•

Deadwood Dick

$500 Reward: For the apprehension and arrest of a notorious young desperado who hails to the name of Deadwood Dick. His present whereabouts are somewhat contiguous to the Black Hills.

So began the first novel of the Beadle and Adams *Half-Dime Library* series, which was published on October 15, 1877. The hero of this thriller was described as "a youth of an age somewhere between sixteen and twenty, trim and compactly built, with a preponderance of muscular development and animal spirits." He rode a black horse, wore black clothing and, like the equally improbable Lone Ranger, wore a black half-mask. Hence the title of the novel: *Deadwood Dick, the Prince of the Road; or, the Black Rider of the Black Hills.*

The author of this dime novel was Edward L. Wheeler, who wrote thirty-three Deadwood Dick novels for Beadle and Adams before his death in 1885. As novel followed novel, Deadwood Dick changed occupations several times, though nothing could change his fearless, eloquent, simple personality. In the first novel he was an outlaw, the leader of a gang, and a would-be lover of Calamity Jane. In Wheeler's fourth Deadwood Dick story—*Wild Ivan, the Boy Claude Duval: or, the Brotherhood of Death*—Dick ended his career as a road agent. In the eighth novel—*Omaha Oll, the Masked Terror; or, Deadwood Dick in Danger*—he became a cattleman.

Two years before Wheeler's death, the author's letter-head read "Studio of Edward L. Wheeler, Sensational Novelist, Philadelphia, 1883." He casually listed himself as the author not only of the Deadwood Dick novels but also of the Rosebud Rob novels, Denver Doll novels, and Sugar Coated Sam novels. Other creations of this pro-digiously prolific, always alliterative novelist included Bo-nanza Bill, Cinnamon Chip, Boss Bob, and Solid Sam. But only Deadwood Dick became a minor immortal.

When Wheeler died in 1885, Beadle and Adams were reluctant to lose such a popular and profitable author, and so they hired ghost writers to carry on in his name. The first of the ghost-written "Deadwood Dick, Jr." novels appeared on January 19, 1886: *Deadwood Dick, Jr.; or, The Sign of the Crimson Crescent*. By 1897, the year before Beadle and Adams ceased publishing, Deadwood Dick, Jr., had appeared in ninety-seven of their novels.[1]

Deadwood Dick was obviously a creation of Wheeler's imagination, as were the mining camps and countryside through which he rode. Wheeler himself was never farther west than Titusville, Pennsylvania, where he spent many of his boyhood years. His descriptions of the West, conse-quently, were uninhibited by observation or experience: "Cheyenne, for example, lay to the east of the Black Hills, and the topographic features described by him near Dead-wood do not exist." [2]

But life is frequently eager to imitate art, even the art of the dime novel. Therefore there have always been a number of men who claimed to be—or were said to have been—the "original" of Deadwood Dick.

One of these was created in the 1920's by the town of Deadwood itself, which decided that its "Days of '76" celebration would be more colorful if a real Deadwood Dick were on hand to greet the tourists. An old stablehand named Dick Clarke agreed to take the part and in 1927 went to Washington to persuade President Coolidge to spend the summer in the Black Hills. For everybody but one, the trip was a publicity stunt, but Dick Clarke somehow got it into his head that he was the real thing. And from that time until his death, "he fully believed that he was the original Deadwood Dick." [3]

Another "one and only" Deadwood Dick is said to have been Richard Bullock, who was born in the county of Cornwall, England, in 1842 or 1843. According to Escott North, this Deadwood Dick showed up in the Black Hills in about 1877, became "exasperated" over the constant stage robberies, and went out and emptied his gun into the daring bandit Lame Johnnie. "Deadwood Dick" Bullock eventually gained "a reputation for his intrepidity of nerve, his immunity from injury, and his cold ferocity in battle." [4]

Old residents of the Dakotas propose still other candidates for Deadwood Dick honors. Thus R. L. Hildebrand, who was living in retirement in San Marcos, California, in 1954, remembered that the original Deadwood Dick had been Richard Clark, a "white gentleman" who rode into the Black Hills in 1876 and lived out his life working for the Chicago and Northwestern Railroad. [5]

One Deadwood Dick, perhaps inspired by the "Black

Rider of the Black Hills" subtitle of the first Wheeler novel, wrote his own story—the autobiography of a Negro cowboy. It was called *The Life and Adventures of Nat Love: Better Known in the Cattle Country as "Deadwood Dick"—By Himself.* The story had its own subtitle: "A True History of Slave Days, Life on the Great Cattle Ranges and on the Plains of the 'Wild and Woolly' West, Based on Facts, and Personal Experiences of the Author." In his Preface, Nat Love insisted that he was writing for those who "prefer facts to fiction," and he therefore "tried to record events simply as they are, without attempting to varnish over the bad spots or draw on imagination to fill out a chapter at the cost of the truth."

A forthright statement, certainly, and an admirable purpose. But one who reads the book soon wonders whether the author does not protest too much. The internal evidences of style and content seem to owe something, at least, to the dime novel. Nat constantly performed near miracles, almost always before an admiring audience. No horse could throw him, and no cowboy could touch him. His courage rarely faltered, and his gun never missed. By comparison with Nat Love, Natty Bumppo was a tenderfoot and Pecos Bill was a dude. "Horses were shot from under me, men were killed around me," he wrote, "but always I escaped with a trifling wound at the worst." [6] And his skill was phenomenal: "I could read, identify, and place every brand or mark placed on a horse or steer between the Gulf of Mexico and the borders of Canada, on the North and from Missouri to California." [7]

These proud boasts do not automatically discredit his book, for they differ only in degree from the kind of hyperbole to be found in many otherwise credible books of Western reminiscence. But they also lack external verification. Love said that in 1875, he "was known all over the cattle country as 'Red River Dick,' " and he added that "many of the cattle kings of the West as well as scores of bad men all over the western country have at some time or other had good reason to remember the name of 'Red River Dick.' " [8] Perhaps. But it is remarkable that none of these rather articulate men did remember. The cattlemen for whom Ned claimed to have worked do not appear in the records, and none of the cowboys he worked with seem to have ridden with other crews.

Finally, it must be admitted that some of his statements contradict all other accounts. Thus he attributed the near extinction of buffalo to Indian (not white) hide hunters, and he told nearly incredible stories of cowboy gun battles in roundup arguments. He attributed a kind of generosity to his bosses that would have bankrupted a Goodnight, an Iliff or a Slaughter. He described roundup procedures that would have horrified any cattlemen's association: "the calf was branded with the brand of the finder, no matter who it personally belonged to." [9]

Yet his story is a good one, whatever its authenticity. At the very least, he must have talked or worked with some men who had ridden on long drives. At the best, he may have lived part of the life he described. In any event, this is his account:

Nat Love was born in an old log cabin in Davidson County, Tennessee, in June, 1854. He never knew the day of his birth, for "in those days no count was kept of such trivial matters as the birth of a slave baby." His parents were owned by Robert Love: his father was a foreman of the slaves, and his mother presided over the kitchen at the big house. He grew up with very little education, "as smart negroes were not in much demand at that time."

With the end of the war Nat's family gloried in its freedom, but without money or possessions found it difficult to begin a new life. Living became additionally hazardous when Nat's father died, and the teen-ager had to become the head of the family. After three or four years of the hardest kind of struggles, his family was finally able to care for itself, and the young man was ready to go out on his own.

Before he left home Nat got a job which was to prepare him for his future career. A neighbor, Mr. Williams, owned a horse ranch on which there were a number of young colts. Nat was hired to break the colts for ten cents apiece. For a time he made money while having fun. But there came a day when he was asked to break a big stallion with "uncertain temper and wild disposition." This job, he thought, was worth fifty cents, but he compromised for twenty-five—paid in advance. He finally broke Black Highwayman, after a wild ride which took him through several pastures, stampeded a number of horses and stirred up all the dogs in the neighborhood. Then he discovered, at the end of the ride, that he had lost his quarter.

Nat's chance to "see more of the world" came when he won a horse in a raffle. He sold the horse, gave half the money to his mother and went west. He bought some "underwear and other needful articles," and started out for the first time alone in a world he knew very little about.

When Nat Love left home at the age of fifteen in 1869, word of the cattle drives from southern Texas into Kansas had reached the boys in Tennessee. So the young horsebreaker worked his way across Missouri and headed for "trail's end." Arriving in a typical frontier city, he saw saloons, dance halls, gambling houses, cowboys and "very little of anything else." Seeing the cowboys on their prancing horses, Nat decided to make their life his own.

The next morning he found a Texas outfit which had delivered its herd and was preparing to go back down the trail. There were several Negro cowboys among them, he noted, "and good ones, too." After sharing breakfast with the crew, Nat asked the trail boss for a job. The boss agreed, if the young man could break Good Eye, the wildest horse in the outfit. Bronco Jim, a Negro cowboy, gave Nat some pointers, and Nat wore down the horse, although he later admitted that it was the toughest ride of his life. Having won his job, he rode down the trail to Texas to begin a career as a cowboy.

During those first few months with a cattle outfit, Nat learned that the work pushed a man to the limit of his endurance. He rode through hailstorms so violent that they would have discouraged a weaker man. When he first met hostile Indians, he confessed, he was too badly scared to run. But after a series of trials he had so adapted himself to life in the cattle country that he could cope with any of these adversities, particularly because he was born with "a genuine love of the free and wild life of the range." Soon, he admitted, he was known as a good all-round cowboy.

Nat's home ranch was on the Palo Duro River in the Texas Panhandle, where he worked for three years, taking part in all the activities of range life, including the drives to Kansas cattle towns. He learned the value and satisfaction which came from companionship, and he noted that with the earth for a bed and the sky for a covering all men were more or less the same.

As a boy in Tennessee, Nat had gone on rabbit hunts, but

in Texas he discovered that guns were used in a more serious manner. He took every opportunity to practice with his forty-five, and in time he learned to shoot better than his friends.

When Nat left the Texas Panhandle, he rode into Arizona, where he worked for an outfit on the Gila River. By this time he had ridden many of the trails of the Southwest, and felt that his competence as a cowboy was no longer in doubt. In Arizona he proved his worth to his employer by adding two talents, one cultural and one practical. Through his association with Mexican vaqueros he learned, he said, to speak Spanish like a native. More important for his boss, he became especially adept at reading brands, becoming the outfit's chief authority. Sometimes when he had identified a steer, he had to cut it out of the herd, by throwing it if necessary. (This appears to be a rather strange way of working cattle.)

It was not uncommon, according to his account, for trouble to arise over disputed brands, and on such occasions the cowboys sometimes resorted to shooting. Law in Arizona in the seventies was controlled by the man with the most courage or the fastest gun. In Holbrook, Arizona, Nat witnessed an affair which began among his friends when they disputed the ownership of a horse. It was a sad thing, he reported, to see three of his friends dead and others wounded.

Love's descriptions of trailing longhorns to Dodge City are much like accounts written by hundreds of old-time cowmen. He described the preparation for the drive, the selecting of the men, the rounding up of the cattle. He described the different classes of drives, whether the herds were mixed, wet, yearlings or older steers. His figure for the number of cattle in a trailing herd was accurate, and the makeup of his outfit was like that of almost any other.

In his account Love took the reader through all the hazards, pleasures and excitements of a trail drive. His story, in fact, included most of the adventures reported by more than three hundred old-timers who reminisced in *The Trail Drivers of Texas,* published eighteen years after Nat's autobiography was printed. They all rode through violent storms, brought stampedes to a halt, crossed raging rivers, and shot and were shot at by Indians. And then they saw the elephant in Dodge or in similar cowtowns.

Dodge City, Nat remembered, was a town the cowboys sought to paint a "deep red," and where they tried to drink up all the "bad whiskey." They found women and they gambled, but it was all over in two or three nights. Unlike most of the cowboys, Nat did not spend all of his trail pay. Drawing a limited amount, he let it go "free," and when it was gone he went back to camp.

When the boss of Love's outfit bought a herd below the Rio Grande, just across the border in Mexico, Nat was one of the cowboys chosen to go down and drive the herd back. In Mexico the American cowboys fraternized with the vaqueros. Nat, at first, professed to be skeptical of the "greasers," but when the vaqueros proved to be not only a "jolly" lot but also excellent cowboys, his skepticism turned to praise. From the vaqueros the Americans picked up several pointers, and Nat commented that the American cowboys, like men in other trades, were always willing to learn anything new when they found those capable of teaching it.

Because the herd purchased in Mexico was to be delivered in Wyoming, Nat had his chance to go on a really long drive. His crew cut across into Texas, went north through the Panhandle and the Strip into Kansas, veered northwest for Wyoming and finally arrived at the range on the Powder River. On this drive the outfit faced more than the usual number of hazards. They got through the Cherokee country without paying the tolls demanded by the Indians, but they suffered severe losses when they met a herd of stampeding buffalo. The loss of many of their steers was incidental to the death of one of the cowboys. Cal Surcery was thrown from his horse and trampled: when they recovered the body, after the buffalo had passed over it, there was little left. They gave Cal a "Christian burial" and continued the drive. Arriving in Wyoming, the outfit delivered the herd with "genuine relief," rested up for a few days and began the long trek back to Arizona. The return trip was less hazardous; they went down through Colorado and Utah, country which Nat had not previously seen.

Before summer was over he was on another drive, this time taking a herd of horses to Dodge City. Danger also rode with them on that trip. In a skirmish with Indians, Nat's horse was shot from under him, and his partner, James Holley, was killed.

In the spring of 1874, Nat Love again went north with a herd of longhorns, this time the destination being Ogallala, Nebraska. On this drive he reported no harrowing experiences as his crew picked up the Goodnight-Loving Trail in New Mexico and went through Colorado and into Nebraska. He did, however, comment on Ogallala: a "very tough place" populated by the "tough element" of the cow country.

Back at the home ranch in Arizona at the end of the summer, Nat took time to survey his position in life, to marvel that a one-time Tennessee slave boy, now only twenty, could be leading a life so exciting, so "reckless and free." He glorified in the fact that he had a full share of respect from his fellow cowboys and the confidence of his employers. He was, he thought, in a position to "defy the world. What man with the fire of life and youth and health in his veins could not rejoice in such a life?"

In the spring of 1875, after participating in the rounding up, branding and cutting, Nat went on another long drive to the north, this time into the Dakotas. Two memories from that trip were the joys of eating fresh buffalo steak and the mild excitement of becoming involved, with his outfit, in a brawl at a saloon along the trail. There was some shooting, but no one was badly hurt.

Like many another cowboy who wrote about his adventures on the range, Nat bragged of some of his escapades while drunk. Once in Mexico he rode into a saloon while firing his forty-five and enjoyed the exhilarating ride out while the Mexicans were firing at him. On another occasion he rode by Fort Dodge while full of whiskey. He suddenly conceived the "fool idea" that he should rope a cannon. It would not budge, and Love was arrested by the soldiers. When he explained that he wanted to take a cannon back to Texas to use against Indians, they laughed and let him go.

Along with twenty picked men, Nat went out to run down a herd of wild mustangs. He and his crew made a wide circle, ten to fifteen miles across, and surrounded them. Then the men walked their horses while the mustangs ran. When the wild horses came within two miles of a mounted man, the stallion leading the herd turned it around to go off in another direction. In this fashion the cowboys rode about ten miles a day, gradually narrowing the circle, while the mustangs ran sixty or seventy. After ten days the wild horses slowed down considerably, and the cowboys came close enough at times to shoot the stallion that led the herd. But it was thirty days before the mustangs were so completely exhausted that they could be roped. Twenty men worked day and night for a month to capture sixty horses.

In the spring of 1876, Love's outfit received an order for three thousand three-year-old steers to be delivered at Deadwood. The route took them through New Mexico and Colorado, to Cheyenne and into the Dakotas. On June 25, while Nat and the other cowboys were within eight or nine days' drive of their destination, General Custer and his troops, over to the west on the Little Big Horn, were eliminated by the Sioux under Sitting Bull. ("We did not know that at the time," Nat wrote, "or we would have gone to Custer's assistance.") Arriving near Deadwood on July 3, the cowboys delivered the herd and got ready for the fourth. Deadwood, on July 4, 1876, was a brand new town, booming because of the recent discovery of the Homestakes mine.

The town was ready for the cowboys when they rode into it on the morning of the fourth. The mining men and gamblers organized a roping contest, and collected two hundred dollars for prize money. Six of the contestants, Nat reported, were Negroes. Each cowboy was to rope, throw, tie, bridle and saddle a mustang in the shortest possible time; and the horses were not chosen for gentleness. Nat told what happened: "I roped, threw, tied, bridled, saddled and mounted my mustang in exactly nine minutes from the crack of the gun. The time of the next nearest competitor was twelve minutes and thirty seconds. This gave me the record and the championship of the West, which I held up to the time I quit the business."

With the roping contest completed, a dispute arose over who was the best shot. So a shooting contest was arranged for the afternoon. A range was measured off for the rifle contest at 100 and 250 yards. And the range for the Colts was set at 150 yards, a distance which appears to be one of Nat's fancier exaggerations. Each contestant had fourteen shots with the rifle and twelve shots with his Colt. Nat placed all of his rifle shots in the bull's eye and ten of his twelve pistol shots in the center! His nearest competitor hit only eight with the rifle and five with the forty-five. The winner, and "hero of Deadwood," was Nat Love, the Negro cowboy and former slave. Along with the prize money, the grateful and excited men of Deadwood conferred on Nat the title of "Deadwood Dick," a name which he carried with "honor" ever after.

After winning fame in Deadwood, Nat Love returned to the home ranch in the Southwest where—because he did not mention any heroic deeds or exciting escapades—he presumably spent a quiet summer. In the fall, however, there was a change. Early in October the boys were sent out on the range to look for strays, each cowboy traveling alone. As he rode across the range looking for wandering cattle, Nat was suddenly confronted by a group of Indians from Yellow Dog's tribe. Like most cowboys, Nat felt that he could fight off a normal number of Indians, but this band was too large, so he tried to ride away from them. But the Indians succeeded in shooting his horse from under him and then rode in for the capture. Using his dead horse as a breastwork, Nat fired back until he ran out of ammunition, sustaining, in the meantime, bullet wounds in the leg and breast. He passed out from his wounds and came to in one of Yellow Dog's camps, where he discovered that his wounds had been carefully tended and dressed with herbs.

Nat assumed that his life had been spared because he

had fought so courageously and because "there was a large percentage of colored blood in the tribe." For several days he was carefully guarded, but when his wound healed and he began to show an interest in his captors and their activities, the Indians became more friendly. They even made it clear that they expected him to marry the chief's daughter (for Nat, obviously, only the chief's daughter would do). But he was making other plans, preparing to escape. Having picked out a fast horse in advance, he waited until a night when the Indians were not watchful. He crawled 250 yards through the darkness to where the horses were picketed, found the horse he wanted, and rode all night and into the next day, reaching the ranch a month after he had disappeared.

The cowboys, who had given him up for dead, were glad to see him alive. He kept the Indian pony for five years, and in later life he remembered the fight and his capture by Yellow Dog as his closest brush with death.

On another occasion he ran into a severe storm and lost his direction, the only time, he said, that he was ever really lost. After four days of wandering, and at the point of exhaustion and collapse, he stumbled into the cabin of a hide man. After he had a night's sleep and a good breakfast, the buffalo hunter sent him on his way the next morning with directions for his return to the ranch. Nat's bad luck continued, however, for at dark he was still some distance from the ranch, so he bedded down on the ground. During the night his horse became frightened, pulled up his picket and ran off, leaving Nat forty miles to cover on foot. He finally found his way back to the ranch, but only after he shot a buffalo calf for food, spent another night on the open range and walked through a blizzard which nearly froze him.

All of the things which happened to other cowboys happened to Nat Love. On one drive his outfit was fording a river when Boyd Hoedin and his horse went under. When Hoedin came up the second time, Nat threw his rope and snaked both Hoedin and his horse to safety. At trail's end the boys spent their money and then entered a series of horse races with cowboys from other outfits. Nat's group, of course, had the fastest horses, and they soon "cleaned up pretty near all the money" there was around.

Nat Love was also like some other cowboys who later wrote their memoirs of the old West; they arranged their travels throughout the Southwest so that they were in the right place at the right time to have seen Billy the Kid in action. Once having seen or met the Kid (Nat claimed to have met him in a saloon in New Mexico) the old-timer could then include in his reminiscences a chapter about the Kid's escapades. Nat's account of the Kid is a standard one picked up from hearsay; but like all the rest, it offers just enough variation to add to the confusion about the already clouded life of Billy the Kid.

During the 1880's Nat continued to ride the trails, search for strays, shoot buffalo and read brands. One time in Old Mexico he met and fell in love with a beautiful girl. He really loved her, and they would have been married, but "in the spring she took sick and died."

Although much of Nat Love's autobiography reads like a dime novel from the House of Beadle and Adams, there is nothing inherently incredible about any one of his adventures. Other cowboys fought Indians more fierce than Yellow Dog, rode horses no one else could ride, and proved themselves great cowboys. Bose Ikard, for instance, rode through hostile Indian country, carrying thousands of dollars in gold and trading shots with outlaws. Other cowboys, many of them Negroes, won riding, roping and shooting contests, and still others became great vaqueros and won the love of Mexican maidens. Even Nat's prose style, with its unrelieved hyperbole, can find its match in the reminiscences of old-time cowboys equally uninhibited by a pedantic or meticulous concern for truth. But Nat is unique in claiming to have ridden all the ranges, won all the battles and known all the brands.

At the end of the 1880's Nat Love recognized a major change in the way of life in the West. In 1890 he traded his cowpony for an iron horse; in that year he became a Pullman porter. He realized, he said, that "the march of progress" called for a different way of living, and he believed that Pullman service offered a challenge to an ambitious man. Furthermore it was still exciting to ride across the great mountains and wide plains, even if one had to do it for tips. Nat prided himself on his ability to get along with people, and he "came to have a liking for the service." He believed that the qualities which made him a successful cowboy for twenty years made him, in the 1890's, a successful porter. He gloried in the people he met and the tips he earned. He gave no indication that he felt his change from the life of a cowboy to the life of a porter was anything other than the result of the changing times.

When Nat published his memoirs in 1907, he let his "chest swell with pride" because he was an American. Reaching for dramatic effect, he expressed it this way: "Such was life on the western ranges when I rode them, and such were my comrades and surroundings; humor and tragedy. In the midst of life we were in death, but above all shown [sic] the universal manhood. The wild and free life. The boundless plains. The countless thousands of long horn steers, the wild fleet footed mustangs. The buffalo and other game, the Indians, the delight of living, and the fights against death that caused every nerve to tingle, and the every day communion with men, whose minds were as broad as the plains they roamed, and whose creed was every man for himself and every friend for each other, and with each other till the end."

Thus Nat Love ended his autobiography, his "True History . . . Based on Facts." He had, he claimed, ridden into the West on horseback, ridden throughout the rangeland as Deadwood Dick and then ridden into the twentieth century on a train.

·⊰[13]⊱·

The West as Show Business

Cattlemen and cowboys made little effort to convert their talents to commercialized show business until the early years of the twentieth century, but throughout most of the period of the open range the cowboys competed as amateurs. When times were dull or work was slack, it was a common occurrence for one cowboy to try to outdo another in riding or roping. Occasionally the members of an outfit competed for a pot they made up among themselves, but there were always those who tried to rope any steer or ride any bronc just for the hell or the glory of it.

Nat Love claimed to have been in a "cowboy tournament" in Deadwood on July 4, 1876, but there are relatively few accounts of early formalized contests. An "exhibition of skill with the lariat" was held at a state fair in Austin, Texas, in 1882. The cowboys competed for a silver-trimmed saddle by roping, throwing and tying steers. The winner's time was one minute and forty-five seconds.[1] Two years later a Negro in Mobeetie, in the Texas Panhandle, accomplished the feat in one minute and thirteen seconds—said then to be the best time on record.[2]

A cowboy tournament was held in Denver, Colorado, in October, 1887, where both white and Negro cowboys competed before a crowd of more than eight thousand. Some of the more exciting and frustrating attempts to ride wild horses were reported in the Denver *Republican:* Frank Wells, a white cowboy, roped a small dark bay which immediately jerked him to the ground and began to drag him through the dust around and around the corral. Each time he lost the rope he caught it, but the bay again dragged him until he lost his hold. At the end of fifteen minutes the judges called time, deciding that the battered cowboy could not ride the wild bay.

The next contestant was Pinto Jim, a Negro cowboy, whose job was to mount a sorrel. The battle between the man and the horse "was fierce," but when the sorrel began to exhaust itself by constant plunging, Jim was able to saddle and mount it. "Thirteen minutes were consumed, but the crowd cheered the perspiring man, nevertheless, and he deserved it."

Another Negro cowboy, Bronco Jim Davis, drew the wildest horse of all, one that "knew no taming." Jim had the bronc down several times, but each time the horse kicked and escaped. After half an hour, when it became evident that to prolong the struggle meant serious injury or death to the horse or the man, the judges stopped the contest. By that time the crowd, too, had seen enough.[3]

From the earliest days of trail driving it was frequently necessary to rope unruly steers which broke away from the herd. But roping a running steer was not as easy for working cowboys as modern rodeos and movies would have it. It was not uncommon for a cowboy to throw many misses and for the steer to be a long way from the herd before he was brought down. At times a cowboy forgot his rope and attempted to bring down a steer by hand. The most common method was for the cowboy to ride alongside the steer, reach down and grab it by the horns, leave his horse and get his feet out in front. Then by digging his heels into the ground he could slow down the steer; at the same time he began to twist the animal's head and neck. If all went well the cowboy could finally stop the steer and throw it.

At various times during the range days, the term "bulldogging" was used for throwing a steer. Philip Ashton Rollins described a roundup where the steers were dragged up to the fire to be branded, some of them having been bulldogged, others roped. "Bulldogging," Rollins wrote, "involved throwing one's right arm over a steer's or cow's neck, the right hand gripping the neck's loose, bottom skin or the base of the right horn or the brute's nose, while the left hand seized the tip of the brute's left horn. The 'dogger' then rose clear of the ground; and, by lunging his body downward against his own left elbow, so twisted the neck of the brute that the latter lost its balance and fell. It was a somewhat active performance, because, the instant the dogger took hold, the seized beast began to run, and the man's legs, when not touching the ground in flying leaps, were waving outward to avoid his maddened vehicle's knees." Rollins decided that roping would achieve the same results with less effort and concluded that dogging was more appropriate for public exhibitions than for working range cattle.[4]

A contemporary dictionary definition of bulldogging is "to throw a steer by seizing the horns and twisting the neck." But the term originated, apparently, when the cowboy actually grabbed the nose of the steer and hung on in bulldog fashion.

Ed Nichols reported that he saw bulldogging practiced

in Texas in the late 1870's. Bill Hudson, one of the important cattlemen, was traveling through the country buying longhorns in preparation for a spring drive. At the end of one day of buying, Hudson's cattle were all rounded into one herd, and the men sat down to eat. Suddenly a steer broke out of the herd and could not be driven back. A man from each outfit mounted his horse and attempted to rope the steer, but without success. A Negro cowboy named Andy, "one of Hudson's main trail riders and ropers," could not find his lariat, so in desperation he took after the steer without a rope. "Riding up to it, he reached down with both hands and caught its nose in one hand and a horn in the other. He twisted the steer's nose up and threw him, jumping from the saddle as he did so. It was the first bulldogging I ever saw." [5]

Harry Chrisman wrote of the big Negro cowboy Sam Johnson, who bulldogged a Texas longhorn with horns spreading six feet. Those who saw Johnson's performance thought they had seen one of the best cowboy shows in central western Kansas.[6]

The man, however, who most consistently received credit for being the outstanding bulldogger and showman was the Negro cowboy Bill Pickett. According to Pickett's boss, Zack Miller, "Bill Pickett was the greatest sweat-and-dirt cowhand that ever lived—bar none . . . [and] when they turned Bill Pickett out, they broke the mold." [7]

Among eight authors [8] who included the feats of Bill Pickett in their accounts of the cattle days, the one who told the most complete story of Pickett's life was Fred Gipson in *Fabulous Empire*. His book dealt with the Miller brothers, Zachary, Joseph and George, and their "fabulous" 101 Ranch; yet the story of the 101 Ranch without Pickett would have been just another Western yarn.

The story began in 1871, when G. W. Miller left Missouri for Texas to buy cattle. Even then, long before Bill Pickett entered the action, Miller's crew of six men included one Negro cowboy, Perry Britton, who drove the chuck wagon.[9]

Miller bought his cattle and began a drive to Kansas. On the way north from Texas, he passed through the Cherokee Strip and realized the cattle-ranging potentialities of the area. In the Strip, which technically belonged to the Indians, there were hundreds of square miles of rich grazing land close to Kansas markets. Acting quickly, Miller located on the Salt Fork of the Arkansas where he leased 60,000 acres (in two parcels) from the Cherokees. There he founded his 101 Ranch, which continued to prosper until 1892, when the federal government took the Strip away from the Indians by forcing them to accept nominal payment for their land.

The federal purchase compelled Miller to move, for with the Strip about to be opened to homesteaders, there was no place for large cattle ranches. Fortunately Miller did not have to move far. At the eastern edge of the Strip, the Ponca Indians had been allowed to hold their land; and Miller, who had befriended the Poncas several years earlier, was able to lease 100,000 acres from them for an annual rental of one cent an acre.[10]

By now Miller's three sons—Joe, Zack and George—had reached maturity and had learned the cattle business. Although the 101 Ranch was nearly wiped out in the depression that followed the panic of 1893, it survived and began to grow again. Eventually it became one of the most prosperous ranches in the Southwest.

During the 1890's the 101 acquired a number of expert cowhands, men so capable that whenever they competed in local or nearby cowboy contests they invariably won the prizes. Within a few years they were charged with professionalism and barred from amateur rodeos held in places like Wichita and Enid. This was the crew that Bill Pickett joined at the end of the century. Johnny Brewer was the number one bronc buster and Jim Hopkins the outstanding roper; Pickett became the top bulldogger.

But Bill Pickett was no ordinary bulldogger. In 1900 he was a man about forty years old, "a big-handed, wild-riding South Texas brush-popper" with a style of bulldogging so startling and so effective that he is frequently credited with having originated the sport. Today, in the 1960's, the programs of rodeos held in Western towns refer to Bill Pickett as the Negro cowboy who "invented" bulldogging —or, as it is frequently called now, "steer wrestling."

Pickett's technique went beyond that of any other cowboy. "The way Bill went at it, he piled out of his saddle onto the head of a running steer, sometimes jumping five or six feet to tie on. He'd grab a horn in each hand and twist them till the steer's nose came up. Then he'd reach in and grab the steer's upper lip with his strong white teeth, throw up his hands to show he wasn't holding any more, and fall to one side of the steer, dragging along beside him till the animal went down." [11]

This was bulldogging the way bulldogs did it, taking "guts, bull strength, and the same peculiar sense of timing that makes art out of dancing." [12]

Charles Towne and Edward Wentworth, the authors of *Cattle and Men,* attributed the origins of bulldogging to Pickett and then compared the act to the Elizabethan baiting of bulls with bulldogs. They quoted from John Evelyn's diary of June 16, 1670: "One of the bulls tossed a dog full into a lady's lap, as she sat in one of the boxes at

a considerable height from the arena. . . . I am most heart-
ily weary of the rude and dirty pastime." [13] Tradition has
it that Bill, who was probably unaware of the Elizabethan
sport, got mad when a stubborn bull refused to be driven
into the corral; the cowboy leaped from his horse and
wrestled the bull to the ground.[14]

Although he was to become the most famous of the
group, Pickett was only one of two hundred hands on the
101 payroll when G. W. Miller died in 1903. By this time
Miller was running an operation large enough to bring
in as much as $500,000 a year. Of his land 13,000 acres
were in wheat, 3,000 in corn, and 3,000 in forage crops.
Thousands of cattle roamed his ranges, 50,000 acres of
which he was renting from the Indians at $32,500 a year.[15]

G. W. Miller had built a big ranch, but Mrs. Miller and
her sons set out to make it bigger. Mrs. Miller's first act,
with the $30,000 insurance money, was to buy six sections
of land from the Ponca Indians. On this land the Miller
family built their home—a big white house in Southern
plantation style—about five miles from Bliss, Oklahoma,
where they had stockyards on the railroad. Now the Millers
began to build their operation into an empire. Joe supervised the ranch and farm; Zack did the buying, trading and
selling; George kept the records.[16]

As the 101 became known for having some of the best
cowhands on the range, it sought to improve its reputation
by finding more and better specialists. Kurt Reynolds was
the all-round cowhand; Johnny Brewer could ride anything that bucked; Jim Hopkins could lay his rope over
any steer's horns; Bill Pickett and Lon Sealy were un-
matched as bulldoggers; George Hooker, another Negro,
could do almost anything. Then the Miller brothers hired
Tom Mix, who was said to be a better bartender than

horseman. But Mix looked the part and he learned quickly. Soon he seemed more impressive on a horse than the real cowhands.[17]

Will Rogers was not a regular 101 hand, but for several years, at intervals, he put up with and worked with the 101 cowboys. Rogers had once seen Oro Paso, the Mexican trick roper in a Buffalo Bill show, and the Oklahoman vowed he would master the Mexican's roping tricks if it meant wearing out every rope on the Ponca Reservation. Rogers was assisted by a Negro cowboy, Henry Clay, who helped him perfect the art of roping. As Clay, on a fast horse, rode past Rogers, the horseman called out the horse's foot the roper was to pick up. Eventually Rogers "could make his spinning trick ropes do just about anything but talk." [18]

The 101 Ranch put on its first big rodeo for the 1905 convention of the National Editors' Association. The editors, meeting in Guthrie, went up to the Salt Fork for the show. Thirty-five special trains could not carry the crowd. It was a great show, and the newspapermen gave it ample publicity.[19]

For the next several years the Miller Brothers 101 Ranch became famous for putting on one of the finest rodeos in the world, and it played in such places as Chicago, New York, London and Mexico City. One of the programs listed the following events: [20]

1:30 P.M.   GRAND PARADE
            Indians, Cowboys, Prairie Schooners, Ox Wagons, Oklahoma Farmers, Modern Farm Machinery, Steam Plow, Automobiles, 12 Bands
2:15 P.M.   BUFFALO CHASE
2:30 P.M.   INDIAN SPORTS AND DANCES

2:50 P.M.   MISS LUCILE MULHALL AND HER HORSE, "GOV-
            ERNOR"
            MR. GEO. ELSER, Champion Trick Rider of the
            World
3:20 P.M.   RIDING WILD BRONCOS
4:00 P.M.   CHAMPION STEER ROPING CONTEST
4:45 P.M.   THE WONDERFUL NEGRO "PICKETT"
            Throwing Wild Steer by the Nose with His
            Teeth
5:00 P.M.   COWBOYS AND GIRLS IN HORSEBACK QUADRILLE
5:15 P.M.   BURNING EMIGRANT WAGON TRAIN BY INDIANS
5:30 P.M.   RECEPTION BY THE INDIANS
            "Home, Sweet Home"

During the early years of the century the 101 hands rode
and roped for thousands of customers throughout the
United States—in Enid, Oklahoma, in Kansas City, Missouri, in the Chicago Coliseum, at the Jamestown Exposition in Virginia; but one of the liveliest times the boys had
was in New York, where they played in Madison Square
Garden.

The kind of horse show that the Garden had been putting on had been unprofitable, and the management was
looking for something more exciting. When Zack Miller
was asked how much it would cost to bring his outfit to
New York, he decided to come for the fun, the publicity
and expenses.[21] His cowhands had a good time and expenses ran a little high, but New Yorkers were treated to
some incredible feats of riding, roping, and bulldogging.

The first night in Madison Square Garden the cowboys
performed for a small crowd, but only the first night. Bill
Pickett's act was featured, and the steer was unruly. Frightened by the crowd and angered by the noise, the steer
came out of the chute so fast it got the jump on Pickett's

horse. Before Pickett could catch the steer it had crossed the arena and jumped a gate, knocking off the top boards, and landed in the grandstand. Pickett, on his horse, also jumped the gate, intent on bulldogging the steer. Will Rogers was in the act—to do the hazing for Pickett—so he too followed. Amid the screaming customers Pickett rode the steer down and bulldogged it. By this time Rogers had also ridden into the stands and with his spinning rope picked up the steer's heels. With Pickett hanging on the steer's horns, Rogers dragged the animal back down the stairs into the arena.

The newspaper coverage, that first night, was enough to fill the Garden for the rest of the performances. There was no more bulldogging in the stands, but Pickett brought down steers with his teeth, Rogers amazed the crowd with his rope tricks, and Mix thrilled the ladies with his dashing riding.[22]

With a series of profitable shows in 1908—some of which were in Canada—the Miller Brothers optimistically decided to take the outfit to Mexico. After a so-so reception in Agua Caliente, on the border, they moved on to Mexico City, arriving during a fiesta period. The Mexicans were oriented toward bullfighting and somewhat resented the American rodeo.

The 101 men knew little of bullfighting and even less about its importance in Mexican life. When they were met with some hostility, they were surprised. They aggravated that hostility by encouraging newspaper reports that they believed "Bill Pickett's bulldogging act was a greater show than any Mexican bull-fight." [23] In seeking further publicity, Joe Miller enraged the public by announcing that Bill Pickett could throw two steers in the time it would take two Mexican bullfighters to throw one. When no bullfighters accepted this challenge, Miller offered to donate a thousand pesos to charity if any Mexican bullfighter could duplicate Pickett's act.

No bullfighter accepted the offer, but the bullfighters made a counteroffer: they would bet five thousand pesos that Pickett could not hold on to one of their fighting bulls for five minutes. After some hesitation and a conference with his star performer, Miller accepted the bet. The special act was scheduled as part of the 101 show.

When the day arrived, the stands were packed, but not with rodeo fans or friends. The opening acts were booed, for the audience had come to see only one thing—the death of a Negro cowboy who dared to wrestle a fighting bull with his bare hands.[24]

From the outset Pickett was at a disadvantage because, although his horse was expert at chasing steers, it could not work in close enough. Eventually, and only after the bull had gored his horse's rump, Bill slid off over the horse's tail and grabbed the bull's horns. "For the next two minutes," according to Fred Gipson's account, "the bull made a whipcracker out of Bill Pickett. He slammed the Negro's body against the arena wall. He threw up his head to sling the clinging man creature right and left, trying to dislodge him. He whipped him against another wall. He reached with his forefeet and tried to paw him loose. Finally he got down on his knees and drove his sharp horns into the ground, time and again, trying to run Bill through."[25]

Gradually Pickett began to wear down the bull's strength, but then the customers began to throw a variety of things at the bulldogger. When he was hit in the ribs with a beer bottle, he loosened his hold, and thereafter he could only hang on while the bull threw him about in violent fashion. After six minutes it became clear that the timer had no intention of ringing the bell, so the 101 hands rode into the ring and roped the bull. The crowd in its fury threw every available object, and was held back only through the intervention of a troop of Mexican soldiers. Both Pickett and his horse survived, and Joe Miller collected his wager.[26]

Bill Pickett survived, in fact, for many years. In the spring of 1914 the 101 Ranch was invited to take part in the Anglo-American Exposition to be held in London. Zack Miller took half of the New York show, including Pickett and George Hooker, the Negro trick rider, and shipped for England.

The Miller Brothers rodeo performed successfully in London for several months. A special show was arranged for England's royalty, and Pickett put on his bulldogging act for King George V and Queen Mary. After Bill shook hands with the King and Queen, he went to dinner with an English earl.

The success of the Miller Brothers show in London ended abruptly on August 7, 1914. War had come to England, and under a national emergency order the government commandeered all of the Miller Brothers' horses and vehicles except six horses and a wagon. The show was over: it was time to go home.[27]

It was many years before the Miller Brothers could put their show together again, and when they did it was never the equal of the one they had in those years before the war. During the 1920's their luck was both good and bad. The ranch made money in oil, but was nearly wiped out in a flood. Joe Miller died in 1927, and George Miller was killed in an accident in 1929. The depression was too much for Zack to handle alone, and the once-famous 101 Ranch gradually dwindled away.

In 1932 Zack Miller became ill, and Bill Pickett, "the only one of the old 101 bunch still with him," was his companion and nurse. To please the ailing Miller, Pickett, then in his seventies, went to the corral to cut out some horses. When roped, one big sorrel gave Bill trouble by rearing and plunging. "The years stack up on a man; the Negro bulldogger wasn't as fast-moving as he'd once been. He dodged back, but he wasn't quick enough. One of those hoofs grazed the side of his head, knocking him to the ground." The sorrel then stomped and kicked him, fracturing his skull.

Eleven days later Bill Pickett was dead. "They buried him in the soapstone on a high knoll near old White Eagle's monument and covered him deep, where the coyotes couldn't scratch him out." [28]

On the day Bill Pickett died, April 2, 1932, his boss, Colonel Zachary T. Miller, was credited with writing an epitaph. A few of the lines go like this: [29]

> Old Bill has died and gone away, over the "Great Divide."
> Gone to a place where the preachers say both saint
>   and sinner will abide.
> If they "check his brand" like I think they will
>   it's a runnin' hoss
> They'll give to Bill.
> And some good wild steers till he gets his fill.
> And a great big crowd for him to thrill.

Apparently the old cowhand did have the showmanship and ability to thrill a crowd. The various humane societies eventually made it impossible for him to bulldog with his teeth, but according to Fred Gipson, Bill Pickett at his best was really something to watch. "And when old Bill Pickett tied onto a runaway steer's nose with his teeth and busted him against the ground, the crowd reared up on its hind legs screaming. Right down to the last puff of dust kicked up in the arena, that show was wilder than a wolf." [30]

Epilogue: The West as Fiction

The trails end where fiction begins. As the records show, Negroes helped to open and hold the West. They explored the plains and mountains, fought Indians, dug gold and silver, and trapped wild horses and wolves. Some were outlaws and some were law officers. Thousands rode in the cavalry, and thousands more were cowboys. And for a while, at least, some performed in rodeos and others rode on many of the country's major race tracks.

Yet Negroes rarely appear in Western fiction. They are not, for example, in the dime novels. Approximately two thirds of the 3,158 dime novels published by Beadle and Adams between 1860 and 1898 are laid in the trans-Mississippi West, where they deal with frontiersmen, desperadoes, miners and assorted Texas heroes and badmen.[1] Negroes appear only insignificantly in their plots—action-packed stories far more concerned with bloodthirsty Indians, virtuous maidens, ferocious robbers and leering Boucicault villains than with cowhands and six guns. The dime novels were the predecessors, but not the progenitors, of the true Western story.

Today's Western story began in 1902 with the publication of Owen Wister's *The Virginian,* long after the great trail drives, years after barbed wire, railroads and improved cattle breeding methods had changed the West. Even in 1902 *The Virginian* was a novel about a man of the past, about a hero out of a heroic and idealized age. Wister's hero rode proudly through a nearly lawless Wyoming, making his own justice, hanging rustlers and outshooting the villain in scenes that were prototypes for thousands of similar scenes in later stories and motion pictures. But by 1902 that lawless Wyoming had already disappeared. It had ended, for all practical purposes, with the defeat of the cattlemen in the Johnson County War of 1892. The Wyoming of 1902 was still rough and occasionally bloody, but juries, judges and sheriffs dispensed justice. Had a real Virginian been living when the novel was published, he might well have been tried by a Wyoming jury and hanged by a Wyoming sheriff. Certainly that was the fate of Tom Horn, the "regulator" and hunter of rustlers who was hanged in 1903.

Even *The Virginian,* then, was essentially a historical novel, set in a West that was already a memory. It was better than many of its later imitations, for Owen Wister had visited the West as early as 1885 and had hunted and fished with many of the old-time cowmen and cowboys; and he had ridden hundreds of miles through Western country, recording conversations, anecdotes and descriptions of scenery in his journals. He had been, in a sense, one of the first of the Eastern dudes, finding the great, strange West a romantic and exciting spectacle. Many of the cattlemen and cowboys he met seemed like noble savages, exotic and colorful, uninhibited and a little shocking in their speech and action, but nature's noblemen. Years later he described them, sentimentalized and somewhat oversimplified, in *The Virginian.*

There were working Negro cowboys in the West that Wister visited, but there are none in his fiction. He probably saw comparatively few, for his journals show that his Western trips were vacations, essentially social visits or hunting and fishing trips. Just as there are cowboys, but few cows—and rustlers, but few calves or steers—in his stories, so there are few working cowboys of any kind in his journals. While the cowboys were roping, castrating, branding, fencing, driving or loading cattle, Wister was usually riding, hunting or fishing with a cattleman host or guide. He saw cowboys at leisure, but rarely at work.

Although his grandmother, Fanny Kemble, had written one of the greatest pre-Civil War protests against the institution of slavery, Owen Wister shared the racial prejudices of his time and social class. One of his few strong disagreements with his Harvard friend Theodore Roosevelt was caused by Roosevelt's appointment of a Negro to a minor federal post. Their correspondence is eloquent testimony of Wister's attitude toward Negroes. So, too, are occasional passages in Wister's stories and journals.[2]

Yet *The Virginian* is not necessarily an anti-Negro book because it contains no Negro characters. What it expresses, rather, as does most of Wister's work, is an admiration for the Anglo-Saxon, for the conquering white man, for the noble Nordic. It is expressed, for example, in Wister's description of American cowboys in an article published in *Harper's* in 1895: ". . . they came in shoals—Saxon boys of picked courage (none but the plucky ones could survive) from South and North, from town and country."[3] This admiration for the plucky white race was one that Wister shared with another author whom he greatly admired—

Rudyard Kipling. It was, moreover, one that he shared with millions of his countrymen at the beginning of the twentieth century.

One cause of widespread pride in the peculiar virtues of the white race was rationalization of new United States imperialism. In 1900 Americans elected William McKinley and so endorsed a policy by which America would assume its share of "the white man's burden." In the same year, Congress enacted the Platt Amendment, which specifically claimed the right of the United States to interfere in Cuba to protect the liberty or property of American citizens. Puerto Rico had been occupied since the Spanish-American War. United States troops were fighting in the Philippine Islands against Filipinos who were continuing their revolution for independence. And in 1900, American troops were part of the relief expedition sent to suppress the Boxer Rebellion in China. Some of these activities were justified on simple grounds of economic advantage or military necessity, but all were defended on the grounds of white supremacy and of white moral responsibility for Christianizing and educating inferior and colored peoples. So the newspapers and magazines were full of praise of Anglo-Saxon law, Aryan civilization and the Nordic tradition of courage and chivalry. At the same time they preached the duty of defending the spiritual values of a white civilization from the menaces of the yellow peril or black savagery.[4]

Almost inevitably this new exaltation of the Anglo-Saxon and the Aryan involved corresponding denigration of Negroes in America. The decade following 1900 has frequently been called the "nadir" of white-Negro relations in America. It was during this decade that opinions of "sociologists" like Frederick L. Hoffman gained wide currency: he wrote that "all facts prove that education, philanthropy, and religion have failed to develop [among the Negroes] higher appreciation of the stern and uncompromising virtues of the Aryan race." [5] Many novels echoed and amplified this belief; perhaps the most successful of them was Thomas Dixon's *The Clansman* (1905), which later became the basis of the motion picture *The Birth of a Nation*. This novel, which glorified the Ku Klux Klan, described its emergence as "one of the most dramatic chapters in the history of the Aryan race." Both Dixon's message and his prose style are well illustrated by his description of the arrival of the invalided Thaddeus Stevens at the impeachment proceedings against President Johnson: "The negroes placed him in an arm-chair facing the semicircle of Senators, and crouched down on their haunches beside him. Their kinky heads, black skin, thick lips, white teeth, and flat noses made for the moment a curious symbolic frame for the chalk-white passion of the old Commoner's face.

"No sculptor ever dreamed a more sinister emblem of the corruption of a race of empire-builders than this group. Its black figures, wrapped in the night of four thousand years of barbarism, squatted there the 'equal' of their master, grinning at his forms of Justice, the evolution of forty centuries of Aryan genius. To their brute strength the white fanatic in the madness of his hate had appealed, and for their hire he had bartered the birthright of a mighty race of freemen." [6] As Dixon's book gained wide popularity, the status of the Negro in popular literature reached its own nadir.

It was at this time and in this intellectual milieu that Wister published *The Virginian*. Scholars may argue the technical priority of other books as the "original" Western

—Andy Adams, *The Log of a Cowboy* (1903), or B. M. Bower, *Chip of the Flying U* (1906)—but Wister's novel was the great archetype that established the Western as a distinct genre of popular fiction. Certainly it contained all the essential elements: a strong, simple and thoroughly good hero; a villain who was incarnate evil; a heroine who was pure and beautiful as well as stupid or stubborn enough to misunderstand or distrust the hero for at least half the story; large quantities of physical violence; and a final and fatal confrontation of good and evil. Certainly, too, it was enormously successful, going through fifteen printings during the first eight months after its publication; by 1911 it was in its thirty-eighth printing. By 1938 it had sold more than one and one-half million copies.[7]

Wister's book was unlike most other great best-sellers in that it set the pattern for thousands of short stories, novels, motion pictures and television programs. Zane Grey, a New York dentist, was quick to recognize the possibilities of the pattern. He started with such "frontier" novels as *Betty Zane* (1903), but beginning with *Riders of the Purple Sage* (1912) he wrote more than fifty Western novels before his death. In the 1920's there was a great multiplication of Western novels and Western pulp magazines. So phenomenal was their success that they became, at least for a time, America's best-known contribution to popular literature.

The product was successful, and so it seemed foolish to vary the formula. An important part of that formula, just as it had been for Wister, was the Saxon pluck of the hero. Thus when Professor Walter Prescott Webb asked several magazine editors to give their reasons for the popularity of the Western story, here was one answer: "The Western story is the most popular type of action story. In order to give reasons for this, one thing must be recognized immediately: it is understood by us, and should be understood by everyone, that we are dealing with the popularity of Western stories as concerns the readers who are white, who may be called Nordics, using this term advisedly. The white race has always been noted for being hard-drinking, hard-fighting, fearless, fair and square." [8] Quite obviously, the Negro cowboy, in fiction, was confronted with a color line over which he could not ride.[9]

Today that color line cannot be drawn in quite the same way. Since World War II the Negro cowboy has been as infrequently in fiction as he was before the war, but his absence is accounted for in a different way. Most editors and writers have turned away from the kind of thoughtless racism openly expressed during the earlier part of the century. It can no longer be said that the continued maintenance of the color line in Western fiction is an expression of overt and conscious race prejudices.

Neither is it merely a matter of literary inertia, of unthinking repetition of formula. While it is true that popular commercial fiction clings desperately to stereotypes and is restrained by editorial taboos, many of the stereotypes have been shattered and many of the taboos abandoned in recent years. There has even been much talk of "adult" Westerns, in which the heroes have had some impure motives and the villains have been "good guys with emotional problems." Since World War II a bit of this growing up has become evident in some of the Western novels and stories of Ernest Haycox, Clay Fisher and Jack Schaefer.

Perhaps one sign of this new maturity has been the appearance of a few Negroes in stories about the West. One such story is "Stampede!" by Allan R. Bosworth, which appeared in *The Saturday Evening Post* in 1950. The story covers a drive up the Western Trail into Kansas, and Dan

Robie, the Negro cowboy, is treated pretty much as the real Negro cowboy was treated on the actual drives up the Western Trail in the 1870's and 1880's.

On occasion, too, novelists have respected Western history. Walter Van Tilburg Clark in *The Ox-Bow Incident* (1940), set in Nevada in 1885, included in his large cast a Negro who had only a minor role physically but played a major part symbolically as the conscience of the others. *The Aristocrat,* by Genevieve Greer, developed an important secondary character in Abe, the old Negro who wore high heeled boots and a ten-gallon hat and still walked like the cowboy he had once been. In *The Wonderful Country* (1952), set in the Southwest after the Civil War, Tom Lea used Negro troops and a Negro sergeant who had once been a cowboy. But these novels are not "Westerns."

One possible explanation of the nearly complete white monopoly of roles in Western fiction and drama is the unique status of the cowboy as an American folk hero. Unlike other folk heroes, he is a kind of nameless Everyman, a symbol of the real or desired courage, independence and triumph of the ordinary American. As Lewis Atherton said, "virtually any schoolboy can name Daniel Boone as the symbol of the wilderness Indian fighter, Mike Fink and Davy Crockett as kings of the wild frontier, and Paul Bunyan as hero of the lumber camps. All of these characters, except possibly Boone, have been raised to the stature of Beowulfs of old—folk heroes, yes, but credited with feats that put them above the emulation of mortal man. But who is *the* great American cowboy? In answer, one must recognize that he continues to be a composite of many men, a nameles hero in recognition of the fact that his deeds were not beyond the powers of virtually anyone willing to exert his energies. His feats were great but not miraculous, and Americans have been reluctant to endow him with a superhuman personality. As a hero of the American folk, he is truly all of them in one." [10] Such a hero, it was believed, could not be too clearly differentiated from most other Americans. He could not be a Swede, a German or an Englishman—though all of these were real cowboys—and he could not be a devout Mormon, Catholic or Jew. Like an "ideal" Presidential candidate, he was expected to be a white, Protestant American with whom most Americans can identify.

Yet even this explanation has now become unsatisfactory. Certainly recent history has shown a continuous decline in American bigotry. No particular religion is now necessarily a fatal handicap to a candidate for high office, and most of us have cheered for sports heroes of different races and religions. Americans are learning that one of their strengths—one of their glories—is unity in diversity. And in most popular fiction and drama, as well as in sports, show business and public life, that diversity is being represented.

Today, perhaps, ignorance of history is the most important reason that the Negro cowboy does not ride in fiction. Americans have assumed that because Negroes have not been in Western fiction they were never in the West. The prairie was different from the city, said one writer, for there the Jew, Negro and Italian never came.[11] This attitude Americans accept as history, and what they learn is strangely incomplete.

The modern world learns about itself through its fiction, somewhat inaccurately. From reading Faulkner, Hemingway, Dos Passos, Steinbeck and Caldwell, the Frenchman sees the American man becoming immature, being obsessed with fears and having a "mixture of puritan-inspired neuroses and essential loneliness." [12] When the 1957 riots in Little Rock made headlines all over the world, the sales of Harriet Beecher Stowe's *Uncle Tom's Cabin* rose in Helsinki.[13] It is difficult to see how the Finns in reading a novel published in 1852 can have gained much insight into an American problem of 1957.

Writers and casting directors who have studied the old West and who know something of its diversity believe that they must respect the ignorance of their audience. They fear the incredulity of readers and viewers. They know that truth may be stranger than fiction, and hence less credible. They fear that the accurate representation of the Negro's role in the opening of the West would paradoxically seem to be a falsification of history.

Their fear may well be justified. Yet ignorance hurts everyone by impoverishing and cheapening a proud memory. Americans have lost something valuable if they forget that Wild Bill Hickok and George Washington Carver grew up on the Western plains at the same time. Americans need to remember that the West once nearly approached the democracy that they are still striving to achieve: "when a cowman sets out to hire help, he's not much concerned with a man's sex appeal or photogenic qualities; what he's looking for is a man who can get the job done, a *working* cowhand." [14] In Philip Ashton Rollins's words, "The men who made the spirit of the West, who forbade Mason and Dixon's line to extend, who harnessed democracy, wore 'chaps.' " [15] Americans need to remember that the Wyoming pioneers desegregated their first school; then maybe American history and fiction can one day be desegregated.

Perhaps all Americans may someday share in the heritage of the West. They may someday correct the injustice described by Dr. Frank P. Graham, former president of the University of North Carolina, when he wrote, "Negro children in school, in the library, at the moving picture, and over the radio, see and hear, and learn about white people. The picture in the school primer is always a picture of the white child." [16] Eventually those Negro children may also see, hear and learn about some of their own great-grand-fathers who broke wild horses, fought wilder Indians and rode in the choking dust behind great herds of cattle.

Notes

Chapter 1

1. William Brandon, *The American Heritage Book of Indians* (New York, 1961), pp. 137–138.
2. Brandon, pp. 117–118.
3. John Walton Caughey, *California* (New York, 1940), pp. 167–168. An old story also attributes the "founding" of Chicago to Jean Pointe de Saible, a free Negro who started a trading post on the present site of the city in 1790. Helped by his wife Catherine and his daughter Cézanne, he built a homestead and surrounded it with a bakehouse, a dairy, a workshop, and stables and poultry houses. For sixteen years he dealt with the trappers, explorers and Indians who passed his post. "Within the house he built, so runs the legend, Chicago's first marriage was solemnized, the first election held, and the first white child was born. Pottawattomie Indians say: 'The first white man to settle Chicago was a Negro.' " (Roi Ottley, *Black Odyssey: The Story of the Negro in America* [New York, 1948], pp. 86–87.)
4. York was valuable not only because of his size and strength, but also because Indians were fascinated by his color and delighted by his dancing. See James McClellan Hamilton, *From Wilderness to Statehood: A History of Montana, 1805–1900* (Portland, Oregon, 1957), p. 10.
5. John C. Frémont, "A Narrative of the Exploring Expedition to Oregon and North California," *The Daring Adventures of Kit Carson and Frémont among Buffaloes, Grizzlies, and Indians* (New York, 1885), pp. 106–107. See also William Brandon, *The Men and the*

Mountain: Frémont's Fourth Expedition (New York, 1955), p. 80.

6. J. Frank Dobie, *The Mustangs* (Boston, 1952), pp. 80–81; Robert Glass Cleland, *This Reckless Breed of Men: The Trappers and Fur Traders of the Southwest* (New York, 1950), p. 345; James P. Beckwourth, *The Life and Adventures of James P. Beckwourth*, ed. Bernard De Voto (New York, 1931), pp. xxvi–xxvii, xxxii.

7. Ray Allen Billington, *The Far Western Frontier: 1830–1860* (New York, 1962), p. 48.

8. W. Sherman Savage, "The Negro in the Westward Movement," *The Journal of Negro History*, XXV (1940), 533–534.

9. Savage, pp. 534–535.

10. For a unique, though not always trustworthy, account of Negroes in early California, see Delilah L. Beasley, *The Negro Trail Blazers of California* (Los Angeles, 1919). For description of Negro mining activity, see W. Sherman Savage, "The Negro on the Mining Frontier," *The Journal of Negro History*, XXX (1945), 30–46. See also Glenn Danford Bradley, *The Story of the Pony Express*, ed. Waddell F. Smith (San Francisco, 1960); Stanley Vestal, *The Old Santa Fe Trail* (Boston, 1939), pp. 56, 172; Waterman L. Ormsby, *The Butterfield Overland Mail*, ed. Lyle H. Wright and Josephine Bynum (San Marino, California, 1942), p. 51; Roscoe P. Conkling and Margaret B. Conkling, *The Butterfield Overland Mail, 1857–1869* (Glendale, California, 1947), I, 333; John Ross Browne, *A Tour Through Arizona, 1864, or, Adventures in the Apache Country* (Tucson, Arizona, 1951), *passim*.

11. Edward Everett Dale and Morris L. Wardell, *History of Oklahoma* (New York, 1948), p. 141; Kenneth W. Porter, "The Seminole in Mexico, 1850–1861," *The Hispanic American Review*, XXXI (1951), 1–36; Kenneth W. Porter, "Negroes and Indians on the Texas Frontier, 1831–1876," *The Journal of Negro History*, XLI (1956), 293, 297–304; John Marvin Hunter, ed., *The Trail Drivers of Texas*, 2d ed., rev. (Nashville, Tennessee, 1925), p. 560.

Any discussion of Negro-Indian relations must point out the difficulty of defining the word *Negro*—or *Indian*, for that matter. Thus it has been estimated that 29 percent of American Negroes have Indian ancestry (Melville J. Herskovitz, *The Anthropometry of the American Negro* [New York, 1930], p. 279). And the converse is certainly true: many Indians today are part Negro. (See Kenneth W. Porter, "Relations Between Negroes and Indians Within the Present Limits of the United States," *The Journal of Negro History*, XVII [1932], 287–367.)

As Roi Ottley has explained, the word *Negro* "is an inadequate description of the people it is supposed to label. When scratched, they are white, black, red, brown and yellow, and thousands of shades in between, resembling nearly every type of person that inhabits the earth, with caste, class, racial and national differences. After three hundred years of intermingling—African with European, Indian and Mongolian—it would tax the abilities of an anthropologist to pigeonhole the contrasting pigmentations, hair textures, bone structures, varying physiques and facial characteristics. Loosely, one might say, Negro is a state of mind." (Ottley, p. 1.)

Legal definitions of *Negro* are hardly helpful. An 1879 statute of Virginia defined a Negro as anyone with one-fourth or more Negro blood. Later, the general assembly of Virginia redefined *Negro* to mean anyone with one-sixteenth or more of Negro blood. Finally, in 1930, Virginia decided that any person in whom there is "ascertainable any Negro blood shall be termed a colored person." (Ottley, p. 210.) In this last definition, Virginia was merely echoing the formulations of Arkansas ("if he has in his veins any Negro blood whatever"). Virginia was also accepting the definitions used in many Western states which had no Jim Crow laws but had strict laws against intermarriage; most of these defined a Negro as "anyone known to have any Negro ancestry whatsoever." (Richard Bardolph, *The Negro Vanguard* [New York, 1959], p. 12; Gunnar Myrdal, *An American Dilemma: The Negro Problem and Modern Democracy* [New York, 1944], p. 198.) All these states, both in the South and in the West, were caught in the paradox described by Mark Twain in *Pudd'nhead Wilson:* "To all intents and purposes Roxy was as white as anybody, but the one sixteenth of her which was black outvoted the other fifteen parts and made her a negro. She was a slave, and saleable as such. Her child was thirty-one parts white, and he, too, was a slave and, by a fiction of law and custom, a negro." (Samuel Langhorne Clemens, *Pudd'nhead Wilson* [New York, 1955], p. 43.)

So it is with the men described in this history of Negro cowboys. Some were light-skinned and some were dark, some were more Negro than Mexican, and some were more Indian than Negro. But all of them—whatever their white American, Spanish, Mexican or Indian ancestry—were known as "Negroes." Like Roxy, they were given a common label by a fiction of law and custom.

12. Mari Sandoz, *The Buffalo Hunters: The Story of the Hide Men* (New York, 1954), p. 202; Stanley Vestal, *Dodge City, Queen of Cowtowns* (New York, 1954), pp. 59–61.

13. Sidney E. Whitman, *The Troopers: An Informal History of the Plains Cavalry, 1865–1890* (New York, 1962), p. 33.

14. Whitman, p. 37. Negroes also served as scouts with white regiments. One such man was killed at the Battle of the Little Big Horn. Speaking long after the event, a Cheyenne described him: "I went riding over the ground where we had fought the first soldiers during the morning of the day before. I saw by the river, on the west side, a dead black man. He was a big man. All of his clothing was gone when I saw him, but he had not been scalped nor cut up like the white men had been. Some Sioux told me he belonged to their people but was with the soldiers." This Negro had been identified as Isaiah, a Sioux interpreter for Custer's Seventh Cavalry. (Thomas B. Marquis, *Wooden Leg* [Lincoln, Nebraska, 1957], p. 261.)

15. Whitman, p. 32; Theophilus G. Steward, *The Colored Regulars in the United States Army* (Philadelphia, 1904), p. 90.

16. Frederic Remington, *Frederic Remington's Own West,* ed. Harold McCracken (New York, 1960), p. 69.

17. W. Sherman Savage, "The Role of Negro Soldiers in Protecting the Indian Territory from Intruders," *The Journal of Negro History,* XXXVI (1951), 25–34.

Chapter 2

1. Struthers Burt, *Powder River* (New York, 1938), p. 207; J. Frank Dobie, *The Longhorns* (Boston, 1941), p. 46.

2. J. Frank Dobie, *A Vaquero of the Brush Country: Partly from the Reminiscences of John Young* (Boston, 1943), p. 41.

3. John Marvin Hunter, ed., *The Trail Drivers of Texas,* 2d ed., rev. (Nashville, Tennessee, 1925), p. 715.

4. Hunter, p. 479.

5. Hunter, pp. 595–596.

6. Hunter, p. 671.

7. Hunter, p. 821.

8. Joseph L. Clark and Julia Kathryn Garrett, *A History of Texas, Land of Promise,* rev. ed. (Boston, 1949), pp. 380–381.

9. Dobie, *The Longhorns,* p. 309.

10. Wendell G. Addington, "Slave Insurrections in Texas," *The Journal of Negro History,* XXXV (1950), 414.

11. Addington, p. 432.

12. Philip Ashton Rollins, *The Cowboy* (New York, 1922), p. 287.

13. Chris Emmett, *Shanghai Pierce: A Fair Likeness* (Norman, Oklahoma, 1953), p. 23.

14. Roi Ottley, *Black Odyssey: The Story of the Negro in America*

(New York, 1948), p. 173. Compare this attitude to that in Mark Twain's *Huckleberry Finn* where Huck is making up a story about a boat's blowing out a cylinder head. Aunt Sally asks, "Good gracious! anybody hurt?" Huck replies, "No'm. Killed a nigger." Aunt Sally then comments, "Well, it's lucky; because sometimes people do get hurt."

15. Andrew Forest Muir, "The Free Negro in Jefferson and Orange Counties, Texas," *The Journal of Negro History*, XXXV (1950), 185–194.

16. William Frank Zornow, *Kansas: A History of the Jayhawk State* (Norman, Oklahoma, 1957), p. 186.

Chapter 3

1. Joseph Jacinto Mora, *Trail Dust and Saddle Leather* (New York, 1946), p. 13.

2. Edward Douglas Branch, *The Cowboy and His Interpreters* (New York, 1961), p. 7.

3. Wayne Gard, *The Chisholm Trail* (Norman, Oklahoma, 1954), pp. 34, 243.

4. Branch, p. 6.

5. Ernest Staples Osgood, *The Day of the Cattleman* (Chicago, 1960), p. 27.

6. Gard, p. 42.

7. Charles A. Siringo, *Riata and Spurs* (Boston, 1931), p. 150.

8. Siringo, pp. 134–145.

9. Siringo, p. 18.

10. Cordia Sloan Duke and Joe B. Frantz, *6,000 Miles of Fence: Life on the XIT Ranch of Texas* (Austin, Texas, 1961), p. 172.

11. J. Frank Dobie, *The Longhorns* (Boston, 1941), p. 240.

12. Dobie, p. 324.

13. Dobie, pp. 324–329.

14. John Marvin Hunter, ed., *The Trail Drivers of Texas*, 2d ed., rev. (Nashville, Tennessee, 1925), pp. 923–924.

15. Siringo, p. 8.

16. Siringo, p. 17.

17. Charles A. Siringo, *A Texas Cowboy; or, Fifteen Years on the Hurricane Deck of a Spanish Pony* (New York, 1951), p. 43.

18. Siringo, *A Texas Cowboy*, p. 41.

19. Siringo, *A Texas Cowboy*, pp. 95–96.

20. Siringo, *A Texas Cowboy*, p. 159. From "A Note on Charlie Siringo, Writer and Man," by J. Frank Dobie.

21. Hunter, p. 546.

22. Mora, pp. 32–33.

23. J. Frank Dobie, ed., *Legends of Texas* (Austin, Texas, 1924), p. 53.

24. Ramon F. Adams, *Western Words: A Dictionary of the Range, Cow Camp and Trail* (Norman, Oklahoma, 1944), p. 104.

25. Dobie, *The Longhorns,* p. 190.

26. James C. Shaw, *North from Texas: Incidents in the Early Life of a Range Cowman in Texas, Dakota, and Wyoming, 1852–1883* (Evanston, Illinois, 1952), p. vii.

Chapter 4

1. Wayne Gard, *The Chisholm Trail* (Norman, Oklahoma, 1954), pp. 25ff.

2. Wayne Gard (p. 65) explained how McCoy could operate in Abilene, although the town is in the eastern half of Kansas: "In choosing Abilene as the site for his market for Texas cattle, McCoy violated—perhaps unwittingly—the Kansas statute of February 26, 1867. The line which this law established, only west of which could Texans trail their cattle lawfully from southwestern Kansas to the Union Pacific Railroad, ran a mile west of Ellsworth and about sixty miles west of Abilene. But as the country around and below Abilene was thinly settled and as no one seemed interested in enforcing the letter of the new law, McCoy was not hampered much at the start on legal grounds."

3. Gard, pp. 65–67.

4. Gard, p. 75.

5. Gard, pp. 75–76.

6. Edward Everett Dale, *The Range Cattle Industry: Ranching on the Great Plains from 1865 to 1925* (Oklahoma City, Oklahoma, 1960), p. 46.

7. John Marvin Hunter, ed., *The Trail Drivers of Texas,* 2d ed., rev. (Nashville, Tennessee, 1925), p. 221.

8. Hunter, p. 591.

9. J. Frank Dobie, *The Longhorns* (Boston, 1941), p. 85.

10. Ed Nichols, *Ed Nichols Rode a Horse,* as told to Ruby Nichols Cutbirth (Dallas, Texas, 1943), p. 8.

11. Hunter, p. 778.

12. Jack Potter, *Cattle Trails of the Old West,* ed. Laura R. Krehbiel (Clayton, New Mexico, 1939), p. 75.

13. Nichols, p. 9.

14. J. Frank Dobie, *A Vaquero of the Brush Country: Partly from the Reminiscences of John Young* (Boston, 1943), p. 93.

15. Dobie, *A Vaquero of the Brush Country*, p. 96.

16. Hunter, pp. 417–418.

17. Hunter, p. 112.

18. Hunter, p. 252.

19. Hunter, p. 58.

20. Hunter, p. 48.

21. Hunter, p. 988.

22. Hunter, p. 453.

23. Hunter, p. 717.

24. Hunter, p. 880.

25. Hunter, p. 307.

26. Hunter, p. 400.

27. Hunter, p. 157.

28. Hunter, p. 987.

29. Hunter, p. 204.

30. Hunter, p. 113.

31. Charles A. Siringo, *A Texas Cowboy; or, Fifteen Years on the Hurricane Deck of a Spanish Pony* (New York, 1951), p. 64.

32. Hunter, p. 231.

33. Hunter, pp. 252–253.

34. Mrs. George H. Gilland, "The Texas Trail as Followed by a Pioneer in 1882," *Annals of Wyoming*, XII (1940), 257–258.

35. Hunter, p. 378.

36. Hunter, pp. 138–139.

37. Hunter, pp. 645–646.

38. Philip Ashton Rollins, *The Cowboy* (New York, 1922), pp. 218–219.

39. Joe B. Frantz and Julian Ernest Choate, Jr., *The American Cowboy: The Myth and the Reality* (Norman, Oklahoma, 1955), p. 38.

40. Hunter, p. 679.

41. Edgar Beecher Bronson, *Cowboy Life on the Western Plains: The Reminiscences of a Ranchman* (New York, 1910), pp. 42–43.

42. Emerson Hough, *The Story of the Cowboy* (New York, 1897), p. 138.

43. Everett Dick, *Vanguards of the Frontier* (New York, 1941), p. 457.

44. Ramon F. Adams, *Come an' Get It: The Story of the Old Cowboy Cook* (Norman, Oklahoma, 1952), p. 21.

45. Gard, p. 119.

46. Nathan Howard Thorp, *Pardner of the Wind* (Caldwell, Idaho, 1945), p. 251.

47. *Prose and Poetry of the Live Stock Industry of the United States* (New York, 1959), p. 613.

48. Gard, pp. 120–121.

49. Dobie, *A Vaquero of the Brush Country*, p. 131.

50. Dobie, *A Vaquero of the Brush Country*, pp. 131–132.

51. Dobie, *A Vaquero of the Brush Country*, pp. 140–141.

52. Dobie, *A Vaquero of the Brush Country*, p. 139.

53. Dobie, *A Vaquero of the Brush Country*, p. 14.

54. Gard, p. 244.

55. Hunter, pp. 485–486.

56. *Prose and Poetry of the Live Stock Industry*, p. 507.

57. *Prose and Poetry of the Live Stock Industry*, p. 509.

58. Gard, p. 168; Wayne Gard, *Frontier Justice* (Norman, Oklahoma, 1949), p. 274; *Prose and Poetry of the Live Stock Industry*, p. 509.

Chapter 5

1. Wayne Gard, *The Chisholm Trail* (Norman, Oklahoma, 1954), p. 181.

2. Mari Sandoz, *The Cattlemen: From the Rio Grande across the Far Marias* (New York, 1958), p. 135.

3. Gard, p. 214.

4. Frank M. King, *Wranglin' the Past* (Pasadena, California, 1946), p. 73.

5. Mrs. George H. Gilland, "The Texas Trail as Followed by a Pioneer in 1882," *Annals of Wyoming*, XII (1940), 253–263.

6. Charles A. Siringo, *Riata and Spurs* (Boston, 1931), p. 70. The story of "The Exodus of 1879" into Kansas is a somewhat confusing one because adequate statistics are lacking and because the reasons given for the exodus are hardly more than educated guesses. John G. Van Deusen suggests three causes for the move: "(1) the sense of personal insecurity attending the reversion of the South to Democratic rule and political discontent among the blacks resulting from disfranchisement; (2) economic discontent resulting from low prices for cotton and the system of debt-servitude which grew out of the operation of the crop lien system; and (3) attractive propaganda." Other reasons for the movement of the "exodusters" were the lack of schools for the Negroes and the great number of "political mur-

ders." General Philip Sheridan reported that in Louisiana alone 1,884 persons had been killed or injured for political opinions in 1868. General Sherman, according to the Senate Reports of the 46th Congress, stated, "Human life in this state [Louisiana] is held so cheaply that when men are killed on account of political opinions the murderers are regarded rather as heroes than as criminals in the localities where they reside."

Propaganda contributing to the exodus began in the early 1870's, but "The movement started in December, 1877, and continued throughout 1878 and 1879, reaching its flood in the latter year."

The Governor of Kansas estimated that between 15,000 and 20,000 immigrants arrived in his state between April and July of 1879. Other guesses ran as high as 60,000.

Frederick Douglass, incidentally, opposed the exodus with a strongly expressed statement: "The business of this nation is to protect its citizens where they are, not to transport them where they will not need protection."

According to Van Deusen, "The exodus ceased suddenly. Those 'exodusters' who returned from Kansas gave such dismal reports of the barren country, the bleak climate and the harder work necessary to open new lands for cultivation that others were deterred from following their example." Approximately two-thirds of the exodusters returned to their old homes or sought opportunities in other states, while the other one-third remained in Kansas—some to prosper. (John G. Van Deusen, "The Exodus of 1879," *The Journal of Negro History,* XXI [1936], 111, 129.)

7. John Marvin Hunter, ed., *The Trail Drivers of Texas,* 2d ed., rev. (Nashville, Tennessee, 1925), p. 33.

8. Hunter, p. 535.

9. Hunter, p. 469.

10. Hunter, p. 409.

11. Hunter, p. 778.

12. Hunter, pp. 527–528.

13. Hunter, p. 222.

14. Ramon F. Adams, ed., *The Best of the American Cowboy* (Norman, Oklahoma, 1957), p. 233.

15. Hunter, p. 272.

16. Adams, p. 121.

17. Harry E. Chrisman, *Lost Trails of the Cimarron* (Denver, Colorado, 1961), pp. 276–277.

18. Robert M. Wright, *Dodge City, the Cowboy Capital, and the Great Southwest* (Wichita, Kansas, 1913), p. 166.

19. Wright, pp. 168–169.

20. Stanley Vestal, *Dodge City, Queen of Cowtowns* (New York, 1954), pp. 26–31. The author reconstructed the story from Army records.

21. George Bolds, *Across the Cimarron* (New York, 1956), pp. 48–49.

22. Wright, p. 239.

23. Wright, pp. 180–181.

24. Wright, pp. 175–176.

25. Ross Santee, *The Lost Pony Tracks* (New York, 1953), pp. 246–247.

26. Santee, p. 171.

27. Wright, pp. 270–277; Chrisman, pp. 175–180.

28. Chrisman, pp. 179–180.

29. Vestal, p. 14.

Chapter 6

1. Wallace Brown, "George L. Miller and the Struggle over Nebraska Statehood," *Nebraska History*, XLI (1960), 299–318.

2. Donald F. Danker, ed., "The Journal of an Indian Fighter: The 1869 Diary of Major Frank J. North," *Nebraska History*, XXXIX (1958), 117.

3. Robert G. Athearn, *High Country Empire* (New York, 1960), p. 132.

4. Bud Cowan, *Range Rider* (New York, 1930), p. 4.

5. Cowan, p. 10.

6. James C. Shaw, *North from Texas: Incidents in the Early Life of a Range Cowman in Texas, Dakota, and Wyoming, 1852–1883* (Evanston, Illinois, 1952), p. 51.

7. Clifford P. Westermeier, ed., *Trailing the Cowboy: His Life and Lore as Told by Frontier Journalists* (Caldwell, Idaho, 1955), pp. 202–204.

8. Edward Charles Abbott and Helena Huntington Smith, *We Pointed Them North: Recollections of a Cowpuncher* (New York, 1939), p. 34.

9. Mari Sandoz, *The Cattlemen: From the Rio Grande across the Far Marias* (New York, 1958), p. 228.

10. Edward Everett Dale, *Frontier Ways: Sketches of Life in the Old West* (Austin, Texas, 1959), pp. 181–182.

11. John Marvin Hunter, ed., *The Trail Drivers of Texas*, 2d ed., rev. (Nashville, Tennessee, 1925), p. 81.

12. Lincoln A. Lang, *Ranching with Roosevelt* (Philadelphia, 1926), p. 351.

13. Mari Sandoz, *Love Song to the Plains* (New York, 1961), pp. 202–203.

14. Federal Writers Project, *South Dakota Place Names* (Vermillion, South Dakota, 1941), p. 427.

15. Con Price, *Memories of Old Montana* (Hollywood, California, 1945), pp. 19–20.

16. Estelline Bennett, *Old Deadwood Days* (New York, 1928), p. 18.

17. Everett Dick, *The Sod-House Frontier, 1854–1890* (Lincoln, Nebraska, 1954), p. 484.

18. Dick, p. 488.

19. August H. Schatz, *Longhorns Bring Culture* (Boston, 1961), p. 82.

20. Maurice Frink, W. Turrentine Jackson, and Agnes Wright Spring, *When Grass Was King: Contributions to the Western Range Cattle Industry Study* (Boulder, Colorado, 1956), p. 59.

21. Glenn Shirley, *Pawnee Bill: A Biography of Major Gordon W. Lillie* (Albuquerque, New Mexico, 1958), p. 268.

22. Edmond Mandat-Grancey, *Cowboys and Colonels: Narrative of a Journey across the Prairie and over the Black Hills of Dakota* (Philadelphia and New York, 1963), p. 326.

23. Shaw, pp. 50–62.

24. Ike Blasingame, *Dakota Cowboy: My Life in the Old Days* (New York, 1958), p. 180.

25. Blasingame, p. 180.

26. Lang, pp. 286–288.

27. Lang, p. 111.

Chapter 7

1. James Evetts Haley, *Charles Goodnight, Cowman & Plainsmen* (Norman, Oklahoma, 1949), p. 243.

2. Haley, p. 242.

3. Haley, p. 136.

4. Haley, p. 134.

5. Haley, pp. 126–147.

6. Haley, p. 242.

7. Haley, p. 243.

8. Haley, p. 167.

9. Haley, p. 219.

10. Haley, pp. 215–216.

11. Haley, p. 207.

12. Haley, pp. 213–214.

13. Dane Coolidge, *Fighting Men of the West* (New York, 1932), pp. 24–25.

14. Coolidge, pp. 22–23.

15. Lewis Eldon Atherton, *The Cattle Kings* (Bloomington, Indiana, 1961), p. 135.

16. Atherton, p. 127.

17. William Lee Hamlin, *The True Story of Billy the Kid: A Tale of the Lincoln County War* (Caldwell, Idaho, 1959), p. 10.

18. George W. Coe, *Frontier Fighter: The Autobiography of George W. Coe, Who Fought and Rode with Billy the Kid* (Albuquerque, New Mexico, 1951), p. 46; Charles A. Siringo, *A Texas Cowboy: or, Fifteen Years on the Hurricane Deck of a Spanish Pony* (New York, 1951), p. 131.

19. Frank M. King, *Pioneer Western Empire Builders: A True Story of the Men and Women of Pioneer Days* (Pasadena, California, 1946), p. 294.

20. Coolidge, pp. 72–74.

21. Hamlin, p. 24.

22. William A. Keleher, *Violence in Lincoln County, 1869–1881: A New Mexico Item* (Albuquerque, New Mexico, 1957), p. 110.

23. Hamlin, p. 55; Keleher, p. 128.

24. Keleher, p. 128.

25. Hamlin, pp. 81–83.

26. Coe, p. 122.

27. Hamlin, pp. 101–102, 109.

28. Hamlin, p. 114.

29. Keleher, pp. 218–219.

30. Clifford P. Westermeier, ed., *Trailing the Cowboy: His Life and Lore as Told by Frontier Journalists* (Caldwell, Idaho, 1955), p. 178.

31. Westermeier, p. 157.

32. Westermeier, p. 178.

33. Coolidge, p. 55.

34. Nathan Howard Thorp, *Pardner of the Wind* (Caldwell, Idaho, 1945), p. 22.

35. Thorp, p. 285.

36. Thorp, p. 285.

37. Thorp, pp. 22–23.

38. Hamlin, p. viii.

39. Frank Waters, *The Earp Brothers of Tombstone: The Story Of Mrs. Virgil Earp* (New York, 1960), p. 134.

40. Joseph Francis Chisholm, *Brewery Gulch: Frontier Days of Old Arizona—Last Outpost of the Great Southwest* (San Antonio, Texas, 1949), p. 42.

41. Chisholm, pp. 42–43.

42. Chisholm, p. 51.

43. Francis C. Lockwood, *Pioneer Days in Arizona, from the Spanish Occupation to Statehood* (New York, 1932), pp. 286–287. Zane Grey used this historical feud and setting in his novel *To the Last Man.*

44. Lockwood, p. 340.

45. Coolidge, pp. 116–120.

Chapter 8

1. Ernest Staples Osgood, *The Day of the Cattleman* (Chicago, 1960), pp. 9–11.

2. Osgood, pp. 19-21.

3. Osgood, p. 21; Glenn Shirley, *Toughest of them All* (Albuquerque, New Mexico, 1953), pp. 19–29. This event is used by Clay Fisher in his novel *The Big Pasture.*

4. Osgood, p. 60.

5. David J. Cook, *Hands Up; or, Thirty-five Years of Detective Life in the Mountains and on the Plains* (Norman, Oklahoma, 1958), pp. 144–149.

6. Maurice Frink, W. Turrentine Jackson, and Agnes Wright Spring, *When Grass Was King: Contributions to the Western Range Cattle Industry Study* (Boulder, Colorado, 1956), pp. 334–335.

7. Frink, Jackson, and Spring, p. 74.

8. Georgia Burns Hills, "Memories of a Pioneer Childhood," *The Colorado Magazine*, XXXII (1955), 123–125.

9. Cook, pp. 217–218.

10. Charles A. Siringo, *A Cowboy Detective* (New York, 1912), p. 89.

11. Cook, Introduction.

12. John Rolfe Burroughs, *Where the Old West Stayed Young* (New York, 1962), pp. 4, 13.

13. Burroughs, p. 189.

14. Burroughs, pp. 16–17.

15. Burroughs, pp. 49–50, 52.

16. Burroughs, pp. 76–77.

17. Osgood, pp. 91–92.

18. Frink, Jackson, and Spring, p. 47.

19. Osgood, p. 46; Harold E. Briggs, *Frontiers of the Northwest: A History of the Upper Missouri Valley* (New York, 1950), pp. 181*ff*.

20. Quoted in Osgood, p. 47, from the Cheyenne *Leader*, April 11, 1872.

21. Velma Linford, *Wyoming, Frontier State* (Denver, Colorado, 1947), pp. 180–200.

22. *Annals of Wyoming*, XVI (1944), 65–66.

23. Joseph Joffe, "John W. Meldrum, the Grand Old Man of Yellowstone National Park," *Annals of Wyoming*, XIII (1941), 28–29.

24. C. G. Coutant, "History of Wyoming," *Annals of Wyoming*, XIII (1941), 221, 364; Agnes Wright Spring, *The Cheyenne and Black Hills Stage and Express Routes* (Glendale, California, 1949), pp. 50, 69, 79, 147, 245; Joffe, p. 28.

25. Coutant, pp. 142–143.

26. Spring, p. 294.

27. Linford, p. 391. It should be remembered that in Wyoming there was racial violence against the Chinese.

28. *Annals of Wyoming*, XVI (1944), 83.

29. Clifford P. Westermeier, ed., *Trailing the Cowboy: His Life and Lore as Told by Frontier Journalists* (Caldwell, Idaho, 1955), p. 213. Quoted from the Denver *Tribune-Republican*, November 16, 1886.

30. Coutant, p. 363.

31. Spring, p. 135.

32. J. Frank Dobie, *The Longhorns* (Boston, 1941), pp. 246–247.

33. Linford, pp. 240–241.

34. Charles Wayland Towne and Edward Norris Wentworth, *Cattle and Men* (Norman, Oklahoma, 1955), p. 265.

35. William Walker, *The Longest Rope: The Truth about the Johnson County Cattle War* (Caldwell, Idaho, 1947), pp. 48–50.

36. Amanda Hardin Brown, "A Pioneer in Colorado and Wyoming," *The Colorado Magazine*, XXXV (1958), 274.

37. Floyd C. Bard, *Horse Wrangler: Sixty Years in the Saddle in Wyoming and Montana* (Norman, Oklahoma, 1960), pp. 13, 67–69, 82, 91, 102.

38. Jennie Winona Williams, "Allen and Winona Williams: Pioneers of Sheridan and Johnson Counties," *Annals of Wyoming*, XIV (1942), 199.

39. Osgood, pp. 250–251.

40. Bard, p. 44.

41. Osgood, p. 255.

42. Quoted in Osgood, pp. 79–80, from the *Rocky Mountain Husbandman,* December 4, 1879.

43. Paul F. Sharp, *Whoop-Up Country* (Helena, Montana, 1955), p. 170. See also Dorothy Gardiner, *West of the River* (New York, 1963), p. 32.

44. James McClellan Hamilton, *From Wilderness to Statehood: A History of Montana, 1805–1900* (Portland, Oregon, 1957), p. 499.

45. John Xavier Beidler, *X. Beidler, Vigilante,* eds. Helen Fitzgerald Sanders and William H. Bertische, Jr. (Norman, Oklahoma, 1957), pp. 147–148.

46. Con Price, *Trails I Rode* (Pasadena, California, 1947), p. 201.

47. Edna LaMoore Waldo, *Dakota: An Informal Study of Territorial Days Gleaned from Contemporary Newspapers* (Bismarck, North Dakota, 1932), p. 163.

48. Lucius A. Nutting, *Raw Country* (Laurel, Montana, 1948), pp. 5ff.

49. Bard, pp. 145–146, 155.

50. Price, p. 155.

51. Gary Cooper, "Stage Coach Mary," *Ebony,* XIV (October, 1959), 97–100.

52. Cordia Sloan Duke and Joe B. Frantz, *6,000 Miles of Fence: Life on the XIT Ranch of Texas* (Austin, Texas, 1961), pp. 139–140, 142.

53. Duke and Frantz, p. 142.

54. Frink, Jackson, and Spring, p. 109.

Chapter 9

1. Maurice Frink, W. Turrentine Jackson, and Agnes Wright Spring, *When Grass Was King: Contributions to the Western Range Cattle Industry Study* (Boulder, Colorado, 1956), pp. 57–58.

2. James McClellan Hamilton, *From Wilderness to Statehood: A History of Montana, 1805–1900* (Portland, Oregon, 1957), p. 395.

3. Frink, Jackson, and Spring, p. 99.

4. Lewis Eldon Atherton, *The Cattle Kings* (Bloomington, Indiana, 1961), p. 168.

5. Hamilton, p. 395.

6. Quoted in Frink, Jackson, and Spring, p. 99, from T. A. Larson, "The Winter of 1886–87 in Wyoming," *Annals of Wyoming,* January, 1942.

7. Frink, Jackson, and Spring, p. 104.

8. Frink, Jackson, and Spring, p. 110.

9. Atherton, p. 214.

10. Cordia Sloan Duke and Joe B. Frantz, *6,000 Miles of Fence: Life on the XIT Ranch of Texas* (Austin, Texas, 1961), p. 6.

11. Duke and Frantz, pp. 57–58.

12. Duke and Frantz, p. 195.

13. Duke and Frantz, p. 24.

14. Duke and Frantz, p. 190.

15. Duke and Frantz, pp. 84, 171–172.

16. Duke and Frantz, p. 6.

17. Duke and Frantz, pp. 6–7.

18. Tom Lea, *The King Ranch*, II (Boston, 1957), pp. 484–488, 648, 672–681.

19. John C. Devlin, "Of Cowboys and Kings," *The New York Times* (Western Edition), November 21, 1962, p. 8.

20. C. L. Sonnichsen, *Cowboys and Cattle Kings: Life on the Range Today* (Norman, Oklahoma, 1950), p. 8.

21. Sonnichsen, p. xiii.

22. Sonnichsen, p. 8.

23. Sonnichsen, p. 88.

24. Sonnichsen, p. 93.

25. Leslie A. Fiedler, "Montana: or, The End of Jean Jacques Rousseau," *Partisan Review*, XVI (1949), 1243.

26. Quoted in Sonnichsen, p. 32, from Toi Kerttula, "In Memoriam," *The American Cattle Producer*, April, 1949, p. 12.

27. Sonnichsen, p. 93.

28. Sonnichsen, pp. 95, 104, 106.

29. Frank C. Hibben, *Digging Up America* (New York, 1960), pp. 14–17; letter to Philip Durham from Professor Frank C. Hibben, Department of Anthropology, University of New Mexico, dated September 20, 1963.

Chapter 10

1. Roi Ottley, *Black Odyssey: The Story of the Negro in America* (New York, 1948), pp. 203–204.

2. Philip Ashton Rollins, *The Cowboy: His Characteristics, His Equipment, and His Part in the Development of the West* (New York, 1922), p. 22.

3. George Gaylord Simpson, *Horses* (New York, 1961), pp. 82–83.

4. Emerson Hough, *The Story of the Cowboy* (New York, 1897), p. 91.

5. Clifford P. Westermeier, *Man, Beast, Dust: The Story of Rodeo* (published by the author, 1947), p. 173.

6. Harry E. Chrisman, *Lost Trails of the Cimarron* (Denver, Colorado, 1961), p. 75.

7. J. Frank Dobie, *The Mustangs* (Boston, 1952), p. 197.

8. Everett Dick, *Vanguards of the Frontier* (New York, 1941), p. 490.

9. Hubert E. Collins, *Warpath & Cattle Trail* (New York, 1928), pp. 3–4.

10. Lincoln A. Lang, *Ranching with Roosevelt* (Philadelphia, 1926), pp. 286–288.

11. Dobie, p. 303.

12. J. Frank Dobie, *A Vaquero of the Brush Country: Partly from the Reminiscences of John Young* (Boston, 1943), p. 229.

13. Stith Thompson, ed., *Round the Levee* (Austin, Texas, 1935), p. 60.

14. Dobie, *A Vaquero of the Brush Country*, p. 229.

15. Dobie, *A Vaquero of the Brush Country*, p. 228.

16. Dobie, *A Vaquero of the Brush Country*, pp. 228–236; Dobie, *The Mustangs*, p. 245.

17. Dobie, *The Mustangs*, pp. 235–240; J. Frank Dobie and others, eds., *Mustangs and Cow Horses* (Austin, Texas, 1940), pp. 61–66 (a reprint of Florence Fenley, "The Mustanger Who Turned Mustang," *The Cattleman*, September, 1940).

18. Dobie, *The Mustangs*, p. 240.

19. Chrisman, pp. 96–100.

20. Thomas Donaldson, *Idaho of Yesterday* (Caldwell, Idaho, 1941), pp. 120–121.

21. John Fisher's fear of Indians in California, though groundless at the time he came to San Francisco, was one shared by many tenderfeet.

But the fear would have been realistic in earlier times and other parts of California. In 1862, for instance, cowboys and Indians traded shots and arrows in the Owens Valley. Cattlemen were expropriating this rich hunting ground of the Paiute Indians, the valley that stretches from the shadow of Mt. Tom in the north to Mt. Whitney in the south. The Indians were fighting back.

In February, after they had killed several white men, the Indians were met by a force of cowboys and miners who stalked them in the Alabama Hills near the town of Lone Pine. At least thirty Indians were killed, and "Negro Charley Tyler" was credited with shooting four of them. Then the cowboys and miners moved up the valley, again engaging and defeating a number of Indians near the site of the present town of Bishop. Again Charley Tyler killed at least one of the enemy.

A year later, he was less fortunate. He was traveling with two other men and two women and a girl when their party was surprised by Indians at an Owens River crossing. The others cut loose their wagon horses and escaped, but Tyler was unable to catch any of the horses they were driving and was surrounded and killed. Some days later his Colt's powder and ball pistol was discovered on the body of an Indian killed in another encounter. (Willie Arthur Chalfant, *The Story of Inyo* [Bishop, California, 1933], pp. 151–188.)

22. W. Sherman Savage, "The Negro in the Westward Movement," *The Journal of Negro History*, XXV (1940), 539.

Chapter 11

1. Hubert E. Collins, *Warpath & Cattle Trail* (New York, 1928), pp. 76–77.

2. Collins, pp. 76–77.

3. Glenn Shirley, *Toughest of Them All* (Albuquerque, New Mexico, 1953), p. 131.

4. Shirley, pp. 131–132.

5. Shirley, pp. 131–136; Frank M. Canton, *Frontier Trails: The Autobiography of Frank M. Canton,* ed., Edward Everett Dale (Boston, 1930), p. 131.

6. Wayne Gard, *Frontier Justice* (Norman, Oklahoma, 1949), pp. 283–284.

7. Gard, pp. 283–284.

8. Wilbur S. Nye, *Carbine and Lance: The Story of Old Fort Sill* (Norman, Oklahoma, 1938), pp. 311–312.

9. Nye, pp. 313–315.

10. Glenn Shirley, *Heck Thomas, Frontier Marshal: The Story of a Real Gunfighter* (Philadelphia, 1962), p. 48.

11. Shirley, *Heck Thomas,* p. 86.

12. Charles A. Siringo, *Riata and Spurs* (Boston, 1931), p. 6.

13. Frank Eaton, *Pistol Pete, Veteran of the Old West* (New York, 1953), p. 90.

14. James H. Cook, *Fifty Years on the Old Frontier, as Cowboy, Hunter, Guide, Scout, and Ranchman* (New Haven, Connecticut, 1925), p. 162.

15. William Walker, *The Longest Rope: The Truth about the Johnson County Cattle War* (Caldwell, Idaho, 1947), p. 278; Asa S.

Mercer, *The Banditti of the Plains; or, The Cattlemen's Invasion of Wyoming in 1892* (Norman, Oklahoma, 1954), p. 132.

16. John Rolfe Burroughs, *Where the Old West Stayed Young* (New York, 1962), p. 24.

17. Brown's Hole was also known as Coon Hole. *Cf.* Dane Coolidge, *Fighting Men of the West* (New York, 1932), p. 97.

18. Quoted by Burroughs, p. 102, from W. G. Tittsworth, *Outskirt Episodes* (Avoca, Iowa, 1928).

19. Burroughs, pp. 103, 109.

20. Coolidge, p. 96.

21. Burroughs, pp. 104–105.

22. Burroughs, p. 24.

23. Burroughs, p. 30.

24. Coolidge, p. 96.

25. Burroughs, pp. 108–109.

26. Burroughs, p. 109.

27. Dean F. Krakel, *The Saga of Tom Horn: The Story of the Cattlemen's War, with Personal Narratives, Newspaper Accounts and Official Documents and Testimonies* (Laramie, Wyoming, 1954), p. 9.

28. Krakel, p. 10.

29. Krakel, pp. 9–11.

30. Coolidge, p. 98.

31. Krakel, p. 12; see also Burroughs, pp. 23–30, 54–57, 102–109, 132–133, 162, 192, 204–210.

Chapter 12

1. Albert Johannsen, *The House of Beadle and Adams and Its Dime and Nickel Novels* (Norman, Oklahoma, 1950), I, 252, 256–258; II, 293–297.

2. Johannsen, II, 296.

3. Albert N. Williams, *The Black Hills, Mid-Continent Resort* (Dallas, Texas, 1952), p. 93.

4. Escott North, *The Saga of the Cowboy* (London [1942]), pp. 107–108.

5. Letter to Philip Durham from R. L. Hildebrand, P.O. Box 61, San Marcos, California, dated March 9, 1954.

6. Nat Love, *The Life and Adventures of Nat Love, Better Known in the Cattle Country as "Deadwood Dick," By Himself* (Los Angeles, 1907), p. 127.

7. Love, p. 129.

8. Love, p. 77.

9. Love, p. 109.

Chapter 13

1. Clifford P. Westermeier, ed. *Trailing the Cowboy: His Life and Lore as Told by Frontier Journalists* (Caldwell, Idaho, 1955), p. 354, quoted from "Stock Notes," Las Animas *Leader* (Las Animas, Colorado, December 15, 1882).

2. Westermeier, p. 354, quoted from "Live Stock Notes," Fort Morgan *Times* (Fort Morgan, Colorado, November 13, 1884).

3. Westermeier, pp. 363–366, quoted from "Cowboys and Wild Horses," Denver *Republican* (Denver, Colorado, October 15, 1887).

4. Philip Ashton Rollins, *The Cowboy: His Characteristics, His Equipment, and His Part in the Development of the West* (New York, 1922), p. 233.

5. Edwin Nichols, *Ed Nichols Rode a Horse*, as told to Ruby Nichols Cutbirth ([Austin,] Texas, 1943), pp. 13-14.

6. Harry E. Chrisman, *Lost Trails of the Cimarron* (Denver, Colorado, 1961), pp. 170–171.

7. Frederick Benjamin Gipson, *Fabulous Empire: Colonel Zack Miller's Story* (Boston, 1946), p. 226.

8. Ramon F. Adams, *The Old-Time Cowhand* (New York, 1961); Ramon F. Adams, *Western Words: A Dictionary of the Range, Cow Camp and Trail* (Norman, Oklahoma, 1944); Ellsworth Collings and Alma Miller England, *The 101 Ranch* (Norman, Oklahoma, 1938); Charles Wellington Furlong, *Let 'er Buck: A Story of the Passing of the Old West* (New York, 1921); Gipson; Ross Santee, *The Lost Pony Tracks* (New York, 1953); Glenn Shirley, *Buckskin and Spurs: A Gallery of Frontier Rogues and Heroes* (New York, 1958); Charles Wayland Towne and Edward Norris Wentworth, *Cattle and Men* (Norman, Oklahoma, 1955); Clifford P. Westermeier, *Man, Beast, Dust: The Story of Rodeo* (Denver, Colorado, 1947); Westermeier, *Trailing the Cowboy.*

9. Collings and England, p. 8.

10. Gipson, p. 82.

11. Gipson, p. 225.

12. Gipson, p. 226.

13. Towne and Wentworth, p. 76.

14. Westermeier, *Man, Beast, Dust*, p. 234.

15. Collings and England, p. 28.

16. Gipson, pp. 183–184.

17. Gipson, pp. 224–226, 233–234.

18. Gipson, pp. 232–233.

19. Gipson, pp. 227–231.

20. Shirley, p. 108.

21. Gipson, p. 232.

22. Gipson, pp. 232–242.

23. Gipson, p. 264.

24. Gipson, pp. 264–268.

25. Gipson, pp. 271–272.

26. Gipson, pp. 273–276. The reception of cowboys among the bullfight fans of Mexico City was less pleasant than the reception that had been given bullfighters in Kansas nearly twenty-five years before. Then Dodge had lost much of its glory as a trail end and shipping point, and the businessmen were trying to recapture some of the color of the 1870's by putting on an unusual Fourth of July celebration in 1884.

Although bullfighting was illegal, the city fathers ignored the law and imported matadors and fighting bulls. The bullfight went on, and the visiting bullfighters performed brilliantly. When the crowd began to yell "throw him" as a bull charged past the leading matador's cape, the matador tried. Abandoning the familiar routine of the ring, he made an obviously futile but dangerous attempt to bulldog the fighting bull. The crowd cheered. Then the matador returned to the work he knew well and killed the bull in proper fashion. The crowd cheered even more. (George Bolds, *Across the Cimarron* [New York, 1956], pp. 141–148; Mari Sandoz, *The Cattlemen: From the Rio Grande Across the Far Marias* [New York, 1958], p. 165.)

27. Gipson, pp. 336–354.

28. Gipson, pp. 382–392.

29. Collings and England, p. 172.

30. Gipson, p. 248.

Epilogue

1. Philip Durham, "A General Classification of 1,531 Dime Novels," *The Huntington Library Quarterly*, XVII (1954), 287–291.

2. Owen Wister, *Owen Wister Out West: His Journals and Letters*, ed., Fanny Kemble Wister (Chicago, 1958), p. 158. One such passage from the *Journals* is as follows: "There was a negro named Brock in Brownwood, a kind of pimp as many of them are. He had been employed as a messenger between a man and a certain married woman. This got him the woman's confidence, and she employed

him to gather cavaliers for her. She seems to have been both gregarious and mercenary. One evening she had told him to supply her with a companion, and finding a likely young male in a saloon, he struck a bargain and brought the male into the lady's presence. She screamed, and the male immediately filled Brock full of bullet holes, for he was the husband. But where poetic justice fails is that this husband and wife are now peaceably housekeeping together. Boccaccio or Balzac could have used this theme and embellished it to advantage."

Owen Wister later embellished the theme himself, in a short story called "Skip to My Loo." The story is narrated by Doc Leonard, who has left the Harvard Medical School and has struck out for Texas. The first day in Texas he sees the "sense" in Jim Crow cars. The story follows the journal by having the Negro unfortunately bringing husband and wife together. And when the irate husband shoots the Negro, the hotel clerk comments, "Well, niggers don't count in this section."

3. Wister, p. 257.

4. Richard Hofstadter, *Social Darwinism in American Thought, 1860–1915* (Philadelphia, 1945), pp. 146–173.

5. Quoted in Willis D. Weatherford and Charles S. Johnson, *Race Relations: Adjustment of Whites and Negroes in the United States* (Boston, 1934), p. 329.

6. Thomas Dixon, Jr., *The Clansman: An Historical Romance of the Ku Klux Klan* (New York, 1905), pp. 170–171.

7. N. Orwin Rush, "Fifty Years of *The Virginian*," *The Papers of the Bibliographical Society of America*, XLVI (1952), 99–117.

8. Walter Prescott Webb, *The Great Plains* (Boston, 1931), p. 467.

9. The mold for the Western story was formed during the decade from 1902 to 1912. Until the eve of World War II, there was only an occasional exception to the stereotype. One exception, for example, was Zane Grey's *Knights of the Range* (1936), a Western novel set in New Mexico. Ride-'em Jackson was a Negro cowboy from Texas who was treated more or less like the other cowboys. He was loyal to the boys in his own outfit, and in turn had their loyalty —even to the extent of their taking a "nigger's" word against that of a white man.

At one point in the novel there was a contest between two outfits to see if a cowboy from either group could stay on an apparently unridable horse. One of the "knights" was Brazos, "the equal of any rider who ever straddled a horse; always excepting Ride-'em Jackson, who was in a class by himself."

After several cowboys had been quickly thrown from the wild horse, it came Jackson's turn. He mounted bareback, sank his teeth into the horse's nose and immediately rode the horse to a standstill.

When cowboys from the opposing outfit had paid off the bets, the boss of the group asked Jackson, who had once ridden for the other ranch, why he had not shown his trick to his former employer. "Wal, boss," said Jackson, "I was only a nigger in your outfit."

In *Twin Sombreros* (1940), a sequel to *Knights of the Range,* Grey again used Jackson, this time as the only one of the old hands still left on the ranch. In *Twin Sombreros* Jackson ("bless his white heart") was called "Nigger Johnson."

10. Lewis Eldon Atherton, *The Cattle Kings* (Bloomington, Indiana, 1961), pp. 246–248.

11. Lawrence P. Spingarn, "Historical," *The Carleton Miscellany,* III (Spring, 1962), 88.

12. Thelma M. Smith and Ward L. Miner, *Transatlantic Migration: The Contemporary American Novel in France* (Durham, North Carolina, 1955), p. 190.

13. Philip Durham and Tauno F. Mustanoja, *American Fiction in Finland: An Essay and Bibliography* (Helsinki, Finland, 1960), p. 107.

14. Frederick Benjamin Gipson, *Cowhand: The Story of a Working Cowboy* (New York, 1958), "Author's Note."

15. Philip Ashton Rollins, *The Cowboy: His Characteristics, His Equipment, and His Part in the Development of the West* (New York, 1922), p. 353.

16. Herman Dreer, "What Does the Innocent Teacher Impart as History?" *The Journal of Negro History,* XXV (1940), 483. Quoted from the "Preface" to N. C. Newbold, *Five North Carolina Educators* (Chapel Hill, North Carolina, 1939), p. 5.

Bibliography

Abbott, Edward Charles ("Teddy Blue"), and Helena Huntington Smith. *We Pointed Them North: Recollections of a Cowpuncher.* New York: Farrar & Rinehart, 1939.

Abbott, Newton Carl. *Montana in the Making,* 8th ed., rev. Billings, Montana: Gazette Printing Company, 1943.

Adams, Andy. *The Log of a Cowboy.* Boston: Houghton Mifflin Company, 1931 (1st ed., 1903).

—— *Why the Chisholm Trail Forks, and Other Tales of the Cattle Country,* ed. Wilson M. Hudson. Austin, Texas: University of Texas Press, 1956.

Adams, Ramon F., ed. *The Best of the American Cowboy.* Norman, Oklahoma: University of Oklahoma Press, 1957.

—— *Come an' Get It: The Story of the Old Cowboy Cook.* Norman, Oklahoma: University of Oklahoma Press, 1952.

—— *The Old-Time Cowhand.* New York: The Macmillan Company, 1961.

—— *Western Words: A Dictionary of the Range, Cow Camp and Trail.* Norman, Oklahoma: University of Oklahoma Press, 1944.

Addington, Wendell G. "Slave Insurrections in Texas," *The Journal of Negro History,* XXXV (1950), 408–434.

Aptheker, Herbert. *To Be Free: Studies in American Negro History.* New York: International Publishers, 1948.

—— *The Negro in the Civil War.* New York: International Publishers, 1938.

Arnold, Oren, and John P. Hale. *Hot Irons: Heraldry of the Range.* New York: The Macmillan Company, 1940.

Athearn, Robert G. *High Country Empire.* New York: McGraw-Hill Book Company, 1960.

Atherton, Lewis Eldon. *The Cattle Kings.* Bloomington, Indiana: Indiana University Press, 1961.

Bancroft, Hubert Howe. *The Works . . .* 39 vols. San Francisco: A. L. Bancroft & Company and The History Company, 1882–1890.

Bard, Floyd C. *Horse Wrangler: Sixty Years in the Saddle in Wyoming and Montana.* Norman, Oklahoma: University of Oklahoma Press, 1960.

Bardolph, Richard. *The Negro Vanguard.* New York: Rinehart & Company, 1959.

Beard, Charles A., and Mary R. Beard. *A Basic History of the United States.* New York: The New Home Library, 1944.

Beasley, Delilah L. *The Negro Trail Blazers of California.* Los Angeles: Times Mirror Printing and Binding House, 1919.

Beckwourth, James P. *The Life and Adventures of James P. Beckwourth,* ed. Bernard De Voto from T. D. Bonner's 1856 edition. New York: Alfred A. Knopf, 1931.

Beidler, John Xavier. *X. Beidler, Vigilante,* eds. Helen Fitzgerald Sanders and William H. Bertische, Jr. Norman, Oklahoma: University of Oklahoma Press, 1957.

Bell, Horace. *Reminiscences of a Ranger; or, Early Times in Southern California.* Santa Barbara, California: Wallace Hebberd, 1927 (1st ed., 1881).

Beller, Jack. "Negro Slaves in Utah," *Utah Historical Quarterly,* II (1929), 122–126.

Benedict, Carl Peters. *A Tenderfoot Kid on Gyp Water.* Austin, Texas: The Texas Folklore Society, 1943.

Bennett, Estelline. *Old Deadwood Days.* New York: J. H. Sears & Company, 1928.

Billington, Ray Allen. *The Far Western Frontier: 1830–1860.* New York: Harper and Row, 1962 (1st ed., 1956).

——— *Westward Expansion: A History of the American Frontier.* New York: The Macmillan Company, 1960 (1st ed., 1949).

Blasingame, Ike. *Dakota Cowboy: My Life in the Old Days.* New York: G. P. Putnam's Sons, 1958.

Bolds, George. *Across the Cimarron,* as told to James D. Horan. New York: Crown Publishers, 1956.

Bosworth, Allan R. "Stampede!" *The Saturday Evening Post,* December 2, 1950, pp. 30, 148, 150–152.

Bradley, Glenn Danford. *The Story of the Pony Express,* ed. Waddell F. Smith. San Francisco: Hesperian House, 1960 (1st ed., 1913).

Branch, Edward Douglas. *The Cowboy and His Interpreters.* New York: Cooper Square Publishers, 1961 (1st ed., 1926).

—— *Westward: The Romance of the American Frontier.* New York: D. Appleton and Company, 1930.

Brandon, William. *The American Heritage Book of Indians.* New York: American Heritage Publishing Co., 1961.

—— *The Men and the Mountain: Frémont's Fourth Expedition.* New York: William Morrow & Company, 1955.

Brawley, Benjamin. *A Short History of the American Negro,* 4th ed., rev. New York: The Macmillan Company, 1944 (1st ed., 1913).

Brayer, Herbert O. "The L7 Ranches," *Annals of Wyoming,* XV (1943), 5–37.

Brewer, John Mason. *Negro Legislators of Texas and Their Descendants: A History of the Negro in Texas Politics from Reconstruction to Disfranchisement.* Dallas, Texas: Mathis Publishing Company, 1935.

Briggs, Harold E. *Frontiers of the Northwest: A History of the Upper Missouri Valley.* New York: Peter Smith, 1950 (1st ed., 1940).

Bronson, Edgar Beecher. *Cowboy Life on the Western Plains: The Reminiscences of a Ranchman.* New York: George H. Doran Company, 1910.

Brown, Amanda Hardin. "A Pioneer in Colorado and Wyoming," *The Colorado Magazine,* XXXV (1958), 271–287.

Brown, Wallace. "George L. Miller and the Struggle over Nebraska Statehood," *Nebraska History,* XLI (1960), 299–318.

Browne, John Ross. *A Tour through Arizona, 1864: or, Adventures in the Apache Country.* Tucson, Arizona: Arizona Silhouettes, 1951 (1st ed., 1869).

Burns, Robert H. "The Newman Ranches: Pioneer Cattle Ranches of the West," *Nebraska History,* XXXIV (1953), 21–32.

Burroughs, John Rolfe. *Where the Old West Stayed Young.* New York: William Morrow & Company, 1962.

Burt, Maxwell Struthers. *Powder River: Let 'er Buck.* New York: Farrar & Rinehart, 1938.

Canton, Frank M. *Frontier Trails: The Autobiography of Frank M. Canton,* ed. Edward Everett Dale. Boston: Houghton Mifflin Company, 1930.

Carrington, Margaret Irvin (Sullivant). *AB-SA-RA-KA, Land of Massacre: Being the Experience of an Officer's Wife on the Plains,* 5th ed., rev. Philadelphia: J. B. Lippincott, 1879 (1st ed., 1868).

Caughey, John Walton. *California.* New York: Prentice-Hall, 1940.

—— *History of the Pacific Coast.* Los Angeles: privately published by the author, 1933.

—— ed. *Rushing for Gold.* Berkeley, California: University of California Press, 1949.

Chalfant, Willie Arthur. *The Story of Inyo.* Bishop, California: privately published by the author, 1933 (1st ed., 1922).

Chatterton, Fenimore. *Yesterday's Wyoming: The Intimate Memoirs of Fenimore Chatterton, Territorial Citizen, Governor and States-man.* Aurora, Colorado: Powder River Publishers & Booksellers, 1957.

Chisholm, Joseph Francis. *Brewery Gulch: Frontier Days of Old Arizona—Last Outpost of the Great Southwest.* San Antonio, Texas: The Naylor Company, 1949.

Chrisman, Harry E. *Lost Trails of the Cimarron.* Denver, Colorado: Alan Swallow, 1961.

Clark, Joseph L., and Julia Kathryn Garrett. *A History of Texas, Land of Promise,* rev. ed. Boston: D. C. Heath and Company, 1949.

Clark, Walter Van Tilburg. *The Ox-Bow Incident.* New York: Random House, 1940.

Cleland, Robert Glass. *This Reckless Breed of Men: The Trappers and Fur Traders of the Southwest.* New York: Alfred A. Knopf, 1950.

Clemens, Samuel Langhorne. *Pudd'nhead Wilson.* New York: Grove Press, 1955 (1st ed., 1894).

Coe, George W. *Frontier Fighter: The Autobiography of George W. Coe, Who Fought and Rode with Billy the Kid,* as told to Nan Hillary Harrison. Albuquerque, New Mexico: University of New Mexico Press, 1951.

Collings, Ellsworth, and Alma Miller England. *The 101 Ranch.* Norman, Oklahoma: University of Oklahoma Press, 1938.

Collins, Hubert E. *Warpath & Cattle Trail.* New York: William Morrow & Company, 1928.

Conkling, Roscoe P., and Margaret B. Conkling. *The Butterfield Overland Mail, 1857–1869,* 3 vols. Glendale, California: The Arthur H. Clark Company, 1947.

Connelly, Christopher P. *The Devil Learns to Vote.* New York: Covici, Friede, 1938.

Cook, David J. *Hands Up: or, Thirty-five Years of Detective Life in the Mountains and on the Plains.* Norman, Oklahoma: University of Oklahoma Press, 1958 (1st ed., 1882).

Cook, James H.   *Fifty Years on the Old Frontier, as Cowboy, Hunter, Guide, Scout, and Ranchman.* New Haven, Connecticut: Yale University Press, 1925.

Coolidge, Dane.   *Fighting Men of the West.* New York: E. P. Dutton & Co., 1932.

Cooper, Gary.   "Stage Coach Mary," *Ebony,* XIV (October, 1959), 97–100.

Coutant, C. G.   "History of Wyoming," *Annals of Wyoming,* XIII (1941), 141–155, 217–230, 355–364.

Cowan, Bud.   *Range Rider.* Garden City, New York: The Sun Dial Press, 1930.

Cox, William R.   *Luke Short and His Era.* New York: Doubleday & Company, 1961.

Crawford, Lewis F.   *History of North Dakota.* Chicago and New York: The American Historical Society, 1931.

Crocchiola, Stanley Francis Louis.   *Clay Allison,* by F. Stanley [pseud.]. Denver, Colorado: World Press, 1956.

Culley, John H.   *Cattle, Horses & Men of the Western Range.* Los Angeles: The Ward Ritchie Press, 1940.

Curti, Merle.   *The Growth of American Thought.* New York: Harper & Brothers, 1943.

Dale, Edward Everett.   *Frontier Ways: Sketches of Life in the Old West.* Austin, Texas: University of Texas Press, 1959.

——   *The Range Cattle Industry: Ranching on the Great Plains from 1865 to 1925.* Norman, Oklahoma: University of Oklahoma Press, 1960 (1st ed., 1930).

——   and Morris L. Wardell. *History of Oklahoma.* New York: Prentice-Hall, 1948.

Danker, Donald F.   "Columbus, a Territorial Town in the Platte Valley," *Nebraska History,* XXXIV (1953), 275–288.

——   ed. "The Journal of an Indian Fighter: The 1869 Diary of Major Frank J. North," *Nebraska History,* XXXIX (1958), 87–177.

Debo, Angie.   *Oklahoma, Foot-loose and Fancy-free.* Norman, Oklahoma: University of Oklahoma Press, 1949.

——   *The Road to Disappearance.* Norman, Oklahoma: University of Oklahoma Press, 1941.

Devlin, John C.   "Of Cowboys and Kings," The New York *Times* (Western edition), November 21, 1962, p. 8.

Dick, Everett.   *The Sod-House Frontier, 1854–1890.* Lincoln, Nebraska: Johnson Publishing Company, 1954 (1st ed., 1937).

—— *Vanguards of the Frontier.* New York: D. Appleton-Century Company, 1941.

Dixon, Thomas Jr. *The Clansman: An Historical Romance of the Ku Klux Klan.* New York: Doubleday, Page & Company, 1905.

Dobie, J. Frank. *Coronado's Children: Tales of Lost Mines and Buried Treasures of the Southwest.* New York: Bantam Books, 1953 (1st ed., 1931).

—— ed. *Legends of Texas.* Austin, Texas: The Texas Folk-Lore Society, 1924.

—— *The Longhorns.* Boston: Little, Brown and Company, 1941.

—— *The Mustangs.* Boston: Little, Brown and Company, 1952.

—— *A Vaquero of the Brush Country: Partly from the Reminiscences of John Young.* Boston: Little, Brown and Company, 1943 (1st ed., 1929).

—— and others, eds. *Mustangs and Cow Horses.* Austin, Texas: Texas Folk-Lore Society, 1940.

Donaldson, Thomas. *Idaho of Yesterday.* Caldwell, Idaho: The Caxton Printers, 1941.

Dreer, Herman. "What Does the Innocent Teacher Impart as History?" *The Journal of Negro History,* XXV (1940), 474–483.

Duke, Cordia Sloan, and Joe B. Frantz. *6,000 Miles of Fence: Life on the XIT Ranch of Texas.* Austin, Texas: University of Texas Press, 1961.

Durham, Philip. "A General Classification of 1,531 Dime Novels," *The Huntington Library Quarterly,* XVII (1954), 287–291.

—— "The Lost Cowboy," *The Midwest Journal,* VII (1955), 176–182.

—— "The Negro Cowboy," *American Quarterly,* VII (1955), 291–301.

—— and Tauno F. Mustanoja. *American Fiction in Finland: An Essay and Bibliography.* Helsinki, Finland: Société Néophilologique, 1960.

Eaton, Frank. *Pistol Pete, Veteran of the Old West.* New York: The New American Library, 1953.

Eby, Cecil D., Jr., ed. " 'Porte Crayon' in the Rocky Mountains," *The Colorado Magazine,* XXXVII (1960), 108–121.

Emilio, Luis F. *History of the Fifty-Fourth Regiment of Massachusetts Volunteer Infantry, 1863–1865.* Boston: The Boston Book Company, 1891.

Emmett, Chris. *Shanghai Pierce: A Fair Likeness.* Norman, Oklahoma: University of Oklahoma Press, 1953.

Ernst, Robert. "Negro Concepts of Americanism," *The Journal of Negro History,* XXXIX (1954), 206–219.

Federal Writers Project. *The Idaho Encyclopedia.* Caldwell, Idaho: The Caxton Printers, 1938.

—— *Idaho Lore.* Caldwell, Idaho: The Caxton Printers, 1939.

—— *Montana.* New York: The Viking Press, 1939.

—— *South Dakota Place Names.* Vermillion, South Dakota: University of South Dakota, 1941.

Fergusson, Erna. *New Mexico: A Pageant of Three Peoples.* New York: Alfred A. Knopf, 1951.

Fiedler, Leslie A. "Montana; or, The End of Jean Jacques Rousseau," *Partisan Review,* XVI (1949), 1239–1248.

Fishel, Leslie H., Jr. "Northern Prejudice and Negro Suffrage, 1865–1870," *The Journal of Negro History,* XXXIX (1954), 8–26.

Fisher, Clay. *The Big Pasture.* New York: Pocket Books, 1956 (1st ed., 1955).

Flipper, Henry Ossian. *The Colored Cadet at West Point.* New York: Homer Lee & Co., 1878.

—— *Negro Frontiersman: The Western Memoirs of Henry O. Flipper,* ed. Theodore D. Harris. El Paso, Texas: Texas Western College Press, 1963.

Franklin, William E. "The Archy Case: The California Supreme Court Refuses to Free A Slave," *Pacific Historical Review,* XXXII (1963), 137–154.

Frantz, Joe B., and Julian Ernest Choate, Jr. *The American Cowboy: The Myth and the Reality.* Norman, Oklahoma: University of Oklahoma Press, 1955.

Frémont, John C. *The Daring Adventures of Kit Carson and Frémont among Buffaloes, Grizzlies, and Indians.* New York: Hurst & Co., 1885 (Contains: "A Narrative of the Exploring Expedition to Oregon and North California").

Friedman, Albert B., ed. *The Viking Book of Folk Ballads of the English-Speaking World.* New York: The Viking Press, 1956.

Frink, Maurice, W. Turrentine Jackson, and Agnes Wright Spring. *When Grass Was King: Contributions to the Western Range Cattle Industry Study.* Boulder, Colorado: University of Colorado Press, 1956.

Furlong, Charles Wellington. *Let 'er Buck: A Story of the Passing of the Old West.* New York: G. P. Putnam's Sons, 1921.

Fuson, Henry Harvey. *Ballads of the Kentucky Highlands.* London: The Mitre Press, 1931.

Gann, Walter. *Tread of the Longhorns.* San Antonio, Texas: The Naylor Company, 1949.

Gard, Wayne. *The Chisholm Trail.* Norman, Oklahoma: University of Oklahoma Press, 1954.

—— *Frontier Justice.* Norman, Oklahoma: University of Oklahoma Press, 1949.

Gardiner, Dorothy. *West of the River.* New York: Thomas Y. Crowell Company, 1963 (1st ed., 1941).

Garrett, T. S. "Some Recollections of an Old Freighter," *Annals of Wyoming,* III (1925), 86–93.

"Gazetteer of Pioneers and Others in North Dakota Previous to 1862," North Dakota State Historical Society *Collections,* I (1906), 355–380.

Geer, Theodore T. *Fifty Years in Oregon.* New York: The Neale Publishing Company, 1916.

Gilland, Mrs. George H. "The Texas Trail as Followed by a Pioneer in 1882," *Annals of Wyoming,* XII (1940), 253–263.

Gillett, James B. *Six Years with the Texas Rangers, 1875 to 1881,* ed. M. M. Qualife. New Haven, Connecticut: Yale University Press, 1925 (1st ed., 1921).

Gipson, Frederick Benjamin. *Cowhand: The Story of A Working Cowboy.* New York: Bantam Books, 1958.

—— *Fabulous Empire: Colonel Zack Miller's Story.* Boston: Houghton Mifflin Company, 1946.

Goplen, Arnold O. "The Career of Marquis de Mores in the Badlands of North Dakota," *North Dakota History,* XIII (1946), 5–70.

Greer, Genevieve. *The Aristocrat.* New York: The Vanguard Press, 1946.

Grey, Zane. *Knights of the Range.* New York: Harper & Bros., 1939.

—— *Twin Sombreros.* New York: Collier, 1940.

Hafen, LeRoy R., and Ann W. Hafen. *Colorado: A Story of the State and Its People.* Denver, Colorado: The Old West Publishing Company, 1945.

Haley, James Evetts. *Charles Goodnight, Cowman & Plainsman.* Norman, Oklahoma: University of Oklahoma Press, 1949 (1st ed., 1936).

Halsell, H. H. *Cowboys and Cattleland.* Nashville, Tennessee: printed for the author by the Parthenon Press, 1937.

Hamilton, James McClellan. *From Wilderness to Statehood: A History of Montana, 1805–1900.* Portland, Oregon: Binfords & Mort, 1957.

Hamlin, William Lee. *The True Story of Billy the Kid: A Tale of the Lincoln County War*. Caldwell, Idaho: The Caxton Printers, 1959.

Hanchett, William. " 'His Turbulent Excellency,' Alexander Cummings, Governor of Colorado Territory, 1865–1867," *The Colorado Magazine*, XXXIV (1957), 81–104.

Herskovits, Melville J. *The Anthropometry of the American Negro.* New York: Columbia University Press, 1930 (Columbia University Contributions to Anthropology, XI).

Hibben, Frank C. *Digging Up America*. New York: Hill and Wang, 1960.

Higginson, Thomas Wentworth. *Army Life in a Black Regiment.* East Lansing, Michigan: Michigan State University Press, 1960 [1961] (1st ed., 1870).

Hills, Georgia Burns. "Memories of a Pioneer Childhood," *The Colorado Magazine*, XXXII (1955), 110–128.

Historical and Biographical Record of the Cattle Industry and the Cattlemen of Texas and Adjacent Territory, 2 vols. New York: Antiquarian Press, 1959 (1st ed., 1895).

Hofstadter, Richard. *Social Darwinism in American Thought, 1860–1915*. Philadelphia: University of Pennsylvania Press, 1945.

Hoig, Stan. *The Humor of the American Cowboy*. New York: The New American Library, 1960 (1st ed., 1958).

Hollon, William Eugene. *The Southwest, Old and New*. New York: Alfred A. Knopf, 1961.

Horan, James D., and Paul Sann. *Pictorial History of the Wild West: A True Account of the Bad Men, Desperadoes, Rustlers and Outlaws of the Old West—and the Men Who Fought Them to Establish Law and Order*. New York: Crown Publishers, 1954.

Horn, Tom. *Life of Tom Horn, Government Scout and Interpreter, Written by Himself, Together with His Letters and Statements by His Friends: A Vindication*. Denver, Colorado: for J. C. Coble by the Louthan Book Company, 1904.

Hough, Emerson. *The Story of the Cowboy*. New York: D. Appleton and Company, 1897.

Howard, Joseph Kinsey. *Montana: High, Wide, and Handsome.* New Haven, Connecticut: Yale University Press, 1944.

Hunt, Frazier. *The Long Trail from Texas: The Story of Ad Spaugh, Cattleman*. New York: Doubleday, Doran & Company, 1940.

Hunter, John Marvin, ed. *The Trail Drivers of Texas*, 2d ed., rev. Nashville, Tennessee: Cokesbury Press, 1925.

Jeltz, Wyatt F. "The Relations of Negroes and Choctaw and Chickasaw Indians," *The Journal of Negro History,* XXXIII (1948), 24–37.

Jenkins, Charles. "The Kearney Cotton Mill—A Bubble that Burst," *Nebraska History,* XXXVIII (1957), 207–219.

Joffe, Joseph. "John W. Meldrum, the Grand Old Man of Yellowstone National Park," *Annals of Wyoming,* XIII (1941), 5–47.

Johannsen, Albert. *The House of Beadle and Adams and Its Dime and Nickel Novels,* 2 vols. Norman, Oklahoma: University of Oklahoma Press, 1950.

Kazeck, Melvin E. *North Dakota: A Human and Economic Geography.* Fargo, North Dakota: North Dakota Institute for Regional Studies, North Dakota Agricultural College, 1956.

Keleher, William A. *Violence in Lincoln County, 1869–1881: A New Mexico Item.* Albuquerque, New Mexico: University of New Mexico Press, 1957.

Kelly, Charles, and Hoffman Birney. *Holy Murder: The Story of Porter Rockwell.* New York: Minton, Balch & Company, 1934.

King, Frank M. *Pioneer Western Empire Builders: A True Story of the Men and Women of Pioneer Days.* Pasadena, California: Trail's End Publishing Company, 1946.

—— *Wranglin' the Past.* Pasadena, California: Trail's End Publishing Company, 1946 (1st ed., 1935).

Krakel, Dean F. *The Saga of Tom Horn: The Story of a Cattleman's War, with Personal Narratives, Newspaper Accounts and Official Documents and Testimonies.* Laramie, Wyoming: Powder River Publishers, 1954.

Krogman, Wilton Marion. "The Racial Composition of the Seminole Indians of Florida and Oklahoma," *The Journal of Negro History,* XIX (1934), 412–430.

La Farge, Oliver. *Santa Fe: The Autobiography of a Southwestern Town.* Norman, Oklahoma: University of Oklahoma Press, 1959.

Lang, Lincoln A. *Ranching with Roosevelt.* Philadelphia: J. B. Lippincott Company, 1926.

Lavender, David. *The Big Divide.* New York: Doubleday & Company, 1948.

Lea, Tom. *The King Ranch,* 2 vols. Boston: Little, Brown and Company, 1957.

—— *The Wonderful Country.* Boston: Little, Brown and Company, 1952.

Leakey, John. *The West That Was, from Texas to Montana,* as told to Nellie Snyder Yost. Dallas, Texas: Southern Methodist University Press, 1958.

Lifton, Robert Jay. "Who Is More Dry?" *New Republic*, August 13, 1962, pp. 12–14.

Linford, Velma. *Wyoming, Frontier State*. Denver, Colorado: The Old West Publishing Company, 1947.

Lockwood, Francis C. *Pioneer Days in Arizona, from the Spanish Occupation to Statehood*. New York: The Macmillan Company, 1932.

Lofton, Williston H. "Northern Labor and the Negro during the Civil War," *The Journal of Negro History*, XXXIV (1949), 251–273.

Logan, Rayford W. *The Negro in the United States: A Brief History*. Princeton, New Jersey: D. Van Nostrand Company, 1957.

Lomax, John A. *Adventures of a Ballad Hunter*. New York: The Macmillan Company, 1947.

Lounsberry, C. A. "Early Development of North Dakota," North Dakota State Historical Society *Collections*, I (1908), 299–310.

Love, Nat. *The Life and Adventures of Nat Love, Better Known in the Cattle Country as "Deadwood Dick," by Himself*. Los Angeles: Wayside Press, 1907.

McCauley, James Emmit. *A Stove-Up Cowboy's Story*. Austin, Texas: Texas Folk-Lore Society, 1943.

McCoy, Joseph G. *Historic Sketches of the Cattle Trade of the West and Southwest*. Kansas City, Missouri: Ramsey, Millet & Hudson, 1874.

MacGowan, Kenneth. *Early Man in the New World*. New York: The Macmillan Company, 1950.

McNickle, D'Arcy. *They Came Here First: The Epic of the American Indian*. Philadelphia and New York: J. B. Lippincott Company, 1949.

McPherron, Ida. *Imprints on Pioneer Trails*. Boston: Christopher Publishing House, 1950.

Mandat-Grancey, Edmond. *Cow-Boys and Colonels: Narrative of a Journey across the Prairie and over the Black Hills of Dakota*, trans. William Conn with introd. Howard R. Lamar. Philadelphia and New York: J. B. Lippincott Company, 1963 (1st ed., 1887).

Mann, Edward B., and Fred E. Harvey. *New Mexico: Land of Enchantment*. East Lansing, Michigan: Michigan State University Press, 1955.

Marquis, Thomas B. *Wooden Leg*. Lincoln, Nebraska: University of Nebraska Press, 1957 (1st ed., 1931).

Mattison, Ray H. "The Army Post on the Northern Plains, 1865–1885," *Nebraska History*, XXXV (1954), 17–43.

—— "Roosevelt and the Stockmen's Association," *North Dakota History*, XVII (1950), 73–95, 177–209.

Mercer, Asa S. *The Banditti of the Plains; or, The Cattlemen's Invasion of Wyoming in 1892.* Norman, Oklahoma: University of Oklahoma Press, 1954 (1st ed., 1894).

Mokler, Alfred James. *History of Natrona County, Wyoming, 1888–1922.* Chicago: The Lakeside Press, 1923.

Mora, Joseph Jacinto. *Trail Dust and Saddle Leather.* New York: Charles Scribner's Sons, 1946.

Muir, Andrew Forest. "The Free Negro in Jefferson and Orange Counties, Texas," *The Journal of Negro History*, XXXV (1950), 183–206.

Myers, Henry Alonzo. *Are Men Equal?* New York: G. P. Putnam's Sons, 1945.

Myrdal, Gunnar. *An American Dilemma: The Negro Problem and Modern Democracy.* New York: Harper & Brothers, 1944.

Neider, Charles, ed. *The Great West.* New York: Coward-McCann, Inc., 1958.

Nelson, John Herbert. *The Negro Character in American Literature.* Lawrence, Kansas: Department of Journalism Press, 1926.

Nichols, Edwin. *Ed Nichols Rode a Horse,* as told to Ruby Nichols Cutbirth. [Austin, Texas] Texas Folk-Lore Society and University Press in Dallas, 1943.

North, Escott. *The Saga of the Cowboy.* London: Jarrolds [1942].

Nutting, Lucius A. *Raw Country.* Laurel, Montana, 1948.

Nye, Edgar Wilson. "Bill Nye's Experience," *Annals of Wyoming*, XVI (1944), 65–70.

—— *Bill Nye's Remarks.* New York: F. Tennyson Neely, 1896 (1st ed., 1887).

Nye, Wilbur S. *Carbine and Lance: The Story of Old Fort Sill.* Norman, Oklahoma: University of Oklahoma Press, 1938.

Obets, Bob. "The Deserters," *Rawhide and Bob-Wire,* ed. Luke Short. New York: Bantam Books, 1958.

O'Kieffe, Charley. *Western Story.* Lincoln, Nebraska: University of Nebraska Press, 1960.

Ormsby, Waterman L. *The Butterfield Overland Mail,* ed. Lyle H. Wright and Josephine Bynum. San Marino, California: The Huntington Library, 1942.

Osgood, Ernest Staples. *The Day of the Cattleman.* Chicago: University of Chicago Press, [1960] (1st ed., 1929).

Ottley, Roi. *Black Odyssey: The Story of the Negro in America.* New York: Charles Scribner's Sons, 1948.

Peattie, Roderick, ed. *The Black Hills*. New York: Vanguard Press, 1952.

Pelzer, Louis. *The Cattlemen's Frontier*. Glendale, California: Arthur H. Clark Company, 1936.

Pence, Mary Lou, and Lola M. Homsher. *The Ghost Towns of Wyoming*. New York: Hastings House, 1956.

Porter, Kenneth W. "Negroes and Indians on the Texas Frontier, 1831–1876," *The Journal of Negro History*, XLI (1956), 185–214, 285–310.

—— "Relations Between Negroes and Indians Within the Present Limits of the United States," *The Journal of Negro History*, XVII (1932), 287–367.

—— "The Seminole in Mexico, 1850–1861," *The Hispanic American Review*, XXXI (1951), 1–36.

—— "The Seminole Negro-Indian Scouts, 1870–1881," *The Southwestern Historical Quarterly*, LV (1952), 358–377.

Potter, Jack M. *Cattle Trails of the Old West*, ed. Laura R. Krehbiel. Clayton, New Mexico: Laura R. Krehbiel, 1939 (1st ed., 1935).

Pound, Louise. "The John G. Maher Hoaxes," *Nebraska History*, XXXIII (1952), 203–219.

Price, Con. *Memories of Old Montana*. Hollywood, California: The Highland Press, 1945.

—— *Trails I Rode*. Pasadena, California: Trail's End Publishing Company, 1947.

Prose and Poetry of the Live Stock Industry of the United States. New York: Antiquarian Press, 1959 (1st ed., 1905).

Roosevelt, Theodore. *The Rough Riders*. New York: Charles Scribner's Sons, 1899.

Reddick, L. D. "The Negro Policy of the United States Army, 1775–1945," *The Journal of Negro History*, XXXIV (1949), 9–29.

Remington, Frederic. *Frederic Remington's Own West*, ed. Harold McCracken. New York: The Dial Press, 1960.

Rollins, Philip Ashton. *The Cowboy: His Characteristics, His Equipment, and His Part in the Development of the West*. New York: Charles Scribner's Sons, 1922.

Rollinson, John K. *Wyoming Cattle Trails*. Caldwell, Idaho: The Caxton Printers, 1948.

Rush, N. Orwin. "Fifty Years of *The Virginian*," *The Papers of the Bibliographical Society of America*, XLVI (1952), 99–117.

Sandoz, Mari. *The Buffalo Hunters: The Story of the Hide Men*. New York: Hastings House, 1954.

—— *The Cattlemen: From the Rio Grande across the Far Marias.* New York: Hastings House, 1958.

—— *Crazy Horse, the Strange Man of the Oglalas.* Lincoln, Nebraska: University of Nebraska Press, 1961 (1st ed., 1942).

—— "The Look of the West—1854," *Nebraska History,* XXXV (1954), 243–254.

—— *Love Song to the Plains.* New York: Harper & Brothers, 1961.

Santee, Ross. *Cowboy.* New York: Grosset & Dunlap, 1928.

—— *The Lost Pony Tracks.* New York: Charles Scribner's Sons, 1953.

Saunders, Arthur C. *The History of Bannock County, Idaho.* Pocatello, Idaho: The Tribune Company, 1915.

Savage, W. Sherman. "The Negro in the Westward Movement," *The Journal of Negro History,* XXV (1940), 531–539.

—— "The Negro on the Mining Frontier," *The Journal of Negro History,* XXX (1945) 30–46.

—— "The Role of Negro Soldiers in Protecting the Indian Territory from Intruders," *The Journal of Negro History,* XXXVI (1951), 25-34.

Schatz, August H. *Longhorns Bring Culture.* Boston: Christopher Publishing House, 1961.

Schell, Herbert Samuel. *South Dakota, Its Beginnings and Growth.* New York: American Book Company, 1942.

Schoenfeld, Seymour J. *The Negro in the Armed Forces.* Washington, D. C.: The Associated Publishers, 1945.

Segale, Sister Blandina. *At the End of the Santa Fe Trail.* Milwaukee, Wisconsin: Bruce Publishing Company, 1948.

Sharp, Paul F. *Whoop-Up Country.* Helena, Montana: Historical Society of Montana, 1955.

Shaw, James C. *North from Texas: Incidents in the Early Life of a Range Cowman in Texas, Dakota, and Wyoming, 1852–1883.* Evanston, Illinois: Branding Iron Press, 1952.

Shirley, Glenn. *Buckskin and Spurs: A Gallery of Frontier Rogues and Heroes.* New York: Hastings House, 1958.

—— *Heck Thomas, Frontier Marshal: The Story of a Real Gunfighter.* Philadelphia: Chilton Company, 1962.

—— *Pawnee Bill: A Biography of Major Gordon W. Lillie.* Albuquerque, New Mexico: University of New Mexico Press, 1958.

—— *Toughest of Them All.* Albuquerque, New Mexico: University of New Mexico Press, 1953.

Simpson, George Gaylord. *Horses.* New York: Doubleday & Company, 1961 (1st ed., 1951).

Siringo, Charles A. *A Cowboy Detective*. New York: J. S. Ogilvie Publishing Company, 1912.

—— *Riata and Spurs*. Boston: Houghton Mifflin Company, 1931 (omits pp. 120–268 of 1st ed., 1927).

—— *A Texas Cowboy; or, Fifteen Years on the Hurricane Deck of a Spanish Pony*. New York: The New American Library, 1951 (1st ed., 1885).

Slaughter, Linda W. "Leaves from Northwestern History," North Dakota State Historical Society *Collections*, I (1908), 200–292.

Smith, Thelma M., and Ward L. Miner. *Transatlantic Migration: The Contemporary American Novel in France*. Durham, North Carolina: Duke University Press, 1955.

Sonnichsen, C. L. *Cowboys and Cattle Kings: Life on the Range Today*. Norman, Oklahoma: University of Oklahoma Press, 1950.

—— and William V. Morrison. *Alias Billy the Kid*. Albuquerque, New Mexico: University of New Mexico Press, 1955.

Spingarn, Lawrence P. "Historical," *The Carleton Miscellany*, III (Spring, 1962), 88–89.

Spring, Agnes Wright. *The Cheyenne and Black Hills Stage and Express Routes*. Glendale, California: The Arthur H. Clark Company, 1949.

"Stars behind Bars," *Time*, October 21, 1940, pp. 43–44.

Steward, Theophilus G. *The Colored Regulars in the United States Army*. Philadelphia: A. M. E. Book Concern, 1904.

Still, Bayrd, ed. *The West: Contemporary Records of America's Expansion across the Continent, 1607–1890*. New York: Capricorn Books, 1961.

Strahorn, Robert E. *The Resources and Attractions of Idaho Territory*. Boise City, Idaho: Idaho Legislature, 1881.

Stuart, Granville. *Forty Years on the Frontier*, ed. Paul C. Phillips, 2 vols. Cleveland, Ohio: The Arthur H. Clark Company, 1925.

Taylor, Thomas U. *The Chisholm Trail and Other Routes*. San Antonio, Texas: The Naylor Company, 1936.

Thompson, Stith, ed. *Round the Levee*. Austin, Texas: Texas Folk-Lore Society, 1935.

Thorp, Nathan Howard. *Pardner of the Wind*, as told to Neil M. Clark. Caldwell, Idaho: The Caxton Printers, 1945.

—— *Songs of the Cowboys*. Boston: Houghton Mifflin Company, 1921.

Towne, Charles Wayland, and Edward Norris Wentworth. *Cattle and Men*. Norman, Oklahoma: University of Oklahoma Press, 1955.

Townshend, Richard B. *The Tenderfoot in New Mexico*. London: John Lane, 1923.

Trenholm, Virginia Cole, and Maurine Carley. *Wyoming Pageant*. Casper, Wyoming: Bailey School Supply, 1947.

Trinka, Zena Irma. *Out Where the West Begins*. St. Paul, Minnesota: Pioneer Company, 1920.

Van Deusen, John G. "The Exodus of 1879," *The Journal of Negro History*, XXI (1936), 111–129.

Vestal, Stanley. *Dodge City, Queen of Cowtowns*. New York: Pennant Books, 1954 (1st ed., 1952).

—— *The Old Santa Fe Trail*. Boston: Houghton Mifflin Company 1939.

Walbridge, Earle F. "*The Virginian* and Owen Wister: A Bibliography," *The Papers of the Bibliographical Society of America*, XLVI (1952), 117–120.

Waldo, Edna LaMoore. *Dakota: An Informal Study of Territorial Days Gleaned from Contemporary Newspapers*. Bismarck, North Dakota: Capital Publishing Company, 1932.

Walker, Tacetta B. *Stories of Early Days in Wyoming*. Casper, Wyoming: Prairie Publishing Company, 1936.

Walker, William. *The Longest Rope: The Truth about the Johnson County Cattle War*, as told to D. F. Baber. Caldwell, Idaho: The Caxton Printers, 1947 (1st ed., 1940).

Washington, Booker T. *The Story of the Negro: The Rise of the Race from Slavery*, 2 vols. New York: Peter Smith, 1940 (1st ed., 1909).

Waters, Frank. *The Earp Brothers of Tombstone: The Story of Mrs. Virgil Earp*. New York: Clarkson N. Potter, 1960.

Weatherford, Willis D., and Charles S. Johnson. *Race Relations: Adjustment of Whites and Negroes in the United States*. Boston: D. C. Heath and Company, 1934.

Webb, Walter Prescott. *The Great Plains*. Boston: Ginn and Company, 1931.

Welsh, Donald H. "Pierre Wibaux, Cattle King," *North Dakota History*, XX (1953), 5–23.

Wesley, Charles H. *History of the Improved Benevolent and Protective Order of Elks of the World*. Washington: Association for the Study of Life and History, 1955.

Westermeier, Clifford P. *Man, Beast, Dust: The Story of Rodeo*. Denver, Colorado: published by the Author, 1947.

—— ed. *Trailing the Cowboy: His Life and Lore as Told by Frontier Journalists*. Caldwell, Idaho: The Caxton Printers, 1955.

Whitman, Sidney E. *The Troopers: An Informal History of the Plains Cavalry, 1865–1890.* New York: Hastings House Publishers, 1962.

Wight, Willard E., ed. "A Young Medical Officer's Letters from Fort Robinson and Fort Leavenworth, 1905–1907," *Nebraska History*, XXXVII (1956), 135–147.

Williams, Albert N. *The Black Hills, Mid-Continent Resort.* Dallas, Texas: Southern Methodist University Press, 1952.

Williams, Jennie Winona. "Allen and Winona Williams: Pioneers of Sheridan and Johnson Counties," *Annals of Wyoming*, XIV (1942), 193–199.

Wister, Owen. *Owen Wister Out West: His Journals and Letters,* ed. Fanny Kemble Wister. Chicago: University of Chicago Press, 1958.

—— *The Writings . . .* 11 vols. New York: The Macmillan Company, 1928.

Wood, A. B. "The Coad Brothers: Panhandle Cattle Kings," *Nebraska History*, XIX (1938), 28–43.

Wright, Robert M. *Dodge City, the Cowboy Capital, and the Great Southwest.* [Wichita, Kansas: Wichita Eagle Press, 1913.]

Wyllys, Rufus Kay. *Arizona: The History of a Frontier State.* Phoenix, Arizona: Hobson & Herr, 1950.

Zornow, William Frank. *Kansas: A History of the Jayhawk State.* Norman, Oklahoma: University of Oklahoma Press, 1957.

Index